TRANS/FORMING FEMINISMS

TRANS/FORMING *Feminisms*

TRANS/FEMINIST VOICES SPEAK OUT

EDITED BY

Krista Scott-Dixon

WOMEN'S ISSUES PUBLISHING PROGRAM

SERIES EDITOR BETH MCAULEY

LIBRARY AND ARCHIVES CANADA CATALOGUING IN PUBLICATION

Trans/forming feminisms : transfeminist voices speak out / ed. Krista Scott-Dixon.

ISBN-13: 978-1-894549-61-5
ISBN-10 : 1-894549-61-9

1. Transsexuals–Identity. 2. Transsexuals–Social conditions. 3. Transsexualism. 4. Feminism. I. Scott-Dixon, Krista, 1973-

HQ77.9.T69 2006 306.76'8 C2006-904347-7

Edited by Lisa B. Rundle
Cover and Design by Liz Martin

Sumach Press acknowledges the support of the Canada Council for the Arts and the Ontario Arts Council for our publishing program. We acknowledge the financial support of the Government of Canada through the Book Publishing Industry Development Program (BPIDP) for our publishing activities.

Printed and bound in Canada

Published by

SUMACH PRESS
1415 Bathurst Street #202
Toronto ON Canada M5R 3H8

sumachpress@on.aibn.com
www.sumachpress.com

CONTENTS

Acknowledgements *9*

INTRODUCTION

Trans/forming Feminisms
Krista Scott-Dixon *11*

SECTION I

NARRATIVES & VOICES

Introduction
Krista Scott-Dixon *36*

1/ On the Origins of Gender
Darryl B. Hill *39*

2/ The Language Puzzle:
Is Inclusive Language a Solution?
Alexander Pershai *46*

3/ Female by Surgery
Lesley Carter *53*

4/ Sometimes Boy, Sometimes Girl: Learning to be
Genderqueer through a Child's Eyes
Shannon E. Wyss *58*

5/ Walking in the Shadows:
Third Gender and Spirituality
Gigi Raven Wilbur *65*

SECTION II

IDENTITIES & ALLIANCES

Introduction
Krista Scott-Dixon 74

6/ Feminist Transmasculinities
reese simpkins 79

7/ Where's the Beef?
Masculinity as Performed by Feminists
Kyle Scanlon 87

8/ Our Bodies Are Not Ourselves: Tranny Guys and the
Racialized Class Politics of Embodiment
Bobby Noble 95

9/ The Feminist Cross-Dresser
Miqqi Alicia Gilbert 105

10/ Queer Femmes Loving FTMs:
Towards an Erotic Transgendered Ethics
Susan Driver 112

11/ It's a Long Way to the Top:
Hierarchies of Legitimacy in Trans Communities
Alaina Hardie 122

12/ Miss Whitey Says: A Rant Against Oppression
in Mainstream Feminism
Ros Salvador 131

SECTION III

INCLUSION & EXCLUSION

Introduction
Margaret Denike 136

13/ Acting Queerly: Lawyering for Trans People
barbara findlay 145

14/ Women's Spaces Are Not Trans Spaces: Maintaining Boundaries of Respect
A. Nicki 154

15/ The Ethics of Exclusion: Gender and Politics at the Michigan Womyn's Music Festival
Susanne Sreedhar & Michael Hand 161

16/ Competing Claims From Disadvantaged Groups: Nixon v. Vancouver Rape Relief Society
Joanna Harris 170

17/ Strategic Essentialism on Trial: Legal Interventions and Social Change
Lara Karaian 182

SECTION IV

SHELTER & VIOLENCE

Introduction
Krista Scott-Dixon 194

18/ Understanding Transphobia: Authenticity and Sexual Violence
Talia Mae Bettcher 203

19/ Safe at Home:
Redefining the Politics of Rape and Its Aftermath
Lynnette Dubois *211*

20/ Anti-Violence Work in Transition
Joshua Goldberg & Caroline White *217*

21/ Transforming Values / Engendering Policy
Wolfgang Vachon *227*

CONCLUSION

Towards Transfeminisms
Krista Scott-Dixon *235*

Glossary *242*
Contributors *250*

ACKNOWLEDGEMENTS

All books are collective projects, but anthologies represent a unique challenge and triumph. This book would not have been possible without the generous contributions of each author. A heartfelt thanks to all of them for their honesty, openness and willingness to share their stories and ideas. In particular, I would like to thank Susan Braedley, Joshua Goldberg, Jacqueline Krikorian, Bobby Noble, reese simpkins, Leah F. Vosko and Caroline White for reading draft portions and providing commentary. Talia Bettcher, Lynnette Dubois, Michael/Miqqi Alicia Gilbert, Sophie Mayer, Andrea Nicki, Kyle Scanlon, Shannon Wyss along with Joshua, Bobby and Caroline contributed valuable insights on transfeminism for an article I wrote for *Herizons* magazine.

I would like to thank Lisa Rundle for her able editorial assistance and expert third-wave feminist guidance, and Beth McAuley for bravely steering Sumach Press in this new direction. Although I did ignore her advice never to edit a book, thanks to my dear colleague Linda Briskin for taking on the projects of organizing the trans symposium at York University in 2002 and integrating trans-related material into the women's studies curriculum.

Thanks to all of the interesting and wonderful people I have met as a result of this research — you continue to teach me and challenge me. Thanks, too, to the people doing social justice work in their own spheres of influence: shelters and centres, social services, support networks, classrooms, labour unions, workplaces and other spaces of transformation. Your labour continues to propel us forward.

Finally, thanks to Alaina Hardie, who inspired it all.

INTRODUCTION

TRANS/FORMING FEMINISMS

Krista Scott-Dixon

> I came to theory because I was hurting — the pain within me was so intense that I could not go on living. I came to theory desperate, wanting to comprehend — to grasp what was happening around and within me. Most importantly, I wanted to make the hurt go away. I saw in theory then a location for healing.
>
> — bell hooks, *Teaching to Transgress*[1]

This is a book about questions.

In some ways, "coming out" as a feminist can echo coming out as trans or queer: the "aha" moment of abruptly punctuated reality, when we realize that our world view has been irrevocably altered; anger at social injustice; shame and self-doubt; and a yearning to know more, to gobble up ideas and experiences that speak to a budding consciousness. Sometimes it is painful; sometimes it is freeing. And there are many questions.

When I teach undergraduate women's studies courses, students have plenty of questions about feminism, and they ask them of me and of themselves with varying degrees of confidence. Some questions are rudimentary, even amusing; others so complex that they have yet to be answered satisfactorily even after nearly two centuries of feminist rumination: Do feminists hate men? Can anyone be a feminist? Do you shave your legs?

What does your husband think? Can feminists even *have* husbands? How do feminists deal with power and hierarchies in their own groups? Can a woman oppress another woman? How can a movement based on identifying a group by their gender address the diversity within that group? Their questions reflect a desire to learn more, to "try on" different ideas and to engage with the challenges posed by feminist ways of thinking and acting.

Since Western society remains firmly attached to the notion of two discrete, tidily organized sexes and genders, the subject of transsexuality, transgender or, the term I will use in this book, *trans* also generates questions. How do we know what our gender is? Why would someone want to live as a gender that does not match the one they were assigned at birth? What are the right pronouns and labels to use? Are non-trans feminists and queer communities natural allies of trans people?

Questions that are asked thoughtfully and honestly, out of a desire to broaden and deepen one's understanding of the world, help us begin a discussion across boundaries and differences. This book asks: What ideas, struggles and experiences do trans and feminist political projects share, what related concerns do they raise and how might insights from one area benefit the other? How might trans and feminist ideas inform future struggles for social justice and the enhancement of human dignity, and how might we build solidarity in order to improve people's lives?

QUESTIONS OF LANGUAGE

As contributor Alexander Pershai points out in his chapter in this collection, choosing appropriate language to describe a rich and varied group of identities and experiences is difficult. "Feminism" has many definitions and incarnations, and not all people who support feminist principles would call themselves feminists, yet the term is more or less adequate as a way of conveying a certain set of related politics, identities and world views. I use feminist writer bell hooks's definition: feminism is a movement to end sexism, sexist exploitation and oppression.[2] I also use the term "feminisms" in the title of this book to indicate that feminism takes many forms and has a long, varied history.

Similarly, I have chosen the term trans as a broad, more or less adequate term that suggests many forms of crossing gender boundaries, whether in terms of behaviour, self-presentation or identity, or in terms of how such crossings are experienced and understood. Many people, in fact, would say emphatically that they are *not* trans, but rather that they are simply men or women who are correcting a biological mistake. Nevertheless, the correction of that mistake requires inhabiting, if only briefly, a non-normative[3] gender space. I prefer trans to more specific categories such as transsexual or transgender, in part because meanings accorded to these terms vary regionally (with Americans tending to prefer transgender as an umbrella term), but largely because of the associations that these terms have with clinical classifications of medical and psychotherapeutic practice and with perceived psychological authenticity (in other words, who is seen as a "true transsexual").[4]

Systems of scientific and medical classification and naming have a context, a history and a politic.[5] Although gender diversity and cross-gendered behaviours appear to be as old as humanity, it was in the late nineteenth century in the West that anxieties over gender roles — as women demanded property rights, improved working conditions and the vote — led to a renewed interest in identifying the biological bases to support a norm of rigid heterosexual patriarchal order.[6] Chemists, botanists, sexologists and natural historians of all kinds worked busily at the project of proving middle-class white straight men's cultural and biological superiority by such means as distilling the essence of manhood from horse testicles or playing voyeur to the steamy sex lives of flowers.[7] Medical and scientific practitioners developed classification schema for numerous "deviant" sex, gender and sexual identities, with the intent to organize divergently gendered people (and behaviours) into a few neatly arranged compartments of criminality, illness and Otherness.[8]

From the late nineteenth to the late twentieth centuries, the work of several influential clinicians and psychotherapists such as Magnus Hirschfeld, Harry Benjamin, John Money and Robert Stoller contributed to the development of a classification system of trans identities for use in psychotherapeutic assessment and practice. This system identified types of trans people based on the degree of "gender distress" and associated behaviours and sexual desires. Transsexuals, sometimes called "true transsexuals," were people who expressed long-term cross-gender feelings and behaviour, significant distress at having to live as their birth gender and a desire for permanent physical reconstruction.[9] Transvestites, often referred to as "fetishistic transvestites" in the early literature but who are now commonly called cross-dressers, enjoyed cross-gender performances and dress but did not desire a permanent transition.

Clinicians also viewed sexual fantasies involving cross-gender expression, identities and clothing, as well as heteronormatively gendered behaviour, as crucial to a proper diagnosis. For example, transsexuals who admitted to being aroused by cross-gender dress or performance, who admitted to a sexual orientation that was not heterosexual or who did not adhere fully to hypermasculine or hyperfeminine norms of gender presentation were often diagnosed as "not true transsexuals." Late-twentieth-century models did not question the problematic basis of this typology but simply added other categories such as transgender and "autogynephilic transsexuals."[10] Thus, until quite recently, North American understandings of trans were limited to psychotherapeutic and medical issues such as treatment, therapy, endocrinology and surgery. These issues were situated in a context that was concerned with "gender authenticity" as defined by an external observer, rather than by people themselves.

While there are advantages to a medical context for trans, such as increased (if still inadequate) access to health care and social services, as well as to a certain kind of social legitimacy, relying solely on a clinical model and mindset developed in the operating theatre or on the psychiatrist's couch has had negative consequences for trans people. The available categories such as transsexual, transgender and transvestite attempt to simplify and often erase complex identities, desires, experiences and behaviours. Clinical insistence on using a birth gender rather than a person's self-identified gender, such as the term "male homosexual transsexual" (which actually denotes a male-to-female trans woman who prefers male partners) is at best confusing and at worst insensitive. Using clinical terminology, with its attendant anxieties over correct diagnosis and management of identities, can also lead one down the problematic path of establishing just who is transsexual *enough* to merit the term, who is transgender and who just happens to be wearing a mustache or a tutu that day. But most significantly, placing trans within a medical and psychotherapeutic context alone means that trans people can only be intelligible when they are sitting in a doctor's office needing to be "cured" of their "condition."

Thus, while some trans people opt to claim and use the more clinical terms for themselves, I prefer to use "trans man" to connote someone who identifies or currently prefers to present himself as male, or "trans woman" for someone who identifies or prefers to present herself as female. Some contributors to the book also use "FTM" (female-to-male) or "MTF" (male-to-female) as shorthand. *Self-identification is the basis for terminology*, rather than transition status, passability, biological configuration or any other criteria. I would like to frame trans in this book as primarily a *social* and *political*, rather than a *medical* and a *psychotherapeutic*, category.[11] This shifts the focus away from notions of individual disease, pathology and cure to systems of sex and gender that organize and often oppress our bodies, experiences and identities.

In this and my other introductory essays in the collection, I have also opted to use "non-trans" instead of "genetic male/female," "bio-man/woman," "women-born-women" or any of the other terms used to describe people who do not self-identify as trans nor experience that troublesome label of "gender dysphoria." I prefer non-trans because it elevates trans as the standard of measurement and gives it a sort of linguistic privilege. (The term rather cheekily suggests that non-trans people like me are the ones who don't quite measure up!) Using non-trans also removes the implication that particular indicators of biology such as genitalia or genetics are what really count in assessing proper gender identification. However, current language is laden with the ideological and cultural baggage of only two genders, and even well-meaning attempts cannot fully capture the nuance of trans experiences and identities. There are a host of other terms that people have invented, (re)claimed and chosen for themselves: butch, boi, Two-Spirit, she-male, tranny, genderfuck, boydyke, stud, genderqueer, hijra, birl and so forth. Some people go one step further by refusing labels altogether. In twenty years' time, trans may appear as quaint as "bluestocking" does to today's feminists.[12] I can only hope that in the future, we will have more words to describe the richness of gender.

Thus, to use the term trans is a choice, like any other, with implications and consequences. Yet, for now, I feel it is the best available option. The contributors to this volume use different words to describe the same thing. I did not ask them to standardize their language; rather, they simply used the terminology that felt most natural to them. I also include a glossary at the back of the book that provides some definitions and attempts to translate the varied language used.

I often refer to feminism and trans as though they are separate things. They are distinct in many ways, particularly as bodies of thought and scholarship, but I do not mean to suggest that they are easily defined, homogeneous, clearly divided groups of people, issues or ideas. There are trans and non-trans (and anti-trans) feminists as well as feminist and non-feminist (and anti-feminist) trans people. In this chapter, along with my introductions to each section (aside from the introduction to the third section, "Inclusion and Exclusion," which is written by Margaret Denike), I draw out some of the threads of scholarship, history and activism that characterize particular trans and feminist struggles, attempting to weave them together and show how they are intertwined, while preserving the unique character of each strand. Thus, I use feminism and trans for convenience rather than precision; the distinction is theoretical rather than descriptive.

QUESTIONS OF SEX AND GENDER

Since Simone de Beauvoir asserted "One is not born a woman, one becomes one" in her 1949 work *The Second Sex*, feminists have been interested in questions of how gender systems shape identity and the self, and how gendered identities are produced within systems of power and social regulation. Feminists distinguished *sex* — or the biological configuration of chromosomes, hormones, body structure, genitals and secondary physical characteristics that are understood to be male or female — from *gender*, which they understood as a cultural and social element of an individual's identity and behaviour. As a common saying goes, "Sex is between the legs; gender is between the ears." Feminists further differentiated sex and gender from *sexuality*, or sexual and erotic desires, fantasies, attractions and behaviours. Sex, gender and sexuality are more than individual characteristics: they are systems of social organization and relationships, as well as analytical concepts through which the world can be understood. Though related, these three elements also appear to operate independently of one another. One's apparent sex at birth may not match one's gender identity, nor can gender presentation always predict sexual orientation. For example, a woman who appears masculine by cultural standards may think of herself as fully female and may or may not identify as a lesbian.

Biological sex in humans is generally dimorphic. In other words, most of the time, from conception onward a person's sex is more or less either male or female. However, like gender, which varies over time, place and context, biological sex may be thought of as a spectrum rather than two firmly divided categories.[13] It was not until the Victorian period that females and males were viewed as opposites; prior to this, Western scientists and natural philosophers tended to assume that females were an inferior copy of males.[14] Now we know that there is a lot of diversity even in something as apparently simple as sexual development. Early in development, male and female fetuses look the same, and their reproductive organs diverge from the same common origin. In a small percentage of people, one or more elements of biological sex are ambiguous; people with these indeterminate biological markers are called intersex.[15]

While one chapter in this book concerns intersexed people, and while some elements of trans issues are related to intersex issues, intersexuality is not the primary focus. Rather, this volume is more interested in the individual and structural meanings given to sex, gender and, to a lesser degree, sexuality, how these three things intersect and how they are relevant to trans, feminist and transfeminist struggles for identity and equity. I begin from the premise, outlined by gender theorist Michael Kimmel in his introduction to *The Gendered Society Reader*, that nearly every culture and society we know "is founded upon assumptions of gender difference and the politics of gender inequality."[16]

*

When I first learned about trans issues several years ago, long after I'd come out as a feminist, I had questions too. For example, I was curious to know whether lived trans experience matched the postmodern feminist theory I had read about gender performance, which suggested that gender was what a person *did* rather than who they were.[17] Being trans seemed very glamourous and fun; in the early postmodern literature about gender, trans people seemed to be having a lovely time doing drag, having excitingly kinky genderqueer sex, disrupting normative gender systems and going out to fabulous nightclubs. Not surprisingly, I quickly discovered that the day-to-day lives of trans people were much different. Gender is not just a performance, though that is part of its complex experience. It's not just a social role that can be separated from biology. Gender is a multilayered phenomenon that digs deep down into our guts, shaping our lives in a profound way. It is a system of social relations that organizes our world, and something that helps us make meaning of the differences between people. Disrupting a sex-gender system can be fun. But because of the power that sex-gender systems have, disruption can also have very real and serious consequences.

Gender operates on many levels, and it is the sloppiness of language and conceptual categories that is often responsible for confusion about what gender is and where it comes from.[18] The most innate layer of gender, the core that provides us with a deep sense of who we are, might be called *gender identity*. Gender identity is the one element of gender that has proven resistant to any intervention. Behavioural therapy, negative or positive reinforcement, shock therapy, Freud, good intentions, religion or psychoactive drugs — none appear to have any sway over a person's fundamentally gendered self-concept. Gender identity, like the centre of an onion, is swathed in other layers of gender that change over time and across cultures and context. It is the difference between gender identity and these other gendered layers that often confuses people when a loved one is about to transition. They may ask: "Why can't you just be sweet and sensitive and stay a guy?" or "Why do you have to be a man to like cars?" *Gender role* is what we do and how we act in the world. *Gender performance* is how we tell others who we are (or what we want them to see). *Gender attribution* is how other people "read" us (correctly or incorrectly). Although the immutability of gender identity and the fluidity of other aspects of gender suggest that gender is a complex interplay of biological and social factors, locating the origin of gender is not the point of this book. The real issue is how gender functions as a *system* that has a structure and a set of rules, and which intersects with, responds to and shapes other social systems and people's lives.

Gender is largely experienced as a set of relations that depends on the idea that there are two categories into which people do and should fit. In order to give meaning to "normal" gender, there must be some idea about what is "deviant" or "abnormal." Even if they mean well, non-trans people may assume that *their* gender does not merit examination; after all, it is "normal" and hence invisible. Focusing on trans people alone as subjects of study does not capture the ways in which even normatively gendered people might support or subvert gender roles and regimes. The privilege of being "perfectly" gendered is also racialized, classed and shaped by other elements of social location, such as age, ability and sexuality, all of which affect how we perceive our gender, and how others perceive us. Heteronormative masculinity, for example, depends on the (repeated) rejection of characteristics associated with femininity, such as subservience.

Men whose other social locations place them in subservient roles, such as racially and/or economically marginalized men, must then come up with ways to reassert or reinvent masculine dominance.

Gender, then, is not just about gender. It is a slippery thing that rubs up against other social signifiers in indecent ways. Individual gender expression is embedded in systems and structures of power that include colonialism, capitalism and intersecting oppressions. Just as the critical examination of whiteness within structures of racial inequality enables us to see how the norm is as constructed a social product as the racialized Other (and how the norm depends on the Other to give it meaning and coherency), asking questions about *both* normative and trans genders and observing how they intersect with other social relations facilitate a richer critical analysis of the gender system as a whole. Examining the social anxieties and struggles over trans issues not only assists us to work towards social justice and equity for all people but also provides insight into how normative genders are produced, maintained and reproduced.

Because we are immersed in a gender system, it is often hard for us to see how much of gender is constructed. Like breathing, which we notice mostly when we can't do it, we tend to become aware of gender norms only when they are challenged or transgressed. Being busted in the "wrong" public bathroom not only asks the bathroom intruder to perform a certain gender properly, but also highlights the notion that, at least in North America, there are two types of public bathrooms and two groups to which bathroom-goers must identifiably belong. However, until the bathroom sanctuary is punctured by a perceived interloper, most people go about their business without giving much thought to the matter. Being normatively gendered carries the privilege of social invisibility, and non-trans people, even those who may push the envelope of their gender role, still rarely give the authenticity of their gender a second thought.

Even passing perfectly does not automatically confer a "normal" gender status, for, as Talia Bettcher asserts in her chapter, trans people can still be outed as "not really" that which they appear to be. Trans people often require people in authority (such as medical-care providers) and/or a set of legal and regulatory documents (such as a revised driver's licence or certificate of surgery) to vouch for their authenticity. In my life as a non-trans person, nobody has ever questioned my right to be a woman: not when I shaved my head, wore army boots, swung a sledgehammer, cursed a blue streak or smoked a cigar (at my wedding, no less). When I sit in a woman's bathroom stall, I don't need to worry that I will hear the thunk-thunk-thunk of a security guard's fist pounding on the door to tell me that I am in the wrong place. As a woman, I am still at risk for various oppressions and abuses, but as woman who is not trans, I nevertheless enjoy many privileges. Gender privilege, the privilege of being normatively and unambiguously placed within a mainstream gender system, despite its constraints, is a great social privilege enjoyed by most people who are not trans.

The desire and need to face the world as one's deeply felt gender identity can be overwhelming, and the consequences of accomplishing this can be painful. In the course of my research on trans issues and participation in trans-related initiatives such as workshops and conferences, I met people who had lost their families, friends, jobs and legal protections[19] as a result of deciding to transition. Some had experienced sexual, physical and emotional violence. Those who chose to modify their bodies with medical interventions such as hormones and surgeries dealt with physical trauma, the often rigid processes of obtaining medical services and the financial costs of care. Yet the trans people who generously shared their stories with me were also survivors and agents who made choices for themselves and found much to celebrate in their lives. They navigated the stormy seas of cultural prejudice, daily indignities and political challenges, often with humour, grit, creative coping strategies, unique insights gained from inhabiting different gendered spaces and a desire to see positive change. Some of them were able to use the constraints of the gender system to their advantage; others developed alternative survival plans. Far from being the isolated, loveless and tragic victims portrayed in mainstream media, many trans people I met were active in creating communities and networks of political and social support. They created new rituals and celebrations to mark trans life passages. They found and sustained relationships that both supported and subverted the norm. In her chapter, "Queer Femmes Loving FTMs," Susan Driver movingly describes her relationship as a queer femme with a trans male partner: "It is the constancy of our belief and love in each other's differences that grounds the meaning of our lives."

QUESTIONS OF THEORY AND PRACTICE

While trans scholarship is a growing field, what has been largely missing from the field of trans and feminist writing is the diverse voices of trans people. Much has been written *about* trans people; much less has been written *by* trans people about themselves, in their own voices. Medical and psychotherapeutic literature on trans (which can often be found shelved in libraries next to books on pathological sexual deviance) has historically treated trans people as objects, not subjects, of study. Trans bodies are on display as "specimens" in medical photographs, eyes blacked out, removing any shred of individuality. In these photographs and case files, trans people are literally forced to measure up to a norm: they stand awkwardly against walls with rulers, hold calibration devices against their genitals and the depth of their vaginas are recorded. They are often nothing more than parts and pieces in medical literature: genital skin to manipulate; phalluses to manufacture from forearm flesh; breasts to add or remove; or a series of hormone shots.

Trans people are positioned in psychotherapeutic case literature as inherently pathological, crazy or in need of classification and psychotherapy. No thought, desire or fashion error of theirs is allowed to be private; their fantasies and behaviour are dissected for clues about "what went wrong." The role of clinicians in producing and reproducing gender norms is never questioned, nor is the clinical classification schema that allows for a very limited range of gender expression. Like the duck-billed platypus who so perplexed nineteenth-century taxonomists that they insisted the animal, not their system of classification, had to be wrong, trans people have been viewed in traditional psychotherapy as aberrations in need of correction and cure.[20] With some exceptions, few clinicians have reflected at all on their power over trans people's lives, their role in developing and sustaining relations of inequality and their gatekeeping function.[21]

Feminist theory identifies medicalized typologies of gender that have attempted historically to categorize "unruly" female bodies and behaviours, such as being lesbian, "frigid" or "hysterical." The origin of the feminine disorder of hysteria was physical: a woman's uterus (*hystera*) was prone to running amok through the body or shrivelling when women studied fields such as mathematics.[22] Later, writes Elaine Showalter, when the study of anatomy disproved the uterus's migratory capacity, doctors simply transferred the origin of hysteria to women's nervous system: "Women were then described as a nervous sex, suffering from vapors, spleen, and fainting fits, or eroticized as hysterical nymphomaniacs."[23] Jean-Martin Charcot's photographs of "hysterics" in the nineteenth century, in which institutionalized "madwomen" are recorded in various physical contortions, parallel the photos of trans people from the twentieth century.[24]

Women could also be viewed as pathological simply for being women. Menstruation was assumed to be responsible for a variety of ills, and menstruating women were thought in the Middle Ages to possess various powers of destruction, including the ability to dull mirrors. Menopausal women could transmit "venom" to children "through their glance," and a woman was thought "venomous by virtue of her very physiological mechanism."[25] Twentieth-century practice was less concerned with menopausal women's poison and more concerned with her "abnormal" hormones and loss of feminine vitality. In both the case of trans and female medical subjects, their sexed and gendered bodies and identities were seen by medical and psychotherapeutic practitioners as *inherently* pathological and in need of correction or management. And in both cases, clinicians (though often genuinely sympathetic) played a central role in establishing and maintaining these gendered norms through systems of medical authority.

Despite the obvious parallels between many feminist and trans critiques, such as a concern with sex-gender norms and difference, feminist literature on trans until very recently has not been much more trans-positive than clinical scholarship. At its best, it has been hesitant or scanty; at its worst, it has been openly hostile. Janice Raymond's famous 1979 work *The Transsexual Empire* is a scathing attack on male-to-female transsexuals who, Raymond felt, sought to co-opt and defile womanhood and femininity, as well as to shore up rigid, negative gender constructs. In her model, female-to-male trans people (though barely mentioned) are really just women who are deluded about the value of accessing male power. Though she does point out the clinical insistence on narrowly defined gender roles, she places the blame on trans people for perpetuating a problematic gender system.[26] Bernice Hausman is critical in her 1995 work of trans people's use of medical technologies to reproduce gender norms, and argues that trans people buy into and perpetuate a problematic gender system.[27] Germaine Greer, like Raymond, argues in a chapter of her 1999 book *The Whole Woman* that the cure for "gender role distress is not mutilation of the sufferer but radical change of gender roles."[28]

The desire to blast open gender categories should be one that thrills and excites us as feminists. However, the frisson of liberation is dampened and diluted by the vitriolic portraits of trans people that writers such as Greer create, of a group of cunning, hormonally "deranged," narcissistic, gender-rigid, "pantomime dames" and fakers whose gender transition represents "an exorcism of the mother" who is "the transsexual's worst enemy."[29] In a particularly vituperative passage, Greer writes,

> When a man decides to spend his life impersonating his mother (like Norman Bates in *Psycho*) it is as if he murders her and gets away with it, proving at a stroke that there was nothing to her. His intentions are no more honourable than any female impersonator's; his achievement is to gag all who would call his bluff. When he forces his way into the few private spaces women may enjoy and shouts down their objections, and bombards the women who will not accept him with threats and hate mail, he does as rapists have always done.[30]

It seems from these writings that not only are trans women rapists dressed as Stepford wives, but they may also be lurking in the showers with a knife. The Canadian feminist magazine *Herizons* asked, in a 2001 article on trans and feminism, "Can a Transgender Person be 'One of Us'?" The response from many feminist circles was clear: No. Trans was positioned as something antithetical or irrelevant to or at least outside of feminism, and the notion that trans people could be feminists, feminists could be trans allies or that there could even be something called *transfeminism* has been poorly considered.

However, not all non-trans feminists feel this way. Many are doing their best to struggle through the new challenges that trans raises for political work and thinking about gender. To its credit, five years later, *Herizons* published an article I wrote on trans and feminism that was much more positive.[31] In 2000, the women's literary journal *Fireweed* produced a special issue called "Trans/Scribes."[32] The National Association of Women and the Law (NAWL) held a consultation on transgender and women's substantive equality in 2003, an event that brought together trans and feminist activists and researchers in order to consider how to "develop an inclusive and responsible feminist approach that respects the human dignity of all individuals, within and across our differences, and advances the substantive equality rights of all women."[33] In the discussion paper for the event, Margaret Denike (a contributor to this volume) and Sal Renshaw critique the "zero-sum" model of human rights that views granting rights to one group (i.e., trans people) as a detriment to another group (i.e., women).

Other recent feminist work, such as that of Patricia Elliot, Cressida Hayes, Eleanor MacDonald and Katrina Roen, has also provided some useful starting points.[34] For example, MacDonald argues that "transgender politics and transgendered people's experiences must be taken seriously by more traditional gender identity-based feminism and contemporary postmodern feminism."[35] MacDonald spares no pleasantries in taking feminists to task, arguing that "traditional feminist approaches need to critique their own exclusionary practices, and challenge their own understanding of gender and sexuality," while postmodern feminists who focus exclusively on what they see as the playfulness and performance of gender must address lived trans realities, "the direct and visceral terms in which transgendered people experience the boundaries and instability of identity."[36]

Conversely, while many trans people have allied themselves with feminism, trans scholarship has frequently ignored feminism as a political movement and mode of thinking, though it often draws from queer theory and some of the insights generated by feminists in theorizing sex-gender relations. Many trans male theorists, such as Henry Rubin or C. Jacob Hale, began their research careers with some connection to women's studies; many trans men who are community activists began their activist careers in feminist/lesbian communities and spaces. In the case of trans women, while many may have been aware of and sympathetic to feminist issues before their transition, post-transition experiences of sexism provide new inspiration. However, there remains little scholarship that explicitly situates trans debates within the types of power relations and sex-gender inequities identified in feminist literature. What has occupied me for years since I became interested in this subject, and engaged with the struggles of trans people for recognition and equality, is the congruence between feminist and trans issues, theories and activism. When I sat in groups dedicated to feminist or trans-positive objectives and listened to people speak, I felt a strange linguistic puzzlement: we were speaking the same language and using the same terms, yet we were not speaking to — or even about — *one another* (nor, it appears, were we listening to one another).

As I have noted already, I am not beginning this book from the premise that feminists and trans people share exactly the same needs, questions and concerns, nor am I assuming that feminists and trans people are each homogeneous, easily classified and distinct groups with competing interests. Indeed, it is precisely the richness of feminist and trans experiences, identities and political inclinations that prompts me to call for a framework of theory and activism that productively addresses this diversity. Feminist thought represents a toolbox of ideas and strategies that may then be applied, in modified forms if necessary, to trans people's struggles. These tools may also be used by non-trans feminists who wish to work towards trans-positive alliances. In essence, I hope to avoid reinventing the wheel when formulating activism and scholarship around trans. As Anne Bishop notes in *Becoming an Ally*, "A great source of power for all people is the process of linking our common problems and concerns … Every time it happens, another movement for social change begins, because people are linked in struggle again and we lose our shame."[37]

TOWARDS TRANSFEMINISMS

There are several common and interrelated themes and concerns of interest to feminist and trans scholars and activists. Here is a very brief overview. These themes emerge and interact in various ways throughout the book and include, but are not limited to, the following:

Sex/Gender Systems and Power

Perhaps the most significant potential contribution of feminist theory to trans theory is the focus on and analysis of how gendered structures of power and privilege operate to proscribe and constrain choices, and how gender (and other intersecting dimensions such as race, class, sexuality, age and so forth) serves as a marker of social differentiation, organization and stratification. Sex-gender systems have been one of the most primary focal points for feminist theorists, who are interested in how these systems produce notions of what is "normal and natural" (and by extension what is "deviant and unnatural"), define and give meaning to identities and organize society in general. What does it mean in our culture to be male, female, masculine, feminine? How can gendered ideologies be both productive and repressive? How might such a system be subverted (or reproduced)?

Self-definition and Self-naming

In a gendered system, how do we come to know, speak of and name ourselves and each other? The power to name, authority over language and control over self-representations are significant privileges. Feminist theorists of language and discourse have pointed out, for example, the false neutrality of using "man" to represent everyone (or, in the famous Canadian "Persons" case of 1929, the fact that legally speaking, "persons" did not include women), the problems of relying on "women" as a unified category, the necessity of developing terms such as "sexual harassment" in order to convey and communicate particular types of gendered experiences, the invisibility or derogation of women in language, and the trouble with developing terms that appropriately describe complex identities. Trans theorists have taken up questions such as pronoun use and the challenge of representing richly gendered experiences and identities using the limited binary of "he" and "she," as well as their legal invisibility that depends on other agencies "naming" them as the correct gender.

Intersectionality, Multiple Identities and Differences

Our experience of the world does not depend on our gender alone but also on our income, geographical location, age, sexuality, ability and a host of other intersecting factors. Each of us is located at the centre of intersecting identities, like the spokes of a wheel connected to the hub. These identities are determined in part by our individual makeup, but also by historic and systemic disparities in access to power and resources. This has implications for how we think about identity, political and social alliances, access and opportunity, rights and privileges.[38]

Safety, Shelter and Women-only Spaces

The creation of "safe spaces" for women that were free from violence and abuse (generally from men) has been a central project of the feminist movement. Now, feminist theories of abuse and safety, as well as policies and institutions designed to create shelter and protect those who are vulnerable, are called into question by issues of trans inclusion in service provision. These challenges include defining who women's shelters serve (and who can provide services) and how to address the broader agenda of providing services to diverse people in need.

Groups, Power and Organizing

Questions of power within groups has been central to the feminist project of consciousness-raising and activism. How may collective movements develop strategies to ensure that members are fully represented and protected and that the group's mandate and ground rules reflect an anti-oppression objective? How may groups and institutions develop rules to provide security and inclusion for their members, without excluding or further marginalizing members? Feminists have looked for methods of collaboration, consensus and decision-making that resist traditional patriarchal structures and empower women as part of groups. Additionally, feminists have explored questions of coalition politics. With whom can we build alliances dedicated to social justice, and how? What strategies should we use? How can we address power imbalances and diversity within and between our groups?

Legislation and Discrimination

In the Canadian context, feminists and marginalized groups have often turned to the Charter of Rights and Freedoms for legal guidance, social justice activism and assistance in developing institutional policies. The concept of rights gained through legislation and the institutionalized remedy of discrimination have informed much of moderate Canadian feminism. However, the law is not always sympathetic or straightforward. For example, the significant case of Kimberly Nixon versus the Vancouver Rape Relief Society — which is ongoing — has provided fertile ground for both feminist and trans legal debate. Moreover, in that it depends on things that are specific, concrete and clearly defined, the law has often served to regulate and control how rights, responsibilities and identities are understood. Several pieces in this collection examine the implications of the Nixon case.

Bodies, Ability and Sexuality

We all have bodies with a physical essence. Both trans and feminist thinkers are concerned with the ways in which living, breathing, feeling bodies experience power relations and systems of sex-gender, as well as how these relations and systems shape our understandings of bodily experience such as ability and sexuality. Just as feminists have debated whether acknowledging sexual difference means pathologizing women, trans people have debated whether using a medical diagnosis of Gender Identity Disorder (GID) is an effective strategy for self-understanding and collective self-empowerment. Just as research into sexual difference has been pursued by both feminists and traditional clinicians working in fields such as neurology, evolutionary biology, endocrinology and psychiatry, trans people and clinicians alike have also sought a physiological "cause" for trans behaviours and identities. Just as feminists have challenged mainstream depictions of "normal" women's bodies as white, abled, young and thin, trans people have also challenged notions that to be "really" trans means having particular medical interventions — or conversely, they have claimed these interventions as human rights. Finally, for many people, physical sexual difference is of less immediate concern than getting their bodies fed, clothed, decorated, moved around, housed, protected, cared for and loved.

About This Book

This volume takes up many of these themes common to feminisms and trans and begins a documented discussion across boundaries and within groups. It does not pretend to be the definitive canon of trans and feminist engagement. Rather, it is the collected work of a handful of contributors who are, like me, interested in sharing stories, debating ideas and working towards social justice and equity for all people. We come from different walks of life, occupy different positions in the world and think about the issues in different ways. The collection privileges Canadians but does include American contributors along with one European. Contributors speak in different voices: academic, polemic, personal, political and poetic. They all ask questions; some suggest answers.

Trans/forming Feminisms is laid out in four sections that engage the general themes outlined above in more specific ways, in order to highlight and contextualize more precise intersections between trans and feminist ideas. Each section is prefaced with an introduction that ties the pieces together, provides context and identifies some of the key issues in feminist and trans debates and discussions. The sections are intended to be interlocking and interrelated, and the ideas in the pieces run throughout the book. The first section, "Narratives and Voices," builds on the feminist ideas of consciousness-raising, speaking from experience and representing oneself in language. The second section, "Identities and Alliances," looks more closely at identities, taking up questions such as how identities are produced, maintained and reproduced, and how diverse identities can work collectively. The third section, "Inclusion and Exclusion," examines the feminist notion of "safe spaces" and "women-only spaces" in the context of trans challenges such as the Kimberly Nixon case and the entrance policies of the Michigan Womyn's Music Festival. The fourth section, "Shelter and Violence," builds on the concepts in the third section to explore case studies of shelter and service provision policy, as well as the sex-gender system that undergirds transphobic abuse. The anthology concludes with suggestions for future research and activism.

This book represents my attempt as a non-trans feminist academic to ask questions and begin a dialogue between groups, ideas and communities that could be mutually beneficial for future social justice and equity work. bell hooks argues that fundamentally, social movements based on coalitions must be driven by love, friendship and affinity.[39] Thus, this book emerges not only from my long-standing scholarly interest in feminist and trans theory but also from my experience of struggling to be an ally to the trans people in my life, and my anger at observing the multiple injustices and mistreatment they endure — from both mainstream society and feminists alike — simply for not being gender-normative (or for being seen as *too* gender normative).

This book is for the people who asked why I would bother myself with trans people when I myself am not trans. This book is for the people I have met in my journey: for the trans woman who tells me that a "feminist nazi" judge took away her children in a custody dispute after her transition; for the young, street-active trans man who was shut out of the women's shelter in which he had previously worked; for the First Nations feminist activist who told me that she did not welcome trans women in her women's shelter even though many of the people seeking care identified as Two-Spirited; for the friend who rapped on my bedroom window at three in the morning because her surgical incision was bleeding profusely and she was afraid to go to the hospital alone to face possibly transphobic medical personnel (who, as it turned out, were wonderfully sympathetic); for the young, proudly non-op trans woman who loved to skateboard and who introduced herself to me as "Chili con carne — with meat!" and giggled at the delicious freedom of being able to invent her own identity with humour and without shame; for the gentle gray-haired non-trans male professor who sat in my seminar on trans and feminism and listened — *listened!* — intently to trans people sharing their stories; for the trans man who told me he did not consider himself part of the trans community in his area because they were "all freaks and fags" who gave "normal" (closeted) trans people a bad name; for the therapists, counsellors, and caregivers who would like to help their trans clients move through their gender journey without reproducing sexist norms; for the lesbian partner who feared that she would lose membership and status among her queer friends when her partner transitioned to male and for the straight woman who battled her homophobia when her partner transitioned to female; for the community activist friend who keeps me honest and grounded (my bad day at work usually involves bureaucratic troubles; his bad day at work can involve a trans sex worker's murder or trying to care for a terrified and suicidal genderqueer teenager just off the bus from small town Canada); and for the many, many others who continue to challenge and inspire me.

As hooks says, feminism is for everybody.

NOTES

1 bell hooks, "Theory as Liberatory Practice," in *Teaching to Transgress* (New York: Routledge, 1994), 59.

2 bell hooks, *Feminism Is for Everybody: Passionate Politics* (Cambridge, MA: South End Press, 2000), 1.

3 I use the term "normative" to imply a system of standardized social conventions that not only describes a particular view of the world but also an ideology of how the world should work. In the case of normative gender, this means the notion that there are two easily categorized sexes and genders, male and female, and that they correspond unproblematically to masculinity and femininity in a context of heterosexual reproductive relations.

4 For more on the classification of trans people, see for instance, Ray Blanchard, "The Classification and Labeling of Nonhomosexual Gender Dysphorias," *Archives of Sexual Behavior* 18, no. 4 (1989). Such classification schemes have since been challenged by trans activists.

5 For example, in the mid-eighteenth century, Carolus Linnaeus, the father of modern taxonomy, declared that a group of furry vertebrates should be called *Mammalia*, literally "of the breast." His decision to highlight the "natural" process of breastfeeding as the basis for a grouping of organisms was grounded in his political stance on maternal wet nursing and population control. It is also worth noting that Linnaeus was not the only taxonomist duking it out for control. During this period, competing

classification schemes vied for supremacy. See Londa Schiebinger, *Nature's Body: Gender in the Making of Modern Science* (Boston, MA: Beacon Press, 1993).

6 This was also a time of classifying "normal" and "deviant" identities based on race-ethnicity, class, sexuality and ability in order to support political projects such as colonialism or eugenics.

7 Nelly Oudshoorn, *Beyond the Natural Body: An Archaeology of Sex Hormones* (New York: Routledge, 1994), and Schiebinger, *Nature's Body*.

8 Michel Foucault, *The History of Sexuality*, trans. Robert Hurley (New York: Vintage Books, 1990).

9 Blanchard, "The Classification and Labeling of Nonhomosexual Gender Dysphorias."

10 Ray Blanchard, "Early History of the Concept of Autogynephilia," *Archives of Sexual Behavior* 34, no. 4 (2005), 439–446.

11 In this project I draw on the insights of critical disability and social determinants of health theories, which challenge the notion of disability and health as an individual deficit and/or capacity, preferring instead to examine the social and physical structures and environments that present obstacles for people. See, for example, Simi Hinton, *Claiming Disability: Knowledge and Identity* (New York: New York University Press, 1998), and Dennis Raphael, ed., *Social Determinants of Health: Canadian Perspectives* (Toronto: Canadian Scholars' Press, 2004).

12 Bluestocking was a term applied in the late nineteenth century to connote a woman-who enjoyed literary or intellectual pursuits. It was also suggestive of early feminist spinsters who prioritized education over conventional feminine interests of marriage and family.

13 Anne Fausto-Sterling, *Sexing the Body: Gender Politics and the Construction of Sexuality* (New York: Basic Books, 2000).

14 Oudshoorn, *Beyond the Natural Body*. It is important to note that this is a North American and European theoretical tradition, and does not necessarily apply elsewhere in other regions or scholarly histories. However, the dominance of Western thought has strongly shaped our current conceptions of gender in Canadian society.

15 Fausto-Sterling, *Sexing the Body*. Some people prefer the term "intersexual." Contributor Gigi Raven Wilbur self-identifies with the term "hermaphrodite," an earlier term derived from the mythical Greek figure Hermaphroditos, the son of Hermes and Aphrodite, who as Ovid recounts in *Metamorphoses* was united with his female lover Salmacis so completely that they generated a single body that combined male and female characteristics.

16 Michael Kimmel, "Introduction," in Michael Kimmel and Amy Aronson, eds., *The Gendered Society Reader* (London: Oxford University Press, 2004), 2. Italics in original.

17 See, for example, Judith Butler, *Gender Trouble: Feminism and the Subversion of Identity* (New York: Routledge, 1989).

18 A similar framework is employed by Eleanor MacDonald in her piece, "Critical Identities: Rethinking Feminism through Transgender Politics," *Atlantis* 23, no. 1 (1998), 3–12.

19 Currently, while the Canadian Charter of Rights and Freedoms protects minority rights on many fronts (such as race/ethnicity and religion), there is no formally stated protection against discrimination based on gender identity or presentation that is intended to apply to trans people. The issue of legal protection is explored in greater detail in section 3, "Inclusion and Exclusion."

20 Interestingly, the humble platypus has a long history of messing with biologists' heads. Its latest antics involve sex chromosomes. Unlike most mammals and many other vertebrates, who have two chromosomes that determine biological sex (in the case of humans, the X and Y chromosomes), platypuses have ten! Laura Carrel, "Evolutionary Biology: Chromosome Chain Makes a Link," *Nature* 432 (2004), 817–818.

21 For more trans-positive scholarship, see for example Ubaldo Leli and Drescher, Jack, eds., *Transgender Subjectivities: A Clinician's Guide* (New York: Haworth Press, 2004), particularly Dallas Denny's chapter, "Changing Models of Transsexualism."

22 Interestingly, however, unlike nineteenth-century social norms that emphasized middle-class women's sexual purity, medieval doctors who endorsed the "wandering womb" theory of women's physical disorder felt that a *lack* of sexual activity could be to blame. However, in both cases, masturbation or genital stimulation by a "qualified practitioner" such as a midwife was one recommended cure. Danielle Jacquart and Claude Thomasset, *Sexuality and Medicine in the Middle Ages,* trans. Matthew Adamson (Princeton, NJ: Princeton University Press), 176; Rachel Maines, *The Technology of Orgasm: "Hysteria," the Vibrator, and Women's Sexual Satisfaction* (Baltimore, MD: Johns Hopkins University Press, 1999).

23 Elaine Showalter, *Hystories: Hysterical Epidemics and Modern Media* (New York: Columbia University Press, 1997), 15.

24 See Georges Didi-Huberman, *Invention of Hysteria: Charcot and the Photographic Iconography of the Salpetriere*, trans. Aliza Hartz (Cambridge: MIT Press, 2003).

25 Jacquart and Thomasset, *Sexuality and Medicine in the Middle Ages,* 75.

26 See also Sheila Jeffreys, *The Lesbian Heresy: A Feminist Perspective on the Lesbian Sexual Revolution* (London: Women's Press, 1994).

27 Bernice Hausman, "Recent Transgender Theory," *Feminist Studies* 27, no. 2 (2001), 465–490, and *Changing Sex: Transsexualism, Technology, and the Idea of Gender* (Durham, NC: Duke University Press, 1995).

28 Germaine Greer, "Pantomime Dames," in *The Whole Woman* (New York: Knopf, 1999), 71.

29 Ibid., 80. Note the use of the word "the" in this context. Trans men are generally absent from this model.

30 Ibid.

31 Krista Scott-Dixon, "Transforming Politics: Transgendered Activists Break Down Gender Boundaries and Reconfigure Feminist Parameters," *Herizons* 19, no. 3 (2006), 21–25.

32 *Fireweed*, Special Issue, "Trans/Scribes" (2000).

33 Margaret Denike and Sal Renshaw, "Transgender and Women's Substantive Equality," paper presented at the National Consultation on Transgender and Women's Substantive Equality, National Association for Women and the Law (NAWL), Ottawa, ON, February 22–23, 2003. Also see the final report prepared September 2003 and available from NAWL at www.nawl.ca/transfinalreport.htm.

34 Patricia Elliot and Katrina Roen, "Transgenderism and the Politics of Embodiment," *GLQ: A Journal of Gay and Lesbian Studies* 4, no. 2 (1998), 231–261; Cressida Hayes, "Reading Transgender, Rethinking Women's Studies," *National Women's Studies Association Journal* (2000), 170–180; and MacDonald, "Critical Identities."

35 MacDonald, "Critical Identities," 4.

36 Ibid., 4–5.

37 Anne Bishop, *Becoming an Ally: Breaking the Cycle of Oppression* (Halifax, NS: Fernwood Books, 1994), 85.

38 For example, as Margaret Denike and Sal Renshaw point out, this has implications for anti-discrimination initiatives and legal protections, as courts and jurisprudence typically focus on a single, exclusionary ground, such as race but not sex nor sexual orientation. See Margaret Denike and Sal Renshaw, "Transgender and Women's Substantive Equality," in National Association for Women and the Law, *National Consultation on Transgender and Women's Substantive Equality* (Ottawa, ON: NAWL, 2003), 9.

39 hooks, *Feminism Is for Everybody.*

SECTION I

Narratives & Voices

INTRODUCTION

Krista Scott-Dixon

Writing from people's lived realities is where this book begins, and the majority of pieces in this anthology build on the feminist notion of speaking from experience in order to effect change. For second-wave feminists in the 1960s and 1970s, political action began from consciousness-raising (CR) sessions in which women shared narratives of their lives, put names to previously nameless phenomena (such as sexual assault), identified common ground with other women and tested ideas of social organizing against their experiences.[1] In her work on violence against women, Anne Bishop suggests that liberation struggles emerge from story-telling: "Story-telling leads to analysis, where we figure out together what is happening to us and why, and who benefits. Analysis leads to strategy, when we decide what to do about it. Strategy leads to action, together, to change the injustices we suffer."[2] Feminists engaged in CR elevated the role of experience and questioned the authenticity of "official" accounts of their lives that did not draw from day-to-day reality, in order to develop a political practice.[3]

This interest in storytelling and life narratives developed into collecting oral histories and the critical study of knowledge production. Feminists interested in issues of representation and experience saw narrative as a means of translating theory into reality, with individual world views a filter for discussing larger issues. To achieve this goal, they used fiction, autobiography, visual art, poetry, songs, films and other forms of representation. They also rejected the idea of the "objective knower" and argued that all viewpoints were necessarily partial and situated in a particular context.[4] The famous slogan that emerged from CR sessions, "The personal is political," which alluded to the public and social dimension of apparently "private" issues, is frequently misinterpreted as the idea that the authenticity of someone's political position could be determined through individual choices. This contention has informed feminist discussions about who can be a feminist, whether it is feminist to engage in certain kinds of relationships, body modifications or sexual practices, and so forth.

Feminists used the experiential-knowledge approach to explore and critique the authenticity and validity of personal accounts about women. This is a salient issue for trans people, in that their stories and identities are also often judged inauthentic or false by mainstream society or medical discourses, particularly if these stories and identities don't match authoritative schema that privilege white, heterosexual, and middle-class ideals and norms. Whose stories are "heard" and whose interpretations of reality are seen as authoritative and "true" depends heavily on who is allowed to be the expert on peoples' experience.

A problem with the use of experience and narrative in feminist practice is how to deal with competing versions of the truth. Many feminists attempted to develop a concept of "women's ways of knowing" that suggested that women had access to particular points of view or ways of understanding the world.[5] This viewpoint could be a result of biology, gendered socialization, the experience of social marginalization, women's position in relationships, or perhaps all of these things. But how could this concept make sense of disagreements among women or the power imbalances between women? Moreover, an exclusive focus on the authority of experience carried the danger of assuming that theorizing from one's experience was a straightforward thing, that experience was unmediated truth and required minimal self-reflection. The risk of constant inward-looking is that (limited) experience can often be privileged over self-critique or an awareness of one's position in a broader context. While consciousness development in the individual is important for self-healing, critical collective consciousness, which involves questioning one's own point of view, and understanding oneself as part of a larger social context, is also important.[6] Nevertheless, the use of narrative, various forms of representation, and self-expression as well as the strategy of speaking from lived experience provide tools for political activism for many marginalized groups.

The diverse stories told by trans people defy easy categorization. Until recently, this has been seen as the fault of trans people, not the theories developed about them. Feminists tested ideas about women against their own experiences; trans people are now testing clinical and feminist theories about gender in the same way. Decades later, this feminist practice of telling stories and speaking out is still relevant for trans liberation movements.

NOTES

1 As feminist Kathie Sarachild wrote in 1978, "The purpose of hearing people's feelings and experience was not therapy, was not to give someone a chance to get something off her chest … The idea was to take our own feelings and experience more seriously than any theories which did not satisfactorily clarify them, and to devise new theories which did reflect the actual experience and feelings and necessities of women." "Consciousness-Raising: A Radical Weapon," in *Feminist Revolution* (New York: Random House, 1978), 144–150.

2 Anne Bishop, *Becoming an Ally: Breaking the Cycle of Oppression* (Halifax, NS: Fernwood Books, 1994), 83.

3 As feminist Himani Bannerji notes, "There is no better point of entry into a critique or a reflection than one's own experience. It is not the end point, but the beginning of an exploration of the relationship between the personal and the social and therefore the political." *Thinking Through: Essays on Feminism, Marxism, and Anti-Racism* (Toronto: Women's Press, 1995), 55.

4 See, for example, Lorraine Code, *What Can She Know? Feminist Theory and the Construction of Knowledge* (Ithaca, NY: Cornell University Press, 1991), and Nancy Hartsock, *The Feminist Standpoint Revisited and Other Essays* (Boulder, CO: Westview Press, 1998).

5 See, for example, Mary Field Belenky, *Women's Ways of Knowing: The Development of Self, Voice, and Mind* (New York: Basic Books, 1986).

6 Bishop, *Becoming an Ally*, 80.

CHAPTER 1

ON THE ORIGINS OF GENDER

Darryl B. Hill

A CLASSIC QUESTION IN GENDER STUDIES INVOLVES THE BASIC NATURE OF gendered identities — is gender the expression of an inner essence or a social construction? In other words, what are the origins of gender? Many dismiss such questions as irrelevant and irresolvable philosophical quandaries — *as if* we could ever know the answer or there actually *was* an origin. However, these questions are central to feminist gender theory, especially to those who study trans lives. Amid all this speculation, few have documented what trans persons actually say on the issue. This essay examines debates on the origins of gender — both in feminist theory and the words of everyday Canadian trans men and women — and reveals that the essentialism/constructionism debate (we are born with our essential gender versus our gender is socially constructed) is too simplistic to fully capture the range of positions on the issue.

THE DEBATE

Classical philosophers debated the central question: What exists? Answers to this question varied, but some argued that each entity on earth had a basic essence. That is, "things" were distinguished by a set of basic defining characteristics that would describe the essential elements of that object or being. This is the fundamental premise of the perspective referred to as *essentialism* in gender theory. Essentialism proposes that there are basic, unchangeable essences that distinguish the different kinds of beings in our world. In this perspective, men and women have fundamentally different essences. There is something, at the heart of one's being, that makes one a woman or a man, and since these essences are distinct, they comprise the basic defining characteristics of being gendered. Thus, because there are only two options for gender — woman or man — gender is dichotomous (literally, "of two forms").

Essentialist feminist theory takes many different approaches to considering what makes a man and a woman. Most commonly, and perhaps most obviously, one of the basic differences between women and men is biological: for example, their genetic codes, hormones and anatomies. There are many who believe that these fundamental biological disparities have wide-ranging implications for women's and men's lives, especially in terms of the roles men and women play in reproduction and perhaps extending into other realms of life such as interests, preferences and abilities. Since the genetic essence is constant throughout life, and one's body and hormones remain mostly constant (although they can change during menopause or after medical interventions), biological essentialists believe that the male and female forms are natural and mostly fixed origins of gender present at conception or birth.

In contrast, social constructionism proposes that gender is something that emerges in a social context, produced through social interaction, including language (e.g., learning what "she" and "he" mean), cultural beliefs, social norms and roles. We are not born into our genders; rather, we are gendered by our society. Clearly, this perspective offers a much more fluid basis for gender, with the possibility of slight or even radical change across the history of one's life. Since there is nothing inborn that shapes one's gender, social constructionists propose that gender is often a choice based on the options presented to an individual by their society, their experiences in that culture, and ultimately, how they play the roles offered to them by their world.

Trans Positions on Gender

Theories of gender have become increasingly sophisticated, surpassing initially simplistic dichotomous models in favour of conceptions that integrate the essentialist/constructionist dialectic. At various times, both essentialist and constructionist models were demonized as simplistic and overly deterministic, with one or the other dominating feminist theory over the last thirty years. By the 1990s, these debates spread to discussion about the origins of sexual orientation. Then the waters, as they say, got muddy.

However, how much of this is just *theory*? Have these perspectives been adopted by trans communities? Do the lived experiences of trans people match what feminist theorists propose? Is it possible that these more complex ideas of gender are reflected in the explanations trans people offer for the origins of their own gender? When asked how they explain their gender, how would trans people respond? Twenty-eight trans-identified Torontonians were asked these questions as part of a larger oral history project.[1] Eighteen participants commented directly and substantively on this issue.

It seems clear to most sensible thinkers that the essentialism/constructionism dichotomy is a false one. It is false for some because both essentialism and constructionism may share similar assumptions.[2] Many confuse essentialism with innateness and constructionism with choice, but an essentialist might believe that one's gender is chosen after early experiences, becoming an intrinsic fact of one's person. Thus, we could be nurtured to be gendered in a particular way, but then these choices become an essential aspect of one's being. Another general problem with the essentialism/constructionism dichotomy is that there are weaker and stronger forms of either position. The positions described at the outset of this chapter are now seen as "strong" views, seeing the world in absolutes. Weak constructionists, however, see gender as learned in particular social, historical and political circumstances, but these constructions may develop into essences (for example, sociological essentialism).

Four respondents (Sherry, Sherry Denise, Veronica and Laura) support strong essentialist views, believing they are born with their gender, but that their gender doesn't match their body. Veronica, when asked about the source of her gender, says that she was born with it. When asked to elaborate, she says:

> I don't know if it comes through, you know, different hormonal changes during pregnancy ... and whether it's born or not, and there's some research on brain differences and ... things like that, but ... either way ... it's just something that I have naturally had.

Her gender is something created by hormones or something in the brain; but whatever it is, it is natural and was present at birth.

Three respondents espouse a strong constructionist version of the origin of gender (David, Susan and BC). BC, who has been reading gender theory, is particularly eloquent on this issue:

> I personally see gender as ... something socially constructed … I think that I'm really strong on the nurture side of the nature versus nurture argument … [I] strongly believe that the differences ... between men and women in society are taught to us.

BC supports a strong social constructionist position: she believes there isn't much difference between gender and sex. She says:

> There are problems with this whole idea that … sex is biological and gender is socially constructed … there's a lot of things that don't clearly fall into one area or the other. Do women walk differently than men because they were trained to, or because their thighs are shaped differently?

She flatly and explicitly rejects any essentialist notions of her gender: "I don't have this essentialist idea that there's … this root or this inner spirit [that] … I'm conjuring up and bringing out and channelling ... I don't believe that." However, she allows that there are some biological differences between males and females: "I think that there are some real biological differences relating to reproduction ... But for the most part ... gender is something that we're really ... well trained in."

Most gender studies graduates today integrate both essentialist and constructionist views using either additive or interactive models. Additive models simply assert that biology, in terms of one's "sex," is the foundation and built on top of that is gender, the culturally specific expectations for the sexes. Gender, the construction, is rooted in biological essence. Interactive theories model gender and sex as both born and made, the consequence of biological sex and one's experiences in the world that both interact in complex and multiple ways. An excellent example of an interactionist theory is Devor's analysis of gender blenders,[3] which contends that individuals are assigned a sex and gender identity based on their biology, which then influences how the individual interprets prescriptions for gender in their culture.

Five respondents (Melisa, Jenniffer, Miqqi, Dawna and Donna) offer explanations that are consistent with an additive model. In this view, sex is the biological foundation, but society and culture adds gender. Whereas social constructionists like BC see little difference between sex and gender, those who support an additive model see gender and sex as two different things.

Melisa articulates a classic additive explanation of gender when asked: Is gender born, made, or both? She responds:

> Both. I'd say born because it's always been a conflict, and I think that's been there. I think it's made in the sense that ... I've made it into what it is today ... but I don't think that's a biological thing.

I ask Miqqi about her thoughts on the origins of gender. At first she replies that she really has no idea because no one knows which theory is correct. Then she offers a classic quote from the drag queen RuPaul: "You're born naked and all the rest is drag." Simple, but to the point, this statement illustrates the basic premise of an additive model of gender: you're born with your biology, and everything else is gender.

An illustration of an interactive model is the notion of psychological essentialism, in which one's feelings and emotions, one's sense of self, is at the core of one's being. In this sense, gender is something we use to explain our needs and desires, to make our lives intelligible to others and to guide social interactions. Most who adopt this position see their consciousness as partly socially constructed and mostly stable, but it can and does change.

Five respondents (Glen, Betty, Zena, Sarah and Phyllis) espouse opinions that reflect a psychological essentialist view, in which one's psychological sense of gender identity results from a consideration of one's social role and who one is as a human being. The main thrust of this view is an integration of both essentialist and constructionist elements. Glen is one of the strongest proponents of this view. His notion of psychological essentialism combines the humanistic notion of self-determination with the social role. He believes that we figure out how to play the role of gender based on who we are as human beings. The single best articulation of the psychological essentialist position is his statement "If you really want to know what my gender is, I don't have one. If I have any gender at all, it's Glen. It's Glen in whatever form that I could put myself together ... this is who I am." His is not a socially defined gender role; he is himself.

Betty, who is a post-operative male-to-female transsexual, explains that her sense of identity is based on a sense of comfort with how she plays her role in society. She reflects on her beliefs about gender and who she is in the world saying, "I don't know ... I don't know what I am. I don't even know if I'm a woman right now. I'm just me." She explains why she became a woman: "'Cause I can just be myself. It's easier to be myself in the female role than it is the male role. I don't know if that's female, but it's me." In Betty's understanding, the essence of her self hasn't changed, just other peoples' reactions to her: "From my point of view, I'm still the same person. But the way that people treat me and see me, and the whole world around me, has changed, right?" This illustrates another key element of psychological essentialism: there is a psychological sense of self that remains consistent throughout life.

Perhaps Zena offers the most cogent summary of the psychological essentialist perspective: "Because your gender is what's in your mind, and how you feel inside, and gender is ... the gender you prefer." At the heart of psychological essentialist views are beliefs in the importance of personal desires and preferences.

*

Philosophers have had little luck definitively resolving questions about the nature of our person. Examining the question of whether the nature of persons is constructed or an essence in trans discourse leads to an appreciation of some of the key assumptions underlying each position, the diversity of positions in this debate, and how to synthesize the essentialism/constructionism dialectic.

The above analysis shows that essentialism/constructionism is a false dichotomy. Few positions can be considered absolutely essentialist or constructionist. A few trans persons are hard and fast social constructionists, a few are strong essentialists, but for most respondents, the issue is more complex than earlier theories of gender proposed. Many subscribed to interactive positions, a mix of essentialist and constructionist views, leading to innovative answers on the origins of gender.

Complicating the issue of the origins of gender should encourage gender theorists, especially those working on trans issues to carefully articulate the assumptions underlying their theories and the kinds of essentialism or constructionism they are using. Moreover, it seems that interactive models of gender offer the strongest hope for a fully dynamic and multidimensional conceptualization. A more useful approach to articulate the nature of gender would be to figure out what essences go with what constructions, how and under what conditions.

NOTES

1 Darryl B. Hill, "Genderism, Transphobia, and Genderbashing: A Framework for Interpreting Anti-Transgender Violence," in Barbara Wallace and Robert Carter, eds., *Understanding and Dealing with Violence: A Multicultural Approach* (Thousand Oaks, CA: Sage, 2002), 113–136.

2 Edward Stein, "Conclusion: The Essentials of Constructionism and the Construction of Essentialism," in Edward Stein, ed., *Forms of Desire: Sexual Orientation and the Social Constructionist Controversy* (New York: Oxford University Press, 1990), 325–353.

3 H. Devor, *Gender Blending: Confronting the Limits of Duality* (Bloomington, IN: Indiana University Press, 1989).

CHAPTER 2

THE LANGUAGE PUZZLE: IS INCLUSIVE LANGUAGE A SOLUTION?

Alexander Pershai

No matter what terms one uses, negotiates or invents to talk about transgender issues and experiences, they are sure to suffer from a linguistic deficiency of one kind or another. There are no adequate terms and categories to define and discuss transgender, trans(s)exuality, genderqueer, cross-dressing, et cetera. Every time we try to find such terms, we fail — partly because transgender is very diverse and cannot fit into traditional categories of "the world of men and women" and partly because language offers us a limited set of terms and meanings of gender-related identities and practices.

Some transgender persons try to avoid traditional definitions and categories because these definitions lock them into spaces they don't belong. For them, the application of traditional names and definitions (such as he, she, man, woman) would be violent and offensive. To them, being transgender means freedom from an identity that is defined by such terms. Other transgendered people are happy to be defined and recognized by and within a female/male binary and would find it derogatory if anything else apart from the terms of women and men were used to address them.[1] No matter what position one takes, one ends up with an artificial and unsatisfactory homogenization of transgender people into a generalized "common" category.

Tackling the issue of language means dealing with individual choice of self-identification, limited linguistic resources and the desire to develop a new language that would give a place and an adequate category for everyone. In this essay, I address the concept of inclusive language regarding transgender and question what would be gained and lost by introducing new terms.

*

The question of language reform has been central to feminist thought for about thirty years. Current language structures are viewed as androcentric (male-oriented), sexist formations that exclude and oppress women, as well as other marginalized groups, and make them invisible.[2] Feminist language reform aims to change exclusive "man-made" language into non-sexist language. Some projects, such as *The A–Z of Non-Sexist Language* by Margaret Doyle, suggest inclusive language as an alternative to exclusive language.[3] Inclusive language provides a space and a place for all groups of people and makes everyone visible and (self)identifiable in adequate and respectful terms. Following that logic, it is possible to assume that inclusive language would make space for transgender experience.

However, inclusive language is complicated and contradictory. Linguist Deborah Cameron points out two basic problems of the projects of feminist language reform. The first one is a "lack of inclusiveness." The second is "inoffensiveness as a political goal." The result is a list of "words to avoid rather than discussing shades or meaning within current feminist usage," and an inclusive language that gives a space only for normative women, ignoring minorities of all types.[4] At the same time, "non-sexist language is one of those feminist ideas that has somehow managed to achieve the status of orthodoxy, not just among feminists, but for a great mass of well meaning people and vaguely liberal institutions."[5] That is, using non-sexist language became a matter of sensitivity and being up-to-date when inclusive language itself is reduced to polite and inoffensive definitions of the norm.

The inclusive language project challenges the representation of linguistic resources of and within a male/female binary. Sexism in this context is women's disadvantaged position in society. The creation of non-sexist categories still concern a binary of women and men. The issues of transgender are still erased and so is the repressive mandatory character of sex and gender.

Language has an infinite creative capacity, but at the same time this freedom of creation has to follow particular rules of grammar and semantics.

Linguistic freedom is ambiguous: everybody is free to create but only within the spaces and resources that the existing language provides. Feminist thinker Dale Spender defines this duality of language, the freedom of creation and its limitations to linguistic sources as a language trap.[6] "Once certain categories are constructed within the language, we proceed to organize the world according to those categories. We even fail to see evidence which is not consistent within those categories ... New names systematically subscribe to old beliefs, they are locked into principles that already exist, and there seems no way out of this even if those principles are inadequate or false."[7]

The lack of terms for transgender means we have to generate semantic hybrids by putting together the notions of *sex*, *sexuality* and *gender* together with prefixes such as *trans-*, *inter-* or *cross-*. Language locks us up within the structure that, first, demands that one have a sex/gender, and second, gives us a limited number of categories for that sex/gender, namely, male or female. Of course, to some degree one could use *person* or *one* as a substitute. But such substitutions are problematic because as soon as we come to defining one's relationships to the world the grammar pushes us to use personal pronouns *he* and *she*, *his* or *her*.

Transgender goes beyond the limits of socially and culturally constructed spaces and categories. Transgender shakes up and subverts the "usual," culturally acceptable visions of sex and gender, male and female, femininity and masculinity, normativity and deviation and so on. Transgender is a much more complicated notion than just crossing borders, changing sex or playing with cultural stereotypes. Still we (have to) define transgender by available and not necessarily applicable linguistic resources. We keep on following pre-given meanings and visions of sex and gender and try to inscribe transgender into normative spaces.

As the definitions of normative and culturally recognizable sex and gender are not acceptable for some transgender people, trans communities coin new terms such as *hir* and *s/he* to identify and define transgender. Using such terms helps to make transgender people definable, recognizable and visible, and includes them in social and cultural structures. *Hir* and *s/he* provide transgender individuals with the possibility of a proper self-identification, and of having a name. But *hir* and *s/he* also turn transgender into a social category that can result in mechanisms of both recognition and marginalization. It is possible that the use of *hir* and *s/he* might become mandatory in speech to signify the "correct" gender of a transgender individual. Will a transgender person *hir*self be happy to expose (or be exposed) that *hir* sex and/or gender is modified? Would it be equally desired by all members of a trans community?

The category of transgender emerges into already functioning social structures of male-oriented society where positions of sex and gender are normative, well-definable and recognizable, and where the category of "male" is supreme and all the rest is subordinate. Having a recognizable category for transgender, and unmistakable relevant pronouns such as *hir* and *s/he,* will indicate peoples' place in a social hierarchy. From this perspective *hir* and *s/he,* from the very beginning, would indicate the *difference from the male norm* and signify a subordinate position of transgender in society.

The question of emphasizing difference thus accompanies the construction of a new category. *Hir* and *s/he* help to create a canon, to homogenize the category. Is there a linguistic canon of transgender? No, there is none; transgender is so diverse that even in a rough sense, we can hardly find common ground. Does transgender need a canon? If yes, then what for? Why is there a desire to give transgender a proper, unmistakable definition? Why does one need to know who exactly — he, she or s/he — one is talking to?

Sheilla Jeffreys, specialist in sexual and queer politics, points out that gender is necessary for the construction of heteronormative male supremacy and patriarchal structures. Gender as a category is used to underline the power of heterosexuality and normative society.[8] Transgender as a settled social category might become another resource to create and reinforce patriarchal discrimination. *Hir* and *s/he* will be another position in a hierarchical heterosexual structure; instead of a binary of *he* and *she,* there will be the triplet *he, she* and *s/he*, in which *he* would still be in a supreme position. Trying to invent a new category in and for the already existing structure doesn't change anything in terms of meanings, it just clarifies definitions of the Other, while positions of power remain the same.

At the same time, even without proper definitions, transgender already exists and occupies the very same space as gender. It uses the infrastructure of gender — the basic male/female border — and bodylines, particularly visual, behavioural, verbal and sexual cues. What is unique to transgender is that it uses the cultural abstractions of gender and its individual applications as empty shells, which it then fills with new meanings. And in some cases, the introduction of new terminology or of better, more appropriate and more precise definitions is not necessary, because existing social structure allows manipulations with gender. Thus, this is not a question of outdated meanings. It is a matter of their reappropriation by some transgender individuals who are happy to stay within existing frameworks. It might be the case that transgender could do without "proper" labels.

What is clear is that the choice of introducing, negotiating and using definitions should belong to trans communities. More attention should be given to self-definitions of transgendered people. As anthropologist Don Kulick points out, it is important "to start collecting data about how transgendered persons actually talk — how they use language in a wide variety of social situations to engender themselves and others."[9] And for these purposes it is important that transgender individuals could use adequate definitions such as *hir* and *s/he* but not on a mandatory basis. It should be a matter of individual choice.

I support the desire of the transgender community to have adequate terms to talk about themselves, to be recognizable as transgender individuals, if desired. My doubt concerns the practical outcome of creating a common category of transgender. By creating or negotiating categories, we exercise existing power relations: new categories cannot exist on their own when they are given meanings and conditions within functioning social structures.

As Deborah Cameron points out, instead of replacing sexist terms with non-sexist ones it is more important to focus on meaning and to try to understand the functioning of linguistic resources.[10] Thus far we've discussed the introduction of new definitions and the recreation of already existing categories. By doing so we have not addressed the social system that oppresses transgender, but have merely tried to upgrade it. Perhaps it is more reasonable to focus our efforts on creating a community that would be structured along categories other than sex and gender; a society where the question of having a mandatory gender would be removed or possibly replaced by something else, where the pronouns *he*, *she* or *hir* would be less important in terms of interpersonal communication and social organization.

However, this is clearly a long-term project since our very language is structured along the gender binary in which existing linguistic meanings stand for the specific division of resources of who one can and cannot be or become according to one's gender. I am not sure if it is possible to outline a clear-cut solution for this problem: language and the social infrastructure that marginalize transgender cannot be changed overnight. My concern is to recognize the problems and potential dangers of creating a "homogenized" category for transgender. I believe that gender (self-) identification — both for transgendered and non-transgendered individuals — should not be categorized and should be a voluntary decision for everyone.

NOTES

1 See, for example, works by David Valentine, where he argues the problem of violence of categories for transgender people and gives examples of how identities and practices could be understood differently within a transcommunity. David Valentine, "'The Calculus of Pain': Violence, Anthropological Ethics, and the Category Transgender," *Ethnos* 68, no. 1 (March 2003), 27–48; David Valentine and Riki Anne Wilchins, "One Percent on the Burn Chart: Gender, Genitals and Hermaphrodites with Attitude," *Social Text* 52/53 (Winter 1997), 215–222.

2 Sexism in language is a complicated and heterogeneous issue. There are different and contradictory tendencies to look at the possibilities, advantages and disadvantages of non-sexist language reform. See, for example, Dale Spender, *Man Made Language* (London: Routledge and Kegan Paul, 1980); Deborah Cameron, *Feminism and Linguistic Theory* (New York: St. Martin's Press, 1985); Deborah Cameron, *Verbal Hygiene* (London: Routledge, 1995); and Ann Pauwels, *Women Changing Language* (London: Longman, 1998).

3 See Margaret Doyle, "Introduction to *The A–Z of Non-Sexist Language*," in Deborah Cameron, ed., *The Feminist Critique of Language: A Reader* (London: Routledge, 1998), 149–154.

4 Deborah Cameron, "Lost in Translation: Non-Sexist Language," in Cameron, ed., *The Feminist Critique of Language*, 161, 156, 159.

5 Ibid., 155.

6 As Dale Spender puts it: "This makes language a paradox for human beings: it is both a creative and an inhibiting vehicle. On the one hand, it offers immense freedom for it allows us to 'create' the world we live in ... But, on the other hand, we are restricted by that creation, limited to its confines, and, it appears, we resist, even though they are 'arbitrary,' approximate ones. It is this which constitutes a language *trap*." Dale Spender, "Extracts from *Man Made Language*," in Cameron, ed., *The Feminist Critique of Language*, 96.

7 Ibid., 96, 98.

8 See Sheila Jeffreys, "Heterosexuality and the Desire for Gender," in Diane Richardson, ed., *Theorizing Heterosexuality: Telling it Straight* (Buckingham, UK: Open University Press, 1996), 75–90.

9 Don Kulick, "Transgender and Language: A Review of Literature and Suggestions for the Future," *GLQ: Journal of Lesbian and Gay Studies* 5 (1999), 615.

10 Cameron, "Lost in Translation," 160–163.

CHAPTER 3

FEMALE BY SURGERY

Lesley Carter

I HAVE NO PROFESSIONAL QUALIFICATIONS FOR WHAT I HAVE TO SAY, BUT I am one who successfully crossed the gender line. In early 2002, at age sixty-three, I exchanged the awkward and embarrassing male role that had been forced upon me for my natural and comfortable role as just another woman in the community.

Let me explain what I think certain terms mean. Trans means "across" or "on the other side." In this context it could refer to one of several things: a transvestite or cross-dresser, who likes dressing up in clothing of the "opposite" sex; a transgendered person, who wants to be able to move back and forth from one role to the other, sometimes seeing him/her self as a more or less equal mixture of man and woman; or a transsexual, who is convinced that born gender and felt gender are irreconcilable and must be fixed. Of these three, only transsexuals really and truly believe that they belong in the social role of a woman (male to female, MTF) or a man (female to male, FTM) and live it twenty-four hours a day, every day of the year. This means the MTF transsexual has to cope using the skills and insights of a woman — or not at all.

Feminism, defined as "the movement aimed at equal rights for women" is one of the great unfinished works of our times. Ask any man about it and he will probably say it has gone too far already. Ask any woman and she will know just how much has to be done to gain equal rights for all. The binary gender system supports and enforces the age old traditions of inequality. I know someone born a woman can be a feminist — she holds the copyright — but how about a woman made female by surgery? For one who has seen both sides of the gender scene, the case in favour of feminism is crystal clear. The weight of all history is on the side of subjugating women to men, and it's plainly wrong. The biological argument that only women can bear children is trotted out to justify maintaining a comfortable position for men by making women cater to men's needs. Women are expected to conform and enable men to stay on top — in more ways than one.

When I first began to try out my social role as a woman in 1997, I quickly found out just how differently a woman is treated. For example, an amusing incident happened after I got an oil change at a very good local service centre in 2003, after my sex reassignment surgery. The young technician assumed (correctly) that I was just another (stupid) woman. He brought a little plastic square decal showing the date and kilometrage and placed it in the upper-left corner of the windshield. I noticed it was facing the wrong way and I couldn't read it when inside the car, so I mentioned it. He assured me it would only stick that way. Being a kind-hearted sort of girl, I didn't press the issue, but once back home I turned it the right way around. The poor young chap just couldn't admit that a mere woman would know better than him. He put it on the right way, though, at future oil changes.

I "grew up" very quickly as a woman. It was a necessity. After a few false steps I decided that I was not going to provide free entertainment for any man, yet they all expected it. One man who said he was too shy (or cheap?) to take me out to dinner told me I owed him sexual favours because he was a "gentleman." Others made it quite clear that if I didn't guarantee them sex they weren't even interested in buying me a coffee. My worst experience on a date was when the windshield wiper fell off my car on the way to meet him. When I reached the very full coffee-shop parking lot, I located my date and showed him the wiper blade. I knew my efforts to install it had obviously been ineffective, and he thought he could do a better job. It was winter, and he indicated that I could sit in his car while he snapped the wiper back on. Afterwards, he got into his car and we took off — he didn't even ask me if that was okay. He said he wanted to show me his limousine garage. It was true that he was the owner of a small fleet. Short of jumping out of a moving vehicle I didn't have much choice but to accompany him. Within five minutes of arriving, he grabbed me and tried to kiss me. I pushed him away, and he took the hint. If I hadn't sent such a clear message that I'd put up a fight, I'm sure I would have been raped. My only comfort was that if he had overpowered me he would have found appropriate anatomy between my legs. Pre-op transsexuals often get murdered when their inappropriate genitals are discovered.

I found it interesting that men were unable to understand one simple fact: when they were attracted to me it didn't automatically mean I was attracted to them. I had never realized that many men behaved that way during the time I spent attempting to live in the wrong gender.

My experiences with women were very different. From women, I experienced friendship, help, advice and care. When I told some of my girlfriends about my surgery date, all they wanted to know was whether I was sure about my decision. On being told that I had given it careful thought and was quite certain it was right for me, they just wished me good luck. A girlfriend drove me to the airport to go to Thailand where my surgery took place, and a transsexual girlfriend picked me up when I got back. A few days before leaving for my surgery I visited a dear woman friend and told her about how I would have to wear sanitary pads for a few weeks due to post-operative bleeding. She got her own supplies out, and demonstrated how much they would hold using water. I was really touched. She had no daughters, but she was teaching me in the same way a mother would initiate her daughter into the mysteries of menstruation.

Come to think of it, women were the only choices I had for assistance, as I wasn't close enough friends with any man to ask for that kind of favour. It's not that I hate men, but they just don't fit into my life in the same supportive way. I've never had any problem in relating to women. When approaching that most radical of surgeries — the "sex change operation" — one of the reasons I wanted it was so that no woman would ever need to fear that I had male designs on her. I think that women have always seen femininity in me. The surgery was just something I had to do to bring closure to the old me.

So, I think I'm a feminist. I haven't joined any group, but I feel more empathy with women than men. I never understood men, and I still don't. Women seem to understand why I had to have surgery to make my anatomy conform to my felt gender. Men usually just clutch their genital region and turn pale. Women understand me in a supportive way that men generally don't seem capable of.

Gay men are an exception. They have proven that they really are a girl's best friend. I was forced out of my home in early 2002 as a result of a dysfunctional family coming to a boil. A gay couple I knew took me in and sheltered me for over two months. They advised me when I wanted advice and helped me move. There was never any pressure. I learned that some gay committed relationships put many heterosexual marriages to shame with the constancy of their love and support.

I'll never know whether I would have come to feminism if I hadn't realized that I was a woman and started living like one. I firmly believe that I was born a woman but lived in an uncomfortable denial for many years. I thought I was very sympathetic and supportive to the woman's movement. It was only after my transition that I realized just how far short of the mark I had been! When a man feels challenged by a strong and capable woman, he may assert himself and try to put her in her place, often without being aware of it himself. If she won't accept his "authority," there is a whole library of uncomplimentary expressions he can use to describe her. He cannot lose. Either he makes his point and dominates her, or he leaves the situation knowing that he only lost the battle and will win the war since he has the weight of patriarchal privilege throughout history on his side.

One interesting illustration of this is the difficulty many transsexuals have in speaking in an effective female voice. Pitch is the least of the qualities that distinguish the differences between the way the sexes speak. Vocabulary, inflection, gestures and the like are much more important. I've heard some trans women who can speak fairly well until they get into a threatening situation. Then the commanding baritone returns — they have simply reverted to the authoritative male way of speaking that they are so comfortable with so that they can regain control of the situation. I've noticed how my own voice becomes husky sometimes, but I've trained myself to keep it true to who I know I am.

How do I know that I'm seen as a woman by women? I'm not talking about looking like a woman but about being accepted as one of them in essence. In daily life, in the community, I have few problems. For example, I campaigned with a political candidate and knocked on hundreds of doors with her, always getting a favourable reception. I handed out hundreds of ballot papers as an election official. There were no questioning looks or challenging questions.

There have also been other, more intimate, examples of acceptance. A couple of years ago, before my surgery, I took a female friend visiting from abroad to Montreal to enjoy Quebec culture just before she went back to her homeland. Since we were both fairly poor, I arranged for us to stay with a former student of mine. I expected that we would occupy the hostess' sons' twin beds and had told my friend that, while we might have to share a room, we would have separate beds. Imagine my embarrassment when our hostess said we could use her queen size bed, since she worked nights. I found that the boys shared a double bed anyway! I didn't know what would happen, but my friend just took it in her stride, changed in the bathroom, we climbed into bed and we went off to sleep. I was greatly relieved that she treated the situation exactly the same as if I been a natal-female friend.

Natal women who know me see me as a natural ally. They see me as more similar to them than different and well within the norms of natal females. I like that.

Now that leaves me with one final problem and no answer — how to explain a too-common complaint. Many trans women report that they are regularly rejected as being women and are treated as men. In the 1999 movie *Better Than Chocolate* (directed by Anne Wheeler), the main transsexual character is physically assaulted in a woman's washroom by a hostile and angry lesbian. There was once a gay bar in Whitby, Ontario, now closed, which banned all transsexuals from the women's washroom, at the insistence of some lesbians. Many of my friends are woman and some are lesbian, yet they never had any problem with me even before my surgery. Am I just lucky? I refuse to speculate on the reason. All I can say is that discrimination has never been my experience. Are women just being kind to me? I'd like to think it goes a lot deeper than that, but you must be the judge.

CHAPTER 4

SOMETIMES BOY, SOMETIMES GIRL: LEARNING TO BE GENDERQUEER THROUGH A CHILD'S EYES

Shannon E. Wyss

"Would you be my pretend daddy?"

So asked the adorable little girl who was sitting on my lap and whom i'd known since she was a baby. I'll call her Shante here. She was four years old. I was in my mid-twenties. And i was stunned. Sure, she'd never really been able to tell what gender i was. Sometimes she referred to me as "she"; sometimes she talked about me as "he." Occasionally, the other adults at the organization where i volunteered would try to correct her and tell her what the "right" pronouns were. But she always returned to using "she" and "he" interchangeably for me.[1]

In response to her question, i wrapped my arms around her as tightly as i could. I ached inside that she felt so deeply, at her young age, the absence of a biological father in her life. I kissed her and told her that, yes, i would be her pretend daddy. We went on playing school, she, her sister and i. As far as i could tell, Shante promptly forgot about it and, five minutes later, was treating me like she always had.

Her question, however, burned in my mind for days, weeks, months afterwards. Indeed, it still burns there today, six years later. It is one of the few *moments* in my life that i can recall with deep clarity and that i can name with absolute certainty as a crucial, instantaneous "turning point." What did it mean, i wonder(ed), for this child to ask me to be her "pretend daddy" when she is black and i am white? What kind of "daddy" could i be as a gentle, affectionate, unconditionally loving, unmacho, nurturing human being? As someone who is attentive to children's needs, who doesn't laugh in front of them at the cute things that they say, and who insists on respecting them as people who have both a humanity and rights equal to my own? Could i give Shante another idea of what masculinity is and can be? Or had she already incorporated the ways in which i interacted with her into what her vision of a daddy was?

When this girl asked me to be her pretend daddy, i had been studying transgender and becoming an ally of the trans community in the U.S. for five years. But all my reading and analysis had never really been about me. Sure, dressed in jeans, a sweatshirt and tennis shoes, i cut a somewhat ambiguous figure. Add to that my shaved head, my 4-foot-11-inch frame and my skinny body, small breasts, makeup-less face and unabashedly hairy legs and you have a person who gets stared at on those rare occasions when i wear a skirt. I'm too unfeminine-looking to be a woman, people's eyes seem to say. But if i was a pre-pubescent boy, i wouldn't have all that hair on my legs. So i get the "Is it a boy or a girl?" stare a lot.

Mostly i just ignore people. And before Shante, i had never really stopped to reconsider, to own, to take further responsibility for my dyke identity. In that one instant, however, this child crystallized for me the issues that had been lurking in the back of my mind for a year or more: How did i see my own gender? How did i wish to be gendered? Did i really want to keep trying to fit into a tiny gender box? Could i do my gender another way? Weren't folks' reactions to me — including Shante's — evidence of the fact that i was already doing it another way?

Suddenly, the boundaries of my feminism were pushed even further. I had claimed feminist as an identity since sixth grade, when my best friend at the time informed me that women earned less than men. My politics had only grown more radical in the ensuing years. My feminism had changed and evolved to encompass not only issues specific to the generic middle-class white woman, but to the situations faced by men, people of colour, those who are economically disadvantaged, immigrants, folks here in the U.S. who don't speak English, lesbians & gays,[2] bisexuals, S&M folks, youth, disabled people, fat people, trans people, intersexed folks and those in the polyamory community. In college and afterwards, feminism for me became a politics about the liberation of all people through the elimination of gender stereotypes and compulsory, binary gender boxes.

My own personal brand of feminism included mainstream women's issues (like equal pay for equal work and reproductive freedom). But it had also morphed until it was about the right of every person to decide what to do with their bodies; the freedom of all people to engage in any consensual sexual activity, social permission for children to learn about sex and sexuality whenever they are ready to ask about it; the right of immigrants to work for decent wages and not to be terrified of harassment, rape or being deported in retaliation for asserting their claims to just treatment; the freeing of men to be feminine, to experience the full range of human emotions and of women to be masculine and aggressive and to learn how to fight; and a whole host of other issues that touch the lives of women and of all other people.

When Shante asked me her question, my feminism mushroomed to encompass gender non-conformity in a way that it never had before: genderqueerness (which refers to people who are neither men nor women, neither masculine nor feminine, but are a gender for which we have no word in the English language) was now about *me*. I had, in short, become the nightmare of the religious right and, sadly, of many feminists, especially second-wave middle-class American women who grew up in the 1960s and 1970s. It was and continues to be frustrating to me that baby-boomer feminists,[3] lesbian feminists of the 1970s and many others can't see that the things that concern me also affect the lives of all women. It is even harder to know that these same feminists will unleash such vitriol against us radical Generation X and Generation Y queers.

Each of us stands on the shoulders of those who have come before us. If it wasn't for lesbian feminists' struggle to have lesbianism accepted as a legitimate sexual orientation, i wouldn't be able to fight for the recognition of genderqueerness. If it wasn't for other feminists' insistence that women control their bodies, i wouldn't be able to advocate for the rights of trans people and intersexed folks to make their own decisions about their bodies. Unfortunately, many feminists who are older than i am seem to see my world view not as a building upon theirs but as a turning away from what they have stood for and as a threat to their very identities and existence. And while i have deep respect for their beliefs, even if i don't always agree with them, it is hard to believe that many of them have an equal amount of respect and open-mindedness for my points of view.

For instance, i have heard feminists allege that trans men are traitors to the feminist cause or that they have abandoned butch lesbians. Others lay exclusive claim to the definition of womanhood, arguing that male-to-female transsexuals are not "true women" because they were born with penises and were raised as boys. Some feminists state that male-bodied people who do a feminine gender are mocking bio-women, not expressing their inner selves. And still others articulate a concern that genderqueer identities undermine their own womanhood. I see such people refusing to consider how their lives and trans lives might be similar, how trans issues might overlap with feminist and bio-women's issues. I see them advocating hatred of gender radicals, wanting us out of "their" feminist community, wishing to silence our experiences and insights and to distance themselves from gender non-conformity. This sort of split is indicative of the generation gaps endemic in the U.S. and of adults' refusal to respect the culture and the contributions of youth to society. But it also signals a fear, a deep and abiding terror that opening our gender boxes, loosening the bonds around our bodies and minds, will somehow unleash a force that will destroy feminism, feminist gains and "the women's community."

To be fair, i can also gladly describe the tremendous amount of support that i have received from many of the feminists in my own life. My best friend, a couple of my co-workers, another radical queer, a straight friend, my girlfriend, all have been tremendously supportive. These people — women, dear friends and feminists all — have fully embraced my identity. They think that my genderqueerness is completely legitimate; they are unwavering allies and they reflect my identity back at me by being at least as enthusiastic about it as i am. All of them know from their personal lives what it's like to be on the fringes of society. They are bisexual, polysexual, polyamorous, queer, working class or of colour; they have dated interracially or have gone out with members of the "same sex"; they have seen war and strife in the Peace Corps. They are all amazing Generation X feminists.

I have also received support from more mainstream women. Since 1995, i have belonged to a local feminist choir, which is populated mostly by middle-aged white women. Some of them identify as straight, some are lesbian, a few are bi. Most of them hold jobs that are not directly connected with social justice work. Few of them have studied feminist or trans theory.

Several years ago, when i decided to come out to them as genderqueer, i was concerned. What would they think? Would they kick me out? I knew that that was possible since my choir had, for over twenty years, defined itself as a feminist *women*'s singing group. I worried about the freak-out factor. This group was the only same-sex one to which i belonged, and it was a group to which i had contributed and of which i had been an integral part since i moved to Washington, DC. I worried that, by coming out as genderqueer, i was jeopardizing my membership in the choir and my relationship with most members. I was not at all sure what kind of response to expect from these strong feminist women.

Much to my surprise, they accepted me totally. More than a few expressed their disappointment that i was worried about their reactions and had, as a result, waited for over a year to come out to them as genderqueer. Since that time, the group as a whole decided, with no prodding from me, to redefine itself. We are now no longer a feminist women's choir but a feminist choir. We have continued to have a very constructive and respectful dialogue about how inclusive to become, and i'm pleased that i have not been the only choir member to speak out in favour of more openness. We are, at least in theory, open to members of any sex or gender. And while no man or trans person has yet tried to join, i feel confident that, when and if such a day comes, the answer to that query about membership will not be "no." Hir[4] presence will undoubtedly cause some discomfort and consternation, for it will force the group to move away from thinking of itself as a women's choir in a much more concrete way than my presence ever could. But i also feel confident that, at least as the group stands now, we will be willing to deal with those challenges and to face the changes that a man's, trans person's, genderqueer's or intersexed individual's presence in the group will bring — and also to embrace the gifts that those types of feminists could contribute.

I look at my choir and see the small revolution that i have unwittingly wrought. I did not come out to them to change the group; i came out to them because i needed their help as we headed to a women's choral festival in the summer of 2001. I was deeply concerned about how i would be received there, and i needed to get the support and encouragement of the women with whom i would be travelling. And yet i not only got my choir's support; i got their endorsement, an endorsement that manifested itself both through individuals' willingness to risk examining their own beliefs and assumptions, and through redefining our group, rewriting our statement of purpose and opening up our membership criteria.

My actions have changed a small corner of my world and, along with other members' support and openness, have made my choir a more welcoming place for any gender non-conformers who come after me. I know from what other singers have told me that my coming out has also created a more welcoming environment for bisexual members and for those who might otherwise not fit the strict rules of 1970s lesbian feminist communities. I look at this accidental accomplishment and i am incredibly proud. I think: maybe if i can change my chorus, then i can help to change "gender-unfriendly" feminists as well.

Support for genderqueers, trans people, genderfuckers, gender warriors — however we define ourselves — can come from all kinds of feminist-identified women as long as we genderqueers are ready to take the risk to talk to non-trans feminists and as long as they are prepared to listen to us. For those other feminists, it only takes an open mind, a willingness to examine one's previously held assumptions, a respect for how other people define themselves and a willingness to stretch one's own world view. Therein lies the feminist genderqueer revolution. It is a revolution, a risk, a challenge and a pleasure to which i call all feminists, no matter what their gender identity, gender expression or gendered experience. We all have something to gain from trans and genderqueer feminist insights and lives.

It appears that Shante already knew that. She never seemed fazed that i didn't fit into one of her preconceived gender boxes. At four years old, she didn't know that i had to be one or the other, that i could never change. So she accepted me as sometimes boy/sometimes girl. And it was wonderful. Shante — this girl with her confusion over which pronouns to use for me — was more right about my gender identity than any of the other children or adults with whom we played. She knew, albeit unconsciously and apolitically, that gender isn't innate and that it's not binary, something that many adults have a difficult time grasping. Yes, i realize that she'll learn a different gender order as she gets older, as more and more messages of gender-conformity and gender-binarism are heaped upon her head. As the truism goes, bigots are taught, not born. And it saddens me to think that someday, should we ever meet again, Shante will likely demand to know "what" i am. She will no longer be content to see me as sometimes boy/sometimes girl. But the fact that she did, at one point in her life, know that gender is messy and fun and flexible, that she could create me in a certain gendered image to fill a deep void in her heart, gives me hope that the rest of us can relearn that, too, for we *all* undoubtedly knew that truth when we were four years old.

Yes, breaking out of our boxes can seem scary. But it can also be a hell of a lot of fun. And it promises to offer all of us much more room to grow than if we stay trapped in those prisons labelled man and woman. Despite what many feminists might believe, my genderqueerness is not an attack on women, a tearing down of their pride in womanhood or a demand that they change how they see themselves; my identity is about me and about wanting to make more options for all of us. But those options are just that: options. Wouldn't you rather that those two genders be rooms that you could choose to enter if they feel comfortable for you instead of cells that we are forced to inhabit from birth? I know that i would. I think that Shante felt similarly. And i hope that you do, too.

NOTES

1 When not at the beginning of a sentence, i leave my first person subject pronouns lowercase. The fact that, in English, we only capitalize the pronoun "I" seems indicative of the self-centredness of much of Western culture: I am more important that you, she, he, it, we or they. As such, my use of "i" signals a rejection of ego-centric cultural norms and values.

2 I join "lesbians & gays" by an ampersand to create a *visual* signal to the reader that highlights the historical conflation of male and female homosexualities, as well as the disturbing tradition of using these words to erase bisexual, trans and genderqueer lives.

3 Baby boomers make up the generation born between 1946 and 1964; Generation Xers were born between 1965 and 1980; and members of Generation Y were born after 1980.

4 "Hir" (pronounced "here") is a gender-neutral, third-person object or possessive pronoun. Its subject equivalent, in my writing, is "ze," although other authors use different gender-neutral subject pronouns, such as s/he.

CHAPTER 5

WALKING IN THE SHADOWS: THIRD GENDER AND SPIRITUALITY

Gigi Raven Wilbur

MY BIOLOGICAL FATHER WAS A MINISTER. I AM A CHANGELING. A CHANGELING is a human baby that is switched out with a faerie[1] infant shortly after birth. Such children are considered to be problem children and full of mischief. Needless to say, my father and I did not mix well. I had a rough time growing up. I was born with undifferentiated genitalia, or in common language, I was born a hermaphrodite, intersex, defined as "a range of anatomical conditions in which an individual's anatomy mixes key masculine anatomy with key feminine anatomy."[2] I do not know whether my parents were informed of this. When I was born, it was common medical practice to take the newborn infant to another room, perform genital reassignment surgery and return the infant to the mother without informing the parents and without documenting it in the medical records.[3]

What I would like to cover here are the emotional components, the moral implications and the gender mysteries of being a hermaphrodite from an intersex perspective. Some concerns and issues overlap with trans issues, some differ and diverge. In my search for the truth, I was taken on many paths that few have ever walked. It has been a spiritual journey, as well as a journey of personal development.

As I grew up, many attempts were made by many people to socialize me as a male. They all failed completely, even though I did try my best to be a male. Even as a child, I knew I was different in many ways. I also knew that I did not have what it took to be male or female. Instinctively, I knew I was something else.[4] It took me over twenty years to learn that I was intersexed.

When I was around ten years old, I went into a severe depression that lasted for several years. Looking back, I know part of this was due to being a hermaphrodite and not having a place to fit into society. Our society allows only two genders to exist, and I was not one of those. Transsexual individuals often report not feeling a "fit" between their bodies and their true gender identity. It is termed gender dysphoria. I certainly felt gender dysphoria, and I think other kids felt something was different about me. They would have little to do with me at that time. I soon started going for long walks in the woods by myself. It was during these walks that I discovered the energies, the goddess and the faeries. Even though I did not know it then, I became a solitary pagan. This new-found spirituality helped me get over my depression and led me to the feminist path I follow now.

On an emotional level, it has been difficult to deal with living in a gender-dualist world. The doctors who performed genital reassignment surgery on me could not cut deep enough to take away my true gender. This has caused some complications. Because of the illusion that the doctors created in my body, many see me as male. It is very difficult to break the illusion. I remember many times going to a transsexual bar dressed in a dress and having people come up to me and say I should make more of an effort to look female. There was an assumption that I was transsexual and making a poor attempt at passing as female. They did not understand that I was going for an androgynous look; I was passing for who I am, a ladyboy. I did not wear a bra or padding, nor did I make any attempt to hide the bulge in my crotch.

Living in a gender-dualist world creates the fertile ground for a concept in the transsexual community called passing, or attempting to look as much like one gender or another as possible. From my experience, there seems to be a split in the transgender community between those who can pass as a gender in which they were not born and those who cannot pass because there are too many masculine or feminine characteristics that cannot be hidden or masked. I see this as dehumanizing and destructive to the transsexual movement.

A healthier approach is to see each individual as a free agent in their gender expression. With some creativity, I could envision a world where a multitude of genders are expressed. Passing creates a judgemental environment littered with standards of what it is to be female and what it is to be male. Who is qualified to determine these standards? Won't these standards always be subjective and easily influenced by social standards?

In modern mainstream American and Canadian society, hermaphrodites have been eradicated from existence. As a result of my unwilling reassignment surgery, I cannot get my true gender documented on a driver's licence or any other legal document. When I fill out forms, I have to lie. I have to choose either male or female. If I were to seek out new surgery, I would have only one option: to be reassigned as a female. When I use a public restroom, I have two choices: to use the men's room or the women's room. Society does not provide a restroom for hermaphrodites.

We are taught that one day we will be attracted to a member of the opposite sex, yet for me, there is no opposite sex. I live in the shadows. I cannot be the gender that I was born. But should this not be a birthright? Why am I not allowed to have both a penis and a vulva? I was born with both — why do I have to choose? When a doctor eradicates a gender, keeps it a secret and sends that infant out to the world, a moral crime has been committed.

I could easily say that I did not create the illusion of my gender presentation; the doctors did. I could further rationalize that since society does not allow my true gender to exist, that I am justified in maintaining the illusion. But I know that this is an illusion and a lie. I cannot live a lie. In the transsexual community, there is a similar dilemma. Should one inform a partner that one is transsexual or keep it secret? It becomes a more difficult question for those who are post-surgery and are attempting to integrate as the reassigned gender. I feel that part of the answer lies in moving away from a dualist gender perspective at a societal level and moving towards a spectrum of gender identities, which is more reflective of what nature actually produces.

*

In my undergraduate and graduate studies, I researched ancient civilizations and ancient religion. I also studied human sexuality. In ancient times, in many cultures, there was a social role for people like me. We were often the shamans, spiritual leaders; we had a function and place in society. Even more importantly, we were acknowledged as a distinctly different gender. We existed.

The ancients believed that people who were intersex, transgender and/or transsexuals — people who were able to bend gender lines — were people who could walk in both the physical world and the realm of the spirit. They felt that bending gender lines prepared these individuals and gave them the ability to experience the non-material realm. In some cultures — Sumerian, Roman and Greek — these were the people who became the sacred prostitute priestesses. Spiritually, I am an eclectic pagan who draws on these traditions. I worship the goddess and follow a matriarchal-egalitarian path that diverges greatly from a patriarchal structure. Paganism is a feminist spirituality that celebrates the goddess as well as the god. In a patriarchal structure, a small group, usually composed of men, has power over the people. In an egalitarian structure, power is shared between all. Each person, regardless of gender, is encouraged to grow and develop. Each person governs his/her own spiritual development. The priest and priestess have no special power-over-others role.

What is it like to be one of the third gender? I am neither female nor male, and I am both female and male. A living paradox, I walk on both sides of our society's gender line. While we do not have an adequate vocabulary for my experience, for me. On a neurological level, I am wired differently from other people. EEGs have shown I have over twice the normal neurological connections between the hemispheres of my brain. While I do not know of any research on this, I do believe that the differences in neurological wiring are tied in with my gender.

My body functions differently than most people's; I am able to have different types of orgasms. While there are many men who are learning techniques to achieve multiple and full-body orgasms (through programs like "The Body Electric" and other techniques like tantra), I started having different types of orgasms from the start of puberty without training. I have male-type orgasms with an erection and ejaculation, and I have female-type orgasms deep within that do not include ejaculation. These can occur with or without an erection. I have full body orgasms and multiple orgasms. On rare occasions, I experience the male-type orgasm simultaneously with the female type orgasm. (These are incredible!) I experience gender from a third gender perspective.

For women and men, sexuality, sacred sex and sex magick[5] can be very powerful. It is said that a woman reaches her full magickal power when she has moon time (menstruation). Many women experience erotic and sexual energy during their moon time too, as well as at other times. Men are able to reach their power through their sexuality in sex magick. While these energies, female and male, are different, they have similarities. Both women and men have cycles in mood, energy and sexual performance. It is something common for all people, no matter what sex or gender we happen to be. In my first year of puberty, I brought the two together when I had moon time combined with my male sexuality and was able to experience different types of orgasms simultaneously.

On a spiritual level, I function as a prostitute priestess. I do a lot of work in sacred sex and sex magick. It is my calling. I work on sexual healing and body-image healing. We all live in a sex-negative society where human sexuality becomes objectified. One of the consequences of living in a sex-negative society is that people tend to repress and deny many of their sexual feelings, especially negative sexual feelings, having been wounded on a psycho-sexual level. When this happens, it can affect sexual functioning. As a hermaphrodite, I am able to work with both female and male energy and assist people in the journey of self healing.

In the ancient sacred sex temples in Greece, people went to the temple not only to worship but also to be worshipped. People went to the temple to learn about sex, sacred sexuality and to practise sex magick. In modern mainstream society, we do not have an institution that provides these services. It is these principles that first drew me to become a prostitute priestess.

I currently run a sacred sex temple. During the day, I give educational workshops on a variety of topics that focus on sex and sacred sexuality. I also do workshops on body-image healing, tantric sex and sexual functioning for both women and men. At night, I open the sacred sex temple. Part of my role is to raise erotic energy, create a sacred space and provide a safe environment for people to explore sexuality and sacred sex. A large part of what I do is to facilitate people joining together with other patrons of the temple and help maintain a sex-positive environment. I open my body and channel sex energy within the temple. I invite each patron to not only worship in the temple but also to be worshipped as a sacred sexual entity. I see the human body as a home for the spirit that resides within and the body is a sacred temple in and of itself. I came up with a phrase for the temple a few years ago that states "If the Goddess had intended for humans to have sex, she would have given us genitals." It was inspired by the phrase "All acts of love are of the Goddess and She gives her blessing to those who perform acts of love."

Unlike the ancient sacred prostitute priestesses, I do not offer direct sexual services, and we do not provide temple prostitutes for sexual services. Instead, we follow a modern approach, helping facilitate sex between temple patrons. The temple is evolving, and I consider it a work in progress. Each time we run the temple, it improves and we discover new techniques to create a safe sex-positive environment for patrons to learn, connect with other patrons and to fly in ecstasy.

*

When a baby is first born, one of the first questions asked usually is: "Is it a boy or a girl?" We are an it, not a person, until that question is answered. Our gender and our sex is an intrinsic part of our identity. I find it interesting that a multi-billion-dollar industry steps in once the question is answered to reinforce the decision. That industry follows us throughout our lives, guiding us in our purchasing decisions, not only for ourselves but for others. A binary gender system puts us all into a set of categories that are unrealistic and harmful, especially when there is inequality between females and males.

Being intersex, the third gender, is not actually all that difficult for me. The hard part is living with the restrictions imposed on me by society. I am who I am, even if there is no name for me. I know who and what I am. The gender mysteries I am talking about don't have anything to do with my body parts or my gender identity, but with the boxes other people try to force me into. But even people who do fit into one of the "normal" categories of gender don't always fit neatly. Wouldn't it be a lot better if we could just be who we are and not have to worry about labels? Perhaps as people learn more about the complexity of gender, we can step away from rigid gender roles and stereotypes and allow people to develop, independent of gender, into fully actualized human beings.[6]

NOTES

1 The Radical Faerie Movement was started by Harry Hay and uses this spelling of "faerie" as part of its tradition.

2 See the website www.isna.org/drupal/node/view/91.

3 For more information about this practice, see Alice Domvrat Dreger, "'Ambiguous Sex' or Ambivalent Medicine?" (March 18, 2006), available online at www.isna.org/articles/ambivalent_medicine.

4 I will not go into all the physiology here, but if you are interested, go to www.isna.org/ to learn more about the physiology of being a hermaphrodite (intersex).

5 In many modern pagan communities the word "magic" is spelled "magick."

6 Recommended reading includes Donald Michael Kraig, *Modern Sex Magick: Secrets of Erotic Spirituality* (Woodbury, MN: Llewellyn Publications, 1998); Colin Spencer, *The Gay Kama Sutra* (New York: Griffin SMP, 1997); Starhawk, *Spiral Dance* (New York: Harper and Row, 1979); John Sulak and V. Vale, *Modern Pagans: An Investigation of Contemporary Pagan Practices* (San Francisco: RE/Search, 2001); Deborah Sundahl, *Female Ejaculation and The G-Spot: Not Your Mother's Orgasm Book!* (London: Fusion Press, 2004); U.D. Frater, *Secrets of Western Sex Magic*, 3rd ed. (Woodbury, MN: Llewellyn Publications, 2001).

SECTION II

Identities & Alliances

INTRODUCTION

Krista Scott-Dixon

POLITICAL ORGANIZING BASED ON SHARED IDENTITIES can foster a sense of solidarity and pride for marginalized groups and provide a foundation for resisting oppression. For oppressed people, "identity politics" can be an active process of self-definition that is then extended into a larger collective project.[1] Formerly shameful and devalued elements of oneself, along with previously pejorative terms such as "dyke" can be transformed and reclaimed as part of group struggles. Famous political slogans such as "Black is beautiful" or "Sisterhood is powerful" provide a focal point for disenfranchised people to locate themselves personally and form a shared political identity.

However, building a political movement on the assumption of a homogeneous, easily distinguished group runs the risk of creating a climate in which policing difference and enforcing sameness within that group feels politically necessary.[2] It can be difficult to theorize an identity that is not relational — that isn't dependent on figuring out who is "us" and who is "them" or on defining oneself as "not-like-them." Identities that may appear straightforward, such as "feminist" or "trans person," may not be an adequate basis for an alliance between people if political positions or world views are not also shared. Turf wars, ideological disputes, battles over strategy and debates over who is to be included under the umbrella of these labels are ongoing in any such group. Feminist organizations continue to struggle over how to understand diverse identities and respond to differences among women in a positive way. Likewise, trans people and organizations have also struggled in their search for organized resistance to multiple oppressions.

Given that we are all complex people with not just one but multiple identities — any combination, for example, of working class, woman, feminist, parent, immigrant or queer — how does one go about deciding which will take primacy? This question has been a divisive one for feminists who have struggled for decades to articulate the links and contradictions between their status as women and their other identities.[3] One danger that feminists identify is that an excessive focus on multiple identities can dilute a focused resistance to structures of power.[4] It can also lead to personal fragmentation. Attempts to name one's many selves can be both empowering and an exercise in frustration, especially if not enough good labels are available.[5] Trans identities in particular may also be time-limited or contingent on shifting circumstances. While the majority of people who decide to identify as feminist will probably do so for life, the same cannot be said of most trans people. Some will reject the identity of trans entirely and argue that he or she is simply a man or a woman who needed corrective medical intervention for a disability or disorder.

Some identities tend to be more visible than others, which shapes people's choices about when to identify as a member of a particular group. People whose skin colour, age or visible disability "marks" them for public scrutiny are not as able to "fly under the radar" as people who can hide elements of themselves. Gender is an identity that is at once *hypervisible* and *invisible.* It's hypervisible because we like to be able to judge a person's gender immediately and those who are non-normatively gendered stand out. It's invisible in that its status as something normal and natural is taken for granted and because many of us can, if we choose, hide our gender identity beneath our gender presentation. Gender may also be temporarily subsumed by our membership in another identity group, and this other identity may be more relevant or immediately felt in certain contexts.

For example, we may identify more strongly with our nationality, Aboriginal status or age group in particular situations, especially those in which we are seen as "different" based on those elements — an older person encountering a gang of teenagers will immediately be seen by the young people as "not like us" on the basis of age. We may be seen to rescind our membership in a gender group through certain behaviours or self-presentations; our status as a "real man" or "real woman" may be called into question. Thus, while gender appears to be an apparently straightforward characteristic of group identity, its coherence can be easily disrupted. Feminists and trans activists have grappled with how to build a movement based on a shared recognition of gender oppression while allowing for a diversity of identities and experiences.

Questions of collective and personal identity are tied to questions of alliances. With whom and how should one ally oneself in order to work towards social justice? Should one seek out others with whom one shares an identity, such as other mothers, other East Asians, other lesbians or other working-class people? Should one seek out political compatriots who share similar political views but whose other identities may be diverse? What strategies emerge from mobilizing around shared or diverse identities?

One approach that feminists have traditionally used is to organize around a shared identity as women. Shared identity can provide a "safer space" in one way but can create problems in another. For instance, women's shelters are based on the notion of women coming together as women for safety. Yet women who seek shelter from abusive partners may find that women's shelters do not meet racialized women's needs for cultural sensitivity, provide accessibility for women with disabilities or understand that lesbians in abusive relationships also require support. The issue of differences among women is addressed further in this book's third section, "Inclusion and Exclusion."

Thus, another approach is to work with others who share affinities rather than identities. Organizing around particular issues has often meant uneasy alliances for both feminists and trans people. For example, in the 1980s and 1990s, some feminist groups, particularly in the United States, allied themselves with the religious right and conservative groups to battle pornography, a decision that has had long-reaching consequences for both freedom of sexual expression and the availability of information and resources on sexuality. Trans people have often sought shelter under the umbrella of gay/lesbian/bisexual organizations. While this strategy has certain advantages, such as the benefit of a more well-developed movement and infrastructure, and many shared interests, it has also has its problems. While queer communities have traditionally provided many spaces for alternative gender roles and identities, some gays, lesbians and bisexuals have expressed hostility towards trans people. Some gays and lesbians may feel that the presence of trans people delegitimizes a gay rights movement that has become largely mainstream, while others feel that queers will not be liberated until a wide spectrum of sexual identities is accepted. Similar discussions emerged around other dimensions of social marginalization, such as race-ethnicity or poverty, that intersect with both queer and trans status. Finally, although plenty of queers are also trans, a great number of trans people not only identify as straight but feel quite uncomfortable about being lumped into a group that is bounded by a sexual orientation that they do not share. They may even be openly homophobic.

Another fraught alliance has been between feminists and men. Despite the presence of many notable male supporters throughout feminism's history, such as W.E.B. Du Bois[6] and Frederick Douglass, pro-feminist men are still often regarded with suspicion and/or hostility. Many feminists argue that only women can be feminists and that female biology and/or life history as a female are key qualifications. Chapters in this section address the question of feminist masculinity as well as women-only spaces and identify how such concepts are based on a certain model of identity.

Activist Bernice Johnson Reagon argues that coalition work means working across differences of identity and this process can result in enduring discomfort in order to achieve shared political aims: "Coalition work is not work done in your home. Coalition work has to be done in the streets. And it is some of the most dangerous work you can do."[7] However, she says, a movement built on the acknowledgement of multiple identities, and differences among women, is key to a sustainable feminist movement. "The reason we are stumbling is that we are at the point where in order to take the next step we've got to do it with some folk we don't care too much about. And we got to vomit over that for a little while. We must just keep going."[8]

NOTES

1 Himani Bannerji, *Thinking Through: Essays on Feminism, Marxism, and Anti-Racism* (Toronto: Women's Press, 1995), 10.

2 As feminist theorist Chris Weedon indicates, the major difficulty with identity politics for long-term organizing is "the tendency to define identity in particular fixed ways which ultimately work to exclude many of those [people] that the group in question want to reach and represent." Chris Weedon, *Feminism, Theory, and the Politics of Difference* (Malden, MA: Blackwell Publishers, 1999), 168.

3 Ibid.

4 Nancy Hartsock, *The Feminist Standpoint Revisited and Other Essays* (Boulder, CO: Westview Press, 1998), 7.

5 As Tania Abdulahad notes, "Confining yourself to labels doesn't help. If you say first that I am Black, and second I am a woman, third I am a Lesbian, fourth I am a feminist, fifth I am a worker, and so on, then, of course, every single time that you think about what you are going to do … it is always along those lines and in that order." Tania Abdulahad, Gwendolyn Rogers, Barbara Smith and Jameelah Waheed, "Black Lesbian/Feminist Organizing, A Conversation," in Barbara Smith, ed., *Home Girls: A Black Feminist Anthology* (New York: Kitchen Table, Women of Color Press, 1983), 301.

6 Phil Zuckerman, *The Social Theory of W.E.B. Du Bois* (Thousand Oaks, CA: Sage, 2004).

7 Bernice Johnson Reagon, "Coalition Politics, Turning the Century," in Smith, ed., *Home Girls*, 359.

8 Ibid., 368.

CHAPTER 6

FEMINIST TRANSMASCULINITIES

reese simpkins

As a mature movement, feminism has had to contend with questions that the trans rights movement, as a newly forming movement, has not. Most feminists agree that being a woman is not the same as being a feminist. In this sense, feminism as a political movement involves something different than being a member of a certain group — one *chooses* a feminist identity. One of the strengths of feminism has been its ability to adapt and to wrestle with questions of identity. It has grown from a movement based upon the enfranchisement of upper-class white women to a movement that struggles to include a multiplicity of individuals with multiple and sometimes competing identities and realities of oppression. As feminism is forced to grapple with race, class, sexuality and gender/sex identification it reinvigorates itself, grows and remains relevant. The trans movement itself is also fraught with competing identities that are still struggling to speak, and trans theory and the trans movement in general have just begun to address questions of race, class and sexuality.[1] And it has yet to separate in what ways being trans differs from being part of a trans movement — it means something to be trans, and it means something else to see that trans-ness as part of an ongoing political project.

While trans and feminist identities may both disrupt sex/gender hegemonies, they are also embedded in discourses of power — as are all identities. Implicit in this is the understanding that identities must both be recognized for what they challenge and for what they reinscribe. It is important, both theoretically and practically, to form political movements that are inclusive in order to allow individuals to challenge power in their own diverse ways. Consequently, it is important to continually interrogate how our own politics and identities impact on a multiplicity of individual subject positions that are not our own. Therefore, we must begin by examining how, and why, the hegemonic[2] sex/gender system ascribes *masculinity* to what it determines to be biological male bodies and *femininity* to what it determines to be biological female bodies.

In order to maintain its dominance, the sex/gender system must maintain the coherency of the sex/gender binary, where hegemonic discourses of femininity and masculinity require that "recognizably" female-bodied subjects become feminine women and male-bodied subjects become masculine men. Since this system is based upon the oppression of women/females/femininities, it is a feminist goal to disrupt this system. Additionally, as this system requires that individuals adhere to hegemonic codes of sex/gender coherency, it is also based upon the oppression of all who do not fit these standards. Hence, it should also be a trans movement goal to disrupt this system.

Power invests itself in bodies. More specifically, discourses of power determine the possibilities of identity. This means that power structures how we think and determines the spaces from which it is possible to challenge power. Discourses[3] of sex/gender work to produce individuals who are part of only two sexes and only two genders, thereby creating the binary categories man/woman, male/female, and masculine/feminine. Furthermore, these discourses also work to produce a coherent sex/gender system based on male = man = masculine.[4] Power not only produces two sex/gender categories, it determines which individuals will go into what categories.

As individuals enter the social world through birth, power interpellates[5] them as boy or girl. The "expert," usually a medical doctor, proclaims one of two categories — "boy" or "girl" — making it appear as if the sex of the individual baby determines the category into which it is placed. From the pronouncement "boy," certain natural/biological sexual traits are "determined" and predicted, such as the presence of a penis, higher testosterone levels and even the amount of hair on the body. Gender predictions follow: *he* will enjoy sports, be good at math, have a good sense of direction. Although there are disagreements over how biology through sex and socialization through gender interact to determine behaviour and identity, biological sex is generally assumed to be immutable.[6]

Judith Butler argues that gender is what naturalizes sex:[7] because hegemonic sex/gender discourses construct gender as the socially constructed part of what it means to be a woman or a man, sex is reified as that which is natural. The result of this is the concept that gender can be changed and questioned, but sex is given and unchangeable. Once we set aside this notion and begin to question sex and how bodies become sexed, it becomes clear that the underlying processes of sexualization are more complex than gender = socialization, sex = natural. Discourses of power construct the concepts of sex and gender to fit individuals into specific categories. If sex is natural and immediately readable off the naked body, it is clear that there can be only two choices, boy or girl. Because an individual's biology does not change throughout their life, biological sex is accepted as an inherent identity — one will always be the boy or the girl one was born. However, intersexed bodies are one example where this model of two sex categories is challenged. Intersexed bodies challenge power's imposition of two sexes/genders by illustrating how power interpellates individuals into one of two sex categories. There are approximately 1 in 100 births where the baby born does not fit into either of the two biological sex categories constructed by power. Moreover, of these cases, approximately 1 in 1,000 babies are given surgery — mutilated in order to make their genitalia fit one of the two categories.[8]

The same discourses of sex/gender that interpellate individuals into male and female bodies also ensure that those coded as male become men, and that those coded as female become women. Although there may not seem to be much difference between being a male or being a man, it means something different to think of yourself as having a male sex and being a man. Dominant discourses of sex/gender define maleness as having a male sex, which means that you have certain biological characteristics, while being a man means that you are both male and that you participate in certain behaviours, which relate to, but are not solely determined by, biology. In other words, one would never say, "he is a good male," because biological traits are somehow separate from goodness.

The process of becoming a man involves entering into masculine behaviour. However, this process changes with different cultural, historical and geographic contexts.[9] Moreover, in the contemporary Western context, there are different types of masculinity and different masculine traits that men can enter based upon their position within other discourses of power, such as race, class, gender, sexuality and ability. An upper-class white business man has access to a different masculinity than some one who is poor, not white and uneducated. The different types of masculinity allow for a flexibility that intersects with other discourses of power, which in turn gives certain masculinities privilege over other masculinities.

The existence of multiple competing masculinities that interact within a hierarchical framework exposes masculinity both as relational[10] and as fragile — something which must be proven. This means that in order to gain legitimacy and higher standing in the masculine hierarchy, masculine beings compete against one another in an ongoing way. This also illustrates that masculine validation is not achieved internally from within a masculine being's own body or sense of self, but rather, masculinity is validated externally, through interaction in the social.[11] In this sense, social validation through sex/gender norms plays an integral role in constructing masculinity and the behaviour of masculine beings.

The specific manner in which masculine beings validate themselves can take many forms, ranging from competition in sports to racial denigration. Hegemonic sex/gender discourses not only create a masculine hierarchy, they also construct masculinity in opposition to femininity. Under these discourses men compete with each other to have more access to hegemonic masculinity, while at the same time this involves oppression of the feminine.

The representative(s) of this feminine category can either be women (who by definition are always not masculine) or other men who are lower in the masculine hierarchy. This means that feminization can take place through other discourses (race, class, ability, sexuality). In other words, the masculine hierarchy feminizes those who have less access to hegemonic masculinity, regardless of why they have less access (whether they are female, homosexual, not-white, poor).[12] Because hegemonic sex/gender discourses oppress those feminized members at the bottom of the masculine hierarchy, both feminists and trans people have a vested interest in destablizing this hierarchy and dismantling hegemonic sex/gender discourses.

*

In order to combat the privileging of men inherent in the masculine hierarchy, Western feminism has historically worked towards women's equality.

Examples of such work include equal pay for equal work, abortion rights, revaluing motherhood, anti-racist campaigns and women's sexual freedom. More recently, feminism's fight for women's equality has come to include a struggle for femininity's equality with masculinity. Consequently, feminists have fought to allow women to include "masculine" behaviours. This has meant women entering those spaces previously reserved for men, thinking through female femininity in ways that do not privilege male masculinity and at times incorporating elements of masculinity into women's behaviour. However, feminism's ability to challenge hegemonic sex/gender discourses has been compromised, because feminism as a whole has failed to challenge how the sex/gender system interpellates masculinity into male bodies and femininity into female bodies.

Although feminism has discussed at length how women of various identities (lesbian, black, poor) inhabit female bodies, feminist political organizing has often taken for granted the biological constructs of male and female even as it challenged the gendered constructs of men and women. The result has been that feminism has fallen short of radically altering the sex/gender system. To fight for women's equality with men, and for access to masculinity as an acceptable part of femininity, is to reinscribe male = man = masculinity.

By disrupting the coherency of the male = man = masculine formula, the trans movement challenges dominant discourses of sex/gender. As such, trans politics are key to feminist politics. The trans movement incorporates multiple trans masculine identities, which engage with different elements of masculinity manhood and maleness and thereby intersect differently with hegemonic discourses of sex/gender. These include butch lesbians, drag kings, pre- and post-operative transsexual men, transsexual men who choose not to define themselves by surgery, and transgendered men, who may or may not have surgery or take hormones.

On the one hand, a post-operative transsexual challenges the ability of the sex/gender system to interpellate individuals into the categories it has constructed by his refusal to become a woman despite 'biological evidence' to the contrary. By fully undergoing sexual reassignment surgery, he illustrates the complex relationship between biology and gender, and between maleness, manhood and masculinity. On the other hand, butch lesbian masculinity challenges the dominant sex/gender discourse, which asserts that those individuals who are the most masculine are biological males or biological men. All trans masculine identities challenge the assumption that there is only one way to be masculine and that only those who are born male under the dominant discourse can become both masculine and men.

Although it is important for the feminist movement to engage with trans masculinities, this does not make all trans masculinities feminist. Since under hegemonic discourses of sex/gender, masculinity consolidates its privilege by oppressing femininity, one of the quickest ways for trans masculine individuals to validate their masculinity is to engage in the oppression of femininity and participate in the misogyny that the sex/gender system demands. However, perpetrating misogynistic oppression is available to all individuals under hegemonic sex/gender discourses. Female CEOs incorporate many elements of masculinity into their behaviour, and while they make no attempt to become men, their representation of masculinity is based upon the oppression of the feminine. It is critical that feminism work with masculine beings to create spaces for feminist masculinities that are grounded in a politics of mutual respect, in which both masculine beings and feminine beings can work together to change the oppression of the feminine in hegemonic sex/gender discourses.

The process of constructing feminist masculinities that challenge the masculine hierarchy is not only important for feminism but for the trans movement as well. The masculine hierarchy's equation male = man = masculine puts trans masculine beings in a precarious position, where their masculinity is always at risk of being not masculine enough. For example, the masculinity of FTMs, by nature of their "female" sexed bodies, is feminized under hegemonic sex/gender discourses. Butch lesbians, whose masculinity conflicts with their womanhood under hegemonic sex/gender discourses, are pathologised as women with a deviant sexuality.[13] This means that those individuals who do not conform to hegemonic sex/gender norms are at risk for being forcibly repositioned into a coherent sex/gender structure through violence, which ranges from rape to bashing to verbal harassment.[14] Violence in this case is used to interpellate individuals into sex/gender norms, re-establish the hegemony of the sex/gender system, maintain the coherency of sex/gender discourses and reinscribe the dominance of male/man/masculine over the female/woman/feminine. As feminist masculinities work to equalize femininity and masculinity, they also work to destabilize sex/gender discourses that force individuals into competition.

Only as allies can the two movements pose a radical challenge to an oppressive sex/gender system. Although the trans movement challenges how the hegemonic discourses of sex/gender interpellate individuals into binary sex/gender categories, without offering a sustained challenge to the masculine hierarchy that inherently denigrates femininity, trans masculine individuals will be forced to continue proving that they are masculine enough to belong. Even though feminism challenges the relationship between masculinity and femininity, this challenge cannot be transformative of hegemonic sex/gender discourses until masculinity's equation with men and male-ness and femininity's equation with women and female-ness are disrupted. Consequently, the trans and feminist movements are most radically challenging to the sex/gender system when they are allied.

However, as alliances are made and the sex/gender system is challenged, both movements must be careful to respect and understand the identities involved. Those feminists and trans people engaging in such politics must be careful not to overwrite less stable, more marginalized identities with those that have more of a purchase on legitimacy. Only through specificity and respect can both movements work together to radically challenge the hegemonic sex/gender system.

NOTES

1 Here it is important to note that grassroots activism around issues such as poverty and sex work has done a much better job at addressing this multiplicity than has academic theory.

2 While it is tempting to understand hegemony as a synonym for dominant, hegemony is based on a complex process that includes both force and consent. Individuals come to see hegemonic interests as their own, regardless of whether it is actually beneficial for them or not.

3 Discourse is used to mean a self-referential account of reality, in which knowledge is structured in very specific ways to produce certain outcomes. In this sense, discourses structure both what and how we "know" what we know.

4 Where male is a scientific/biological category, man is a gendered person and masculinity is a gendered attribute.

5 I use the term interpellate instead of a term like force or manipulate to draw attention to the nuances of identification. It is not a simple matter of power forcing individuals

into categories. Rather through hegemonic discourses of power, we come to identify as members of certain categories because we are pre-figured to fit into pre-existing categories. Hence, there is a complex relationship between identification, agency and power.

6 Leslie Feinberg, *Trans Liberation: Beyond Pink or Blue* (Boston: Beacon Press, 1998), 30.

7 Judith Butler, *Gender Trouble: Feminism and the Subversion of Identity*, 10th Anniversary Edition (New York: Routledge, 1999), 11.

8 "Frequently Asked Questions," *Intersex Society of North America*, retrieved 30 July 2004 from www.isna.org/faq/index.html.

9 R.W. Connell, *Masculinities* (Berkeley: University of California Press, 1995), 77.

10 Masculinity only exists in relation to something else, either femininity or another form of masculinity. In other words, masculine characteristics require some form of opposite (femininity) or something else from which to differentiate itself (another kind of masculinity).

11 Connell, *Masculinities*, 58–59, 77, 83.

12 Ibid., 78–81.

13 Judith Halberstam, *Female Masculinity* (Durham, NC: Duke University Press, 1998), 9.

14 Viviane K. Namaste, *Invisible Lives: The Erasure of Transsexual and Transgendered People* (Chicago: University of Chicago Press, 2000), 135–156.

CHAPTER 7

WHERE'S THE BEEF?

MASCULINITY AS PERFORMED BY FEMINISTS

Kyle Scanlon

THERE ARE MANY ESSAYS OUT THERE IN THE ACADEMIC WORLD THAT EXPLORE the theories and thoughts that feminists have about the existence of FTMs, trans men and "female masculinity." As an FTM who is also a feminist, I would like to hold the magnifying glass over feminists for a change in order to critically examine their relationship to the FTM communities and to challenge them to rethink their positions on FTM identities and experiences.

In my career as a service provider for trans communities, and because of my personal experience as a transsexual man, I receive frequent requests for interviews from academic feminists. Two years ago I said yes to most of those requests. Now I tend to say no. I've grown weary of hearing these young feminist scholars gushing to me about one of two things: the ways in which they too are "FTM trans" and the way that trans men are only transitioning to pursue male privilege.

I'll start with the first. I certainly don't want to dispute anyone's right to own a trans identity, but I do get concerned when FTM identities seem to be worn like a hip, new fashion label. Apparently any postmodern feminist worth her salt is going to write at least one paper on why performing as a drag king at a nightclub is the best way to subvert the patriarchy. Perhaps that's a slight exaggeration; however, when I searched online using the terms "feminism," "drag" and "essay," I found 34,000 sites, including one syllabus for a course titled "Gender and Performance" where a whole section of the course is devoted to "Drag Kings and Masculinity." Newsflash: Being trans is not a fashion statement. Trans-ness is not a fucking playground for the trendy, elite and hip members of academia.

And it isn't just academic feminists exploring the joys of female masculinity. It's also some of the women in queer communities. When I speak to some of my lesbian "drag performance artist" friends and associates, I often hear statements such as:

> "Did you see my new strap-on dildo? It's so realistic! With balls! Oh so fashionable!"
>
> "I'm going by the name Cooper now! And strapping down my breasts when I go out to perform at the dyke bars at night!"
>
> "All my girlfriends love it and I get hit on all the time when I'm in drag!"

They certainly make it sound like fun, don't they? It's a party every night to be FTM, apparently. But these same people are waking up every Monday morning after a weekend gender-bender, removing the fake moustache and packing the dildo back in a drawer. Their families and co-workers only know to call them "Brittany" and "Stacey." How FTM are these people, exactly?

In general, it's irrelevant to me whether academic feminists/lesbians or anyone else has any legitimacy in claiming a trans identity. They can call themselves anything they like so long as they are actually willing to act as a true trans ally. A trans ally is someone willing to stand up and fight for the basic human rights and dignity of all trans people. For too many trans folks out there in Toronto, being trans hasn't been an opportunity for subverting the patriarchy or playing with gender. Instead, being trans has meant fighting for survival, recognition, equality, housing, employment, safety and medical care.

I've been lucky, comparatively speaking. My day-to-day reality is fairly boring. I'm a thirty-three-year-old transsexual man. In other words, I was born female and now live my life as a guy. I'm white, relatively well educated and employed. Yet even still, I was forced to quit my job when I began transitioning because of the constant harassment from my colleagues and employers. And I then had to try to "prove" to Employment Insurance that I quit with good reason or else I would have been denied the benefits I'd been paying into for five years.

Nevertheless, my life is easy compared to the lives of the men and women I frequently work with. I have the pleasure (and the pain) of working as the Trans Programs Co-ordinator at The 519 Church Street Community Centre, a Toronto-based community centre that is located in the heart of the city's queer community. Our trans programs exist in order to support and empower lower-income, street-involved, homeless, substance-using, sex-working and otherwise marginalized transgender, transsexual and Two-Spirit members of the community. At The 519, I experience the visceral reality of trans lives every day. In the past year I've held back the hair of a trans woman who vomited after learning her friend Cassandra Do, a trans sex worker, had been murdered (the murder remains unsolved). I've attended a memorial service for a cross-dressing person of colour who was on the streets when she overdosed (and found myself hoping it was accidental, not purposeful). I've cried with a trans-identified person as ze learned ze was HIV positive; ze'd been sharing a friend's hormone injection needles because ze lived in a shelter where ze didn't have anywhere to safely store clean needles. And last month another trans guy here in Toronto killed himself. I didn't know him well, and now I'll never know him better.

I'm not trying to make us — trans folks — sound like victims. I'm just saying that our lives sure as hell aren't all fun and games, dress-up and "let's subvert the patriarchy for a lark."

I'm frustrated on a number of levels. Clearly. But what relevance does this have for a book on trans and feminisms?

As other contributors to this volume point out, feminists were instrumental in developing the concept of "women-only" spaces. But how has a feminist analysis addressed the issue of FTMs and MTFs in those spaces?

In the case of Toronto, city-funded shelter and hostels are now being pushed towards being trans accessible, thanks to the most recent version of the Toronto Hostel Standards Guidelines. While there are currently a few shelters for women that accept male-to-females, there are still almost no safe spaces for female-to-males. A recent study[1] reports that, when asked, a hundred percent of trans women *and* a hundred percent of trans men reported that women's services were safest for them. One trans man who was interviewed reported being gang-raped in a men's facility, while others described fearing for their lives.

The other difficulty in excluding trans men from "women's" spaces is that most men's facilities and agencies lack relevant services. Anecdotal stories from my clients indicate that a significant portion of trans men have experienced sexual assault, abuse and other trauma as children or young adults. There are no specific statistics to support this statement; no one has cared enough about the issue of trans men's experiences with assault and abuse in Canada to conduct a study that would shed some light on this topic. Only in a women's shelter will a resident be able to find a worker trained in supporting them through their journey as a survivor. Men's services don't provide that. They should, but they don't. This is due in part to the myth that women are "only" victims and men are "only" perpetrators.

A second reason for my frustration when FTM identities and issues are co-opted by feminists/queer women is that I worry about the message being sent to the mainstream world. Yesterday I picked up a recent copy of a queer tabloid. One story caught my eye: Sissy Spacek, Melissa Etheridge and Demi Moore have all signed up to play transsexual men in the fictionalized film version of the documentary *Southern Comfort*. The documentary showcased the real-life tragedy of transsexual man Robert Eads, who died of ovarian cancer. He had been denied appropriate and potentially life-saving health care because of his transsexuality. Robert Eads and his FTM friends will be played by the aforementioned trio of fabulous female icons. I admit that that's sort of cool. But the underlying message of these casting choices is that underneath it all, transsexual men are really just women in fake moustaches. And while part of him might have been pleased to think that the actress who played the title role in *Carrie*, a famous lesbian rocker and Bruce Willis's first wife would be involved in sharing his life and his struggles with a large mainstream audience, I am nevertheless certain that Robert Eads would roll over in his grave if he knew that his entire life journey of living as a man was about to be undone.

For the record, if a movie about *my* life is ever made, I want a biological man or a trans man to play me. I want someone who looks like a man, has a voice deep enough to be taken for a man, facial hair like a man, the musculature of a man and who has himself lived as a man. I want someone the audience will perceive as being a "real man." That's how I perceive myself. I just happen to be a man who has experienced a great deal of gender-based oppression.

Feminism, as I understand it, is fundamentally about eradicating gender-based oppression. And therefore, I proudly call myself a feminist. As much as — if not more than — many of my female feminist friends, I can see the ways in which outdated ideas about gender inhibit, limit and negatively influence our lives. Because of my experience of living as a woman, transitioning and now living as a trans man who is active in queer and trans communities, I can now recognize the extent of oppression on *all* genders/sexes more fully than I could before. Feminism isn't just about fixing the situation for women. Feminist movements have also been concerned with issues of social justice for all. For instance, the early women's movement was also concerned with issues such as the abolition of slavery and better working conditions for all. Presently, feminism represents a way of dissecting and challenging commonplace assumptions and ideologies, and trying to erase barriers to equality of all kinds, including the intersecting dimensions of race, gender, sex, ability, age, religion, sexual orientation and class. Feminism is about addressing and changing *all* situations where a group in power maintains its power through systemic forces that keep other groups disadvantaged.

And any disadvantaged equity-seeking group can benefit from such changes. The queer rights movement, for instance, has many thanks to offer to modern feminist thought. Who else took "homosexuality" out of the sphere of deviant behaviour and brought it into the sphere of valued women's experiences? Who first brought gender studies as a specific area into our universities and colleges? Who else articulated and explored the difference between gender and sex? Who else argued that biology isn't destiny? Feminists, of course. And so, trans liberation will also take much from the work of feminism. I, for one, am grateful for the work done by feminists.

Within the feminist movement, however, there seems to be a great deal of dissent about FTM and trans identities. Many dykes continue to claim Brandon Teena as a lesbian icon who was killed because "she [*sic*] was a lesbian" instead of recognizing that Brandon identified himself as male. This brings me to another concern I have with feminist assessments of FTM and trans men's identities. While recognizing that we all experience the world through various layers of privileges and oppressions due to factors like race, religion, ability, age and sexual orientation, there is one kind of specific form of privilege that I'd like to critique. As a visible trans man, a guy who's really out about being FTM, I continually hear the phrase "male privilege" bandied about. I've even been accused (on numerous occasions) of betraying my lesbian sisters in order to get it.

Privilege is a special right, advantage, benefit or immunity belonging to a person, class or office. Usually privilege accrues by virtue of one's social or economic status; less commonly it is earned. Secretly, I'm amused by the notion that FTMs gain male privilege after transition. Yes, I admit, there will be the odd occasion when a stranger — a bank teller or store clerk maybe — offers me some token or advantage because I am perceived as biologically male. But "male privilege," as it is discussed in feminist circles, is not simply those moments of favour granted to a man but the fact that he accepts it unquestioningly, expects it and, most importantly, views it as "natural."

In my opinion, there isn't an FTM in the world who could spend a whole life in a female body, experience oppression because of it, proceed through transition and suddenly begin to experience a few moments of privilege without any question at all. We're outright stunned, in fact. And many of us do *not* accept the privileges when offered. But even more fundamentally, how much male privilege does a trans man actually have if he is forced to burn his old pictures, avoid old friends and make up a new history to avoid anyone discovering the truth about him? A trans man who transitions at his workplace and who may never become "one of the boys," and that glass ceiling might always be there hovering just above his head. If he tries to change jobs, for the rest of his life he cannot use his old career references and will have to start from scratch.

An FTM-identified person starting transition who begs a gender clinic for hormones may be told he has to live without them for a year as part of a real-life test. Or he may be told at this clinic that he *must* divorce his supportive husband of several years before he can begin transition. Where's the male privilege in these situations? Once he's out about being transsexual, a trans man will definitely lose social status. Worse, he may face a threat to his physical safety. That slide down through the chutes and ladders game of status is exactly the *opposite* of male privilege.

Transsexual men aren't the only ones being accused by feminists of "having male privilege." Transsexual women are often being targeted with that inflammatory phrase as well. I recently heard those two words used, in an extremely accusatory tone, I might add, to explain that "male privilege" was the reason why an MTF transsexual woman wouldn't be able to access services at a shelter. A transsexual woman can't even get a much-used mattress at an overcrowded shelter for one winter night, and you're saying she's got privilege? What's the privilege, exactly? That she'll get to freeze outside, I guess.

Consider another set of examples, also drawn from my experience. A Two-Spirit woman is told that she cannot attend Michigan's Womyn's Festival until and unless she's had costly, painful and invasive medical procedures to remove part of her anatomy. An MTF-identified person who came out about her transsexuality at her place of employment, where she had worked for two years, was fired. A trans woman here in Toronto was recently asked by one of her peers to leave a local lesbian discussion group because it was for "women only." A young transsexual woman with two children is fighting a custody battle because her ex-wife doesn't believe she's fit as a parent anymore.

Where's the male privilege? The common denominator is not privilege but trans oppression. Academic feminists/queer women have used a lens of "oppression and privilege" to view the world and have often urged men, whites, and middle- and upper-class people to consider their own privileges as they move through life. Now it's feminists themselves who need to get real about the kinds of gender privileges they take for granted. I refer to the privilege of being a person whose assigned sex at birth matches their gender identity throughout their lives. I've created a word to describe the assumption that people who "match" in this way are more "real" and/or more "normal" than are those whose assigned sex at birth is incongruent with their gender identity. I call it "biocentrism."

This comes up when, for instance, women's shelters may be uncomfortable serving transsexual/transgendered women for fear that their non-trans clients would be uncomfortable. Underlying this is a biocentric attitude that transsexual women aren't real women. When a service implies that trans women clients should be "grateful" when they are included in "women's only spaces," this is biocentrism. And when some of the drag performance artists and gender theorists out there forget that "playing" with gender is itself a privilege, that too is biocentrism. These feminists need to tackle their own biocentrist attitudes. If they can't, or won't, then, ironically, they are the ones perpetrating gender-based oppression.

My recommendation? Feminist scholars could play a tremendous role in drawing attention to the real-life experiences, needs and issues of trans people if only they could turn their attention away from their own idealized concepts of what fun it must be to explore masculinity. Instead of focusing on how much privilege comes with being accepted as a man in society, female-born feminists and lesbians could instead be critically considering their own privilege and power as women-born- / women-identified women in a world of binary gender systems.

And there's my beef.

NOTES

1 Christina Strang and Deanna Forrester, "Creating a Safe Space for Us All" (Toronto: City of Toronto's Shelter, Housing and Support Services Department, 2005).

CHAPTER 8

OUR BODIES ARE NOT OURSELVES: TRANNY GUYS AND THE RACIALIZED CLASS POLITICS OF EMBODIMENT

Bobby Noble

THE TITLES OF TWO SIGNIFICANT FEMINIST BOOKS ON CLASS — DOROTHY Allison's *Skin* and bell hooks's *Where We Stand*[1] — signal the proposition I want to explore here: that is, they suggest that class may well be constructed as a form of hyperembodiment and hypervisibility, especially for those of us who are working class and racialized white. Making class visible and material within feminist theory is often accomplished through metaphors of the body. One of the few situations in which whiteness is made visible is when it is viewed through the lens of class. Thus, under what conditions can trans-ed[2] bodies, bodies that similarly matter when invisible or fetishized, emerge within the feminist analytical intersections of capitalism, class and race? I want to play in those fields by offering my own trans body, which is white but formerly "off-white," formerly lesbian but now female-to-male transsexual, as a case study in resistance. I want to talk about resistance through a trope of labour; that is, I want to explore the ways in which gender is something we work at and are complicit in making or unmaking for ourselves within contexts of power.

Gender can be an often pleasurable making of self. If gender is also labour, then gender can be unmade, or at least, gender can be remade so that power works through it with less categorical precision. A practice of strategically *un*making one's self, in a context where being a gender means also being embodied in hegemonic ways, is a class, *trans*, anti-racist and union politic I want to cultivate in this era where "self" is the hottest and most insidious capitalist commodity.[3]

The union motto that I want to borrow — *An injury to one is an injury to all* — has been in my life since I was very young.[4] My maternal grandmother was a member of the Canadian Union of Public Employees (CUPE) for her entire working life. She was a hospital worker, back when services such as laundry and food were still provided in-house. She worked in the same hospital laundry for almost forty years. I spent one summer as a young teenager working in that laundry with her and just barely lasted the first month. Conditions were horrific. Unpacking the laundry from the hospital hampers was one of the nastiest jobs I've ever witnessed. Thankfully, I suppose, the staff wouldn't let me near the job of separating the soiled sheets and bloodied towels from the operating rooms. Temperatures were extremely high and very dangerous. Between massive pressing machines that ironed linens and sheets, the huge dryers and washers that laundered sheets at very high temperatures, workers dehydrated on a regular basis.

I remember visiting her on her lunch break when I was much younger. I would wait for her in the hospital cafeteria and when the laundry women came into the room, they certainly were quite a spectacle. Into that otherwise unremarkably populated cafeteria walked a group of white, working-class, big, tough-looking, often hard-drinking women dressed in white dress-uniforms that looked out of place on them. They lumbered into the cafeteria, lit cigarettes, opened home-made lunch boxes and stared down all who dared look. Those women made a mark on me. As a former member of York University's graduate student union, CUPE 3903, I doubt that much of that union's current work on transsexual issues would have made a great deal of sense to all of those women my grandmother worked with, although I suspect a couple might have understood the stakes. Because of the political commitment to social justice issues, CUPE 3903 has passed a number of resolutions that include the struggles of transsexual peoples in their primary mandate. They also support their transsexual members with funding; when I had surgery done, CUPE 3903's Ways and Means fund helped me pay for surgery that has been delisted in the Conservative butchery of Ontario health care.[5]

The men in my family were less union-affiliated but just as affected by the class-based issues of labour activism. My grandfather was one of the "Little Immigrants," groups of white, orphaned working-class British children who were shipped to Canada in the early twentieth century from a series of Reformatory and Industrial Schools known as "Ragged Schools" (because of the ragged clothing of the attendees) for homeless and abandoned children. The schools struck a deal with the Canadian government whereby they would export large numbers of these children to Canada to work as "farm help" and "mother's helpers" in Canadian homes and farms.[6] At its peak, this emigration was responsible for shipping anywhere between eighty and a hundred thousand orphaned or abandoned children to Canada as a ready-made, exploitable indentured domestic servant class.[7] My grandfather was still unable to read and write when he died in 1992.

My grandparents were the primary influences on my gender: I find traces of both of them in the words I use to describe myself ("a guy who is half lesbian") and, in finding these traces, have built a sense of self quite different from their own. The rough and yet somehow vulnerable masculinity of the butches and FTMs brings my grandmother back to me, while, in some kind of temporal and geographical displacement, I find traces of my grandfather's off-white-ness in the class-based traces of manhood I now wear as corporeal signifiers.

For example, to be sure, my family is all white. When I say "off-white," I do not mean to suggest at all that somehow being poor and/or working class means one is no longer white. What I do mean to argue is that whiteness, like gender and class, has a history of invention, construction and utility. The existence of the notion of a white race produces the unconscious (at best) willingness of those assigned to it to place their racial interests above class or any other interests they hold. Entrance into the fiction of whiteness is purchased through an ideological class belief in naturalized whiteness. What white is, then, is a class-based race: the higher up you go, the whiter you get. One is not born white, one buys one's way into whiteness and *becomes* white. This is what the men and women of my ancestry purchased for me off the labour of their class-based whiteness (what I previously called off-white: white, yes, but not middle-class white): entrance, as an educated adult, into a whitened middle class. While I grew up on welfare, we became *whiter* through the generations.

If racialized bodies are the product of both our own labour but also the work of a racial social manufacturing machine, then developing not just a tolerance, but an acquired taste, for destabilizing gender paradoxes within our feminist vocabularies might be one way to trouble that machinery. Female-to-male transsexuals both embody but are also articulated by paradox. My own body as signifier does this too: from the waist up, with or without clothes, I display a white male chest. Naked, from the waist down, my body reads as a conventionally female body even though that is not how I understand it. Clothed, from the waist down, my body displays sufficient signifiers of whiteness and masculinity and I'm just a guy. Given that the surgical production of a penis leaves much to be desired — and the penis they can build costs so much that it is out of reach for most guys — trans men cannot leave the *trans* behind and be *men*.

Self-naming and by implication, self-definition, then, these crucial axioms that feminist movements fought long and hard for, becomes tricky: I find myself at an even greater loss when it comes to finding a language to describe myself. Just recently, I've settled upon the following paradox: "a guy who is half lesbian." I've a long lesbian history that I do not renounce despite tremendous pressure from doctors, sometimes from queer folks, sometimes from straight folks; but have just recently come out as a straight (albeit transsexual) man. Like, *"I am a lesbian man,"* identifying myself through paradox as a *guy who is half lesbian* really comes closest to bringing a number of historical moments together to form *something like an identity*. The tension between *guy* and *lesbian* does the work of articulating in language what my body is currently doing through gender signifiers. The result, of course, is that many FTMs cannot always be read as men in every circumstance (presuming, of course, that any man can).

But masculinity isn't the only subject of un-making found in this No Man's Land that I'm marking as a political site. FTMs hold the potential to do to masculinity what femmes do to femininity: that is, femmes remake femininity through a tremendously potent practice of ironic resignification. My success at passing as a man has become a curious thing with regard to my lesbian-femme partner. One thing I often feel quite compelled to do when we are in queer spaces is to insist that my very out lesbian-femme girlfriend of African descent hold my hand as much as possible.[8] This irony resonates even louder for several reasons. In a historical moment where femmes are accused of not being lesbian enough, or where queer femininity is cast in a suspicious light, it was a bit of an oddity to realize that I passed as *less than bio-guy* when outed as *something else* through my lesbian partner. That is an unusual and very historically specific irony.

Both queer femininity and transsexual masculinity are thinkable in feminist contexts as a result of the work of third wave feminism and are rightly being reconceptualized as political practices even as they are doing different kinds of political work on two different registers of gender. As a trans guy, for instance, it is extremely important to me to be seen as male whereas for my femme partner, it's far more important for her to be seen as lesbian. My partner is also a woman of African descent which means, among other things, a dual battle for her in No Man's Land for visibility. The signifiers most easily read as femme and/or lesbian in our culture are those of white femininity, while *Black* and *femme* are understood as contradictions. For my partner, visibility is frequently conditional: either she is read as her sexuality or she read as her race. Being a racialized, gendered and sexualized subject all at the same time is seen as unthinkable within our current paradigms of identity that privilege, indeed, demand, singularity of identification.

Models of intersectionality, which allow me, for instance, to read myself as raced (white, British), gendered (masculine) and sexualized (hetero-gendered and queerly straight) all at the same time are still sadly missing in our political lexicons. If FTMs wear masculinity as what writer Jay Prosser calls a "second skin"[9] in order to feel visible and, strangely, invisible at the same time, then femmes wear a queer gendered-ness as a second skin that renders them invisible as lesbians. Femmes of colour, to risk an awkward phrase, are hailed as racialized subjects that can leave them invisible as queers *inside* queer communities. Each of these are accomplished through a triangulation, each through the other, and tell us, that despite the work we've done, we've still so much more to do.

One of the most significant things I have done to unmake this supposedly "female" signified body is to have top surgery to remove my breasts, a euphemism for a surgical procedure properly known as "bilateral mastectomy with male chest reconstruction." For several days after the procedure I wore a huge wide binder around my now scrawny looking white chest. Underneath that binder, strangely similar to one I've worn when I wanted to bind my breasts, were two lateral scars where those breasts used to sit. Just above those scars were my nipples, grafted onto my newly configured chest but still healing under dressings to ensure the grafts would take. To be clear: in this type of a procedure — the graft — the nipples are removed completely from the skin. Once the breast tissue is removed, the nipples are then reattached as grafts. After a period of about two weeks, the "new" nipples have attached again to the skin, only this time in a new position on the newly configured chest. But the *metaphor* of grafting is an interesting one and all too relevant to what I've just come through in this "transition."

I prefer the trope of "grafting" to "transition" because it allows me to reconfigure what I mean by transgender or transsexual. All too often, the relation between the "trans" and either "gender" or "sexual" is misread to mean that one transcends the other so that trans people, in essence, are surgically and hormonally given "new" bodies. That is, the terms transgender or transsexual are often misread to suggest a radical departure from birth bodies into squeaky clean new ones. I counter that belief in my second book *Masculinities Without Men?* but also now on and through my body; indeed, even more so now since my nipples were literally grafted back onto my chest: neither of these misreadings are as helpful as they could be.[10] My *gender* now is different from the one I grew up with, yes, but my body is, paradoxically, almost still the same. I have the same scars, the same stretch marks, the same bumps, bruises and birth marks that I've always had. Only it is all different now. The notion of grafting allows me to think through that relation. Not only does this trope allow me to look at the way my "new" body is grafted out of, onto, through my "old," but it is also a way of re-thinking *trans-gendered (read: differently gendered)* bodies as effects of the sex/gender system in crisis and transition. My newish gender is the effect of a productive failure of that manufacturing system, not its success. I'm failing to become the "proper" man that the conservative sex/gender system requires. That is, I'm supposed to become a man who isn't half lesbian and who isn't self-consciously political. In those failings, trans men become remarkably successful "men."

Transsexual and transgender folks do not transcend the sex/gender system; instead, trans folks are an important site where its contradictions and inabilities, as Judith Butler argues, are imploded from within and ultimately, fail to live up to their own idealized imperatives.[11] To return to the paradox I developed earlier, that I am a guy who is half lesbian both makes sense and is utterly impossible all at exactly the same anti-heteronormative but feminist moment.

To say *"I am a lesbian man"* or *"I am guy who is half lesbian"* both materializes and externalizes bodies not always immediately visible yet still absolutely necessary for the performative paradox to work. I remember the day I heard a trans man say, about his former breasts, "It's such a paradox to have to cut some part of myself off in order to feel more like my self." Those words are inscribed painfully across this chest today more than ever. But make no mistake: this is the body not as foundation but as archive; this is same chest, the same body, the same flesh I've always known; only now its text is totally different.[12]

While medicalized interventions do render the gap between self and body less dangerous, they do not, at least for FTMs, render the gap nonexistent. Since my surgery, I'm aware that I signify quite differently and find that I need to begin to transform my own consciousness to keep up. I now find myself asking the question: What kind of *guy* am I presenting? Masculinity as written on a male body is quite different than masculinity as written on a female body. But I'm still a guy who has chosen to keep the *F* on his driver's license, thus inhabiting "normal abnormally."[13] It means, as the best feminist interventions have always told us, that I need to be painfully aware of how I signify, of what kinds of power accrue to my whiteness and masculinity and then work against both of those to challenge those power relations.

As someone who walked the streets, sometimes late at night, in a woman's body, I know all too well the fear of men walking behind me a little too closely. In that same situation now, I cross the street or look away from women, or non-threateningly maneuver the situation so that I put as much distance as possible between myself and a woman out by herself. It means, as someone who walked the streets as a butch lesbian, attempting to challenge heterosexual privilege but also making conversation with gay and lesbian people in public situations rather than with seemingly heterosexual people. It means — as a white man — outing myself whenever and wherever possible as a white race-traitor (someone working against the privileges accorded to whiteness), and then doing the pedagogical work of challenging racism amongst other straight white men. Who better to occupy the space of *guy* but former lesbians who've walked the streets as women, loved as fierce and sometimes stone butches, and who've come of political age in the context of lesbian feminism? For me, that's a proud history that does not get left behind in the operating room.

If class and race are the subject of invention and ideological production, then theorizing transsexual issues as *labour* also doesn't seem that strange to me. Gender identities — that is, gendered selves — are the product of, but also condition, particular kinds of labour. If the sex/gender system works, like any other ideological system, through mis-recognition where we mis-perceive ourselves as natural human beings rather than as ideologically produced subjects, then it requires our complicit co-operation in order to accomplish that misrecognition. What a new century is demanding of feminism is that it also begin to acknowledge its own complicity with the biological essentialisms at the core of the sex/gender systems.

If it is true that gender identities are acts of co-production, then the process of becoming a self, of making a self, which is so much a part of what trans-identities tell us, is also labour that can be used against the sex/gender system. A North Carolina drag king named Pat Triarch calls gender queers and trans folks "deconstruction workers" who, by quite literally putting mis-fitting bodies on the (dis-assembly) line, begin to both resist and re-build the *man-made* gender imperatives that pass as those of nature. These bodies are the labour-intensive archives of a liberation movement, and it is to its sons — sons of the movement — and their allies, that feminist movement needs to turn.[14]

NOTES

1 Dorothy Allison, *Skin: Talking About Sex, Class and Literature* (Ithaca, NY: Firebrand Books, 1994); bell hooks, *Where We Stand: Class Matters* (New York: Routledge, 2000).

2 The pedantic distinction between "transgender" and "transsexual" cannot hold, especially for female to male transsexual men for whom surgeries are always already incomplete. To avoid being repetitive here, I used the prefix "trans-" to signify subjectivities where bodies are at odds with gender presentation, regardless of whether that mis-alignment is self-evident in conventional ways or not. The entire question of what's visible, when, how, and by whom is precisely what's at stake in this essay so policing or prescribing or hierarchizing kinds of political embodiment is a topical identity politic and moral panic that I eschew.

3 There is a curious and undertheorized history of what's come to be known as the "self-help discourse"; there was a time in early second wave feminism, due to the work of rape crisis and battered women's/shelter activists/workers, when recovering from the trauma and violence of the sex/gender system was an inherently political act of resistance. Hegemonic appropriations of these ideas rearticulated this notion of a reconfigured self in extremely conservative ways: self is what cosmetic procedures provide; it's the product of an upper-class leisure-time activity (in most recent years, *Oprah*); self is what's taken up by the beauty myths but also what's used as an advertising strategy (see Subway's new campaign for lighter food consumption which shows a series of people stating why they prefer Subway's new light menu, including a young, blond, white woman from the anorexia demographic saying, "I choose to actually eat"); a newly configured self is what Dr. Phil's diet campaign berates and shames folks into becoming. One of the few feminist texts to begin examining this history is Ann Cvetkovich's *An Archive of Feelings: Trauma, Sexuality and Lesbian Public Cultures* (Durham, NC: Duke University Press, 2003).

4 This is, of course, the primary trope and political rallying cry of Leslie Feinberg's novel *Stone Butch Blues* (Ithaca, NY: Firebrand Books, 1993), one of the most important working-class and trans narratives to call for a practice of strategic un-making.

5 The CUPE 3903 Women's Caucus has not only counted transsexual women amongst its members, but in a truly unprecedented intervention in this border war, recently changed its name (it is now the "Trans Identified and Women Identified" Caucus) to create space for transsexual men as well. It is clear that this local is able to fold the concerns of its transsexual and transgendered members into its mandate as issues of labour, not "lifestyle" as the Ontario Conservative government has so deemed.

6 Kenneth Bagnell, *The Little Immigrants: The Orphans Who Came to Canada* (Toronto: MacMillan of Canada, 1980), 91.

7 Ibid., 9.

8 For the work in this section I am indebted to OmiSoore H. Dryden, my partner, with whom I've spent many pleasurable hours in delightful conversation.

9 Jay Prosser, *Second Skins: The Body Narratives of Transsexuality* (New York: Columbia University Press, 1998).

10 Jean Bobby Noble, *Masculinities Without Men?* (Vancouver: UBC Press, 2004).

11 Judith Butler, "Imitation and Gender Insubordination," in Diana Fuss, ed., *Inside/Out: Lesbian Theories, Gay Theories* (New York: Routledge, 1991), 13–31.

12 See Cvetkovich, *An Archive of Feelings*. On the relation between trauma and countercultural resistance movements as a kind of archive or record of trauma but also of resistance, Cvetkovich writes: "I am interested ... in the way trauma digs itself in at the level of the everyday, and in the incommensurability of large-scale events and the ongoing material details of experience ... I hope to seize authority over trauma discourses from medical and scientific discourse in order to place it back in the hands of those who make culture, as well as to forge new models for how affective life can

serve as the foundation for public but counter-cultural archive as well" (20).

13 Lisa Duggan and Kathleen McHugh, "Fem(me)inist Manifesto," *Women and Performance: A Journal of Feminist Theory* 8, no. 16 (1996), 110.

14 Jean Bobby Noble, *Sons of the Movement: FtMs Risking Incoherence in a Post-Queer Cultural Landscape* (Toronto: Women's Press, 2006).

CHAPTER 9

THE FEMINIST CROSS-DRESSER

Miqqi Alicia Gilbert

CROSS-DRESSING HAS BEEN A PERSISTENT AND LONG-STANDING HUMAN phenomenon. A cross-dresser is someone who officially identifies as one gender but sometimes presents herself or himself in the apparel (and with the demeanour) of the "opposite" gender. For a very long time, it was thought that almost all cross-dressers were males who enjoyed putting on female clothing, wearing makeup, feminine hair styles and so on. These days, however, such a facile assumption is not warranted. There is a great deal of role playing that takes place within the lesbian community involving cross-dressing, and much of it has the same compulsive and sexual undertones as male-to-female (MTF) cross-dressing.

As a lifelong and out MTF cross-dresser, I have had a great deal of interaction with others of my ilk. As a philosopher, I have also tried to be thoughtful about my cross-dressing. The activity itself, if not strange, is unusual at least in a statistical sense, and it certainly goes against the classical gender mores and standards with which I was raised. I have felt strongly for a very long time that cross-dressers need to explore the activity, understand it and discover it as a learning process rather than reduce it to a mere eccentricity. I ask myself: If I do this thing, and if, as it seems, I have very little choice about doing it, then how can I incorporate it into my life in such a way that it becomes a vehicle of growth and knowledge? This has led me to exhort my cross-dressing sisters to explore beyond the limits of the erotic fantasy and fetishistic surface of cross-dressing and use it as a means to better understand womanhood, the meanings of femininity and the importance of feminism. The following is a reworking of two columns entitled "The Feminist Cross-Dresser" (1 and 2) that appeared in 2004 in *Transgender Tapestry,* an international magazine for cross-dressers, transsexuals and other transgender folks.

While my columns aimed to point out the importance of a feminist stance to cross-dressing men, I must point out that many already take active steps to work towards a feminist consciousness. The response to my writings has always been strongly positive, and I am pleased to say that today far more MTF cross-dressers are aware of the issues and challenges facing women and that their own approaches to women are far more sophisticated than they once were.

*

So, you want to be a feminist cross-dresser? You want to use your cross-dressing as a stepping stone to understand the world as a woman lives it, and not just as a pleasurable pastime? Excellent! Read on.

What is feminism? That is at the same time both a simple and a complex question. The basic tenets that are largely common to all flavours of feminism are pretty straightforward. Yet there are different theories of feminism that compete with each other and have, in some instances, dramatically different approaches. Nonetheless, it's possible to come up with a foundational idea that *most* feminist theories would embrace: that sexism is wrong, and that there are no good reasons for men as a group, simply because of their gender, to have advantages, power or rights not available to women. Women and men should have equal access to education and employment, respect for their minds and a full range of choices of roles in life. There is no natural or religious or social justification for women to be relegated to particular roles, to be denied opportunities available to men or to assume an inferior or subservient position to men.

Now most cross-dressers embrace these values and will readily agree that sexism is wrong. Why is it, then, that so many feminists (or, for that matter, so many women) have issues concerning MTF cross-dressers? These objections come from a variety of sources. First, some believe that MTF cross-dressing is a caricature of women. While I honestly believe that this occurs much less than it used to, a significant number of cross-dressers — or

CDs — tend to overdo and hyperbolize those aspects of womanhood that exemplify the idea of woman as an object. A CD with oversize breasts, super high heels, spatula-applied makeup and a micro-miniskirt exhibits just those aspects of being "feminine" that feminists most decry. The fact that there are non-trans women who present in precisely that way does not ameliorate the felt slight. The issue underlying this reaction is, what sort of femininity is one going to embrace?

In many cultures, women's role is to be looked at, to be evaluated first and primarily on the basis of appearance and the degree to which they cause sexual arousal and stimulation. And, yes, we (almost) all want to be sexy and attractive, and there's nothing wrong with that — *unless it becomes the only salient fact about us.* In a context where women are primarily judged as objects, things such as what women say, what they accomplish, what they do, what they feel, what they want, need and envision become secondary or irrelevant. *This is not the case for men.* As a man you are important and your wishes and goals are paramount, they are the most important things about you. Power and choice do not only accrue to studly guys but also to those of us who are overweight and not fabulously handsome. Why? Because our role as sexual objects, most especially post-adolescence, is not viewed as the most important thing about us.

Cross-dressers tend to either look somewhat dowdy, because they model themselves after their mothers, or show exaggerated displays of femininity that appeal to the fetishistic underpinnings of the drive to cross-dress. I believe that one reason younger CDs are less likely to appear at breakfast as if the Queen were joining them is that their mothers were around for the feminist revolution, and they are more likely to have been exposed to both feminist thought and its influence on presentation and attire. Younger CDs are more likely to wear slacks, flat shoes and more comfortable casual clothing than the generation that preceded them. Indeed, the attuned cross-dresser learns that it is easier to pass if one fits in than if one exaggerates one's appearance.

CDs have not had the training, conditioning and day-to-day experience that all women go through. Girls learn about style, clothing, makeup and carriage from each other. Certainly, their mothers play a significant role, though often less than mother would like, but friends and the exemplars of popular icons and their styles are even more important. Boys also go through this, but the regimen regarding what to wear and when to wear it is not nearly so stringent. Boys are lucky if they come out of adolescence knowing what matches, let alone being able to identify taupe and fuchsia.

Another thorny issue that arises for feminists is that men who cross-dress have the privilege of being able to pick it up and put it down. In other words, we can be our woman selves when we want to, but easily drop it when it is not convenient or when it is liable to be costly. I have had the experience of being ignored when people thought I was a woman, and as a feminist cross-dresser I need to pay attention to that and imagine what it would mean to live a life like that rather than play a bit role. My privilege travels with me when I present myself as a man. It is assumed by those relating to me that I have some importance in life, and that what I say and think must be of value. As men, privilege is ours to lose; as women, it must be established and claimed. I've learned for example, that at a conference when I am not dressed I can just introduce myself as Michael Gilbert. However, if I am dressed I know I must introduce myself as Professor Miqqi Alicia Gilbert from York University in order to receive even a similar degree of attention. This is not an isolated case.

Many a cross-dresser fantasizes about dressing en femme to work, of hearing his heels click on the linoleum as he walks down the corridor, of carefully smoothing his skirt out as he sits down by his desk, legs crossed at the ankles, manicured nails picking up his pink flowered tea cup. Sigh. It's funny, but when cross-dressers fantasize about working as a woman, they don't fantasize about being paid less than men. They don't dream of being in a meeting where their ideas are ignored, or of being expected to take on menial or "nurturing" roles. They don't dream about struggling to choose between career and child rearing, or about changing jobs because their husbands got a promotion. No. When we take off our wigs and bras, we put on our male privilege. It's just there, whether we want it to be or not. Not surprisingly, this rankles some women. We don't even have to think about fancy feminist theory here; all we have to do is think about the heterosexual CD who comes home from a night out and leaves a makeup stained bathroom for his wife to clean up. Rankle? You bet. Can you look at your life, and see that your women-self is declaring her sisterhood? Is your femme persona an ally of your wife, girlfriend or partner? Does your inner woman support your partner's needs and aspirations?

How can a cross-dresser be a feminist? First, he can be a feminist in the same way that any other man can. But a CD who is willing to reflect on the realities as well as the fantasies of womanhood can have insights that are not available to many men. These insights range from an intimate awareness of the discomfort of high heels to a shared sense of vulnerability, fear and danger when out alone at night.

Let's begin with a simple example: high heels. There's something sexy and erotic about wearing shoes that are so obviously female and that form your body into a definitely female poise. But, as you know, there's another side to high heels — they hurt. What must it be like to have to wear high heels all the time? Many women have jobs where it is expected that they will wear heels and, in some jobs, for example a dining-room hostess, it is required. How sexy is it to *have* to stand around in three-inch heels no matter how much your feet hurt? The CD has the chance to think about this, to know from experience just how uncomfortable it can be. What makes the CD a feminist is when he begins to think about being forced to present himself in a certain, frequently uncomfortable way. A feminist cross-dresser considers the significance of having no choice, of *having* to be sexy and on display or risk being condemned and even ridiculed. This doesn't mean you can't have fun, but it does mean that you ought to reflect on the underside of those activities you enjoy so much.

At this point you may be thinking about the women you know who are clear that they enjoy getting all dolled up and looking hot; they find male attention welcome in those situations and would feel bad if they were not noticed at all. That's true. I would venture that most people at least sometimes enjoy the experience of feeling and appearing attractive. But wait. First of all, look at the common and ordinary expression I chose: "all dolled up." Men don't get dolled up, women do. And what are dolls? They are objects, play things, toys, and most definitely in the world of children, specifically, little girls. Women, also, are judged much more frequently and much more harshly on their appearance than men. This means that getting it right, looking good, is a pressure that most men don't have to bear.

There is another arena of self-awareness that is open to the CD, and other trans people as well, that is very profound. This concerns the ideas of marginalization and vulnerability. Let's start with marginalization, the fact of not being considered, of being left on the side without a voice, without respect and without the ability to make a difference. This has been the reality for trans people for a very long time. Only recently have we begun to be considered worthy of concern. Our needs have forever been ignored, displaced and assigned a low priority, not only by mainstream heterosexist society but also by gay and lesbian society. We have been misunderstood and misinterpreted by clinical professionals and feminist writers alike. Our rights have long been put on a back burner because adding trans rights to gay and lesbian rights might slow down the gay rights movement. People forget that the "official" beginning of the gay rights movement, Stonewall, was a transgender uprising; that the first legal same-sex marriages were between a genetic woman and a trans woman;[1] and that trans people are regularly beaten, humiliated and murdered. Dealing with us is hard and makes people uncomfortable, so we are pushed aside.

Better yet, don't forget any of that, because this is exactly what women have gone through for centuries. For women the acquisition of status and rights has been a slow and arduous process that is not yet complete, even in the most progressive societies. In less progressive societies, women are no more than chattel whose rights and needs need not be considered at all. CDs need to understand that their own sense of frustration at having to hide and be ashamed is similar to the aspirations of millions of women who also must suppress their desires, hide their true nature, and follow a multitude of rules not of their own making. A cross-dresser who bemoans his inability to dress as he pleases is echoing the complaint of a multitude of women forced to wear veils, burqas or micro-mini cocktail waitress outfits. A CD who goes out dressed risks a beating at the hands of intolerant men for not following the rules of the dress code. Many women must go out following a dress code or risk being beaten by religious zealots. Think about women who are raped, and their violators excused, because these women were seen to be dressed "provocatively."

This brings us to the sense of vulnerability. As a cross-dresser, consider the feeling you get when you are sitting at home alone, all dressed up and minding your own business, when there is a sudden sound outside or a knock at the door. Your stomach lurches as the shot of adrenaline races throughout your system because suddenly you may not be safe, suddenly your carefully guarded sanctuary might be invaded. Or think about the times when you are walking on your own, perhaps from your car to a meeting or an event at a restaurant, and you see a couple of guys coming your way. You try to act natural, confident. You avoid eye contact and hope they will ignore you. Maybe you surreptitiously look around for help or an escape. If they make a comment you keep walking carefully at the same pace, not wanting to signal fear or enrage them. You know that feeling because it has happened to every cross-dresser who has ventured out of his house. And it happens to women all the time.

The feminist cross-dresser is a man who takes his own experience and uses it to open a window into life on the other side. He enjoys himself as a cross-dresser, and hopefully as a man, but he also works at taking a mature and serious look the reality of being a woman as well as the fantasy he enjoys playing out. Most of us have, or had, a "grass is greener" attitude to women. That part of us that embraces things feminine is often very selective and chooses those bits that we experience as fun or interesting or sexy. When we stop to think, when we take a look at the realities, then the difficulties, issues, responsibilities and burdens of womanhood play their role in our psyches as well. That's when you can become a feminist cross-dresser. (But you don't have to burn your bra.)

NOTES

1 Several marriages took place in Ontario between genetic women and trans women in the late stages of transition. The trans woman's birth certificate would subsequently be altered from male to female, thus briging it about that two women were legally married.

CHAPTER 10

QUEER FEMMES LOVING FTMS: TOWARDS AN EROTIC TRANSGENDERED ETHICS

Susan Driver

My lover and I walk the streets with the power of wildly willed desires. Femme woman and transgendered butch, we adore the certainty of our erotic bond. It is a sex/gendered opposition of choice. Living out the mutual joys of sexualized feminine female and masculine male subjectivity, we embrace our contrasting bodies as we move together. These movements feel wonderful, as to us they are the fruition of our histories, experiences and struggles to find romantic happiness. To some we represent the sliding signifiers of gender non-conformity or the material evidence of a stubborn binary system. To others we are seen as confusingly straight, lesbian, queer, perverse, unknown… We have become used to shifting, ambiguous, hostile, fearful and curious receptions. Yet it is the constancy of our belief and love in each other's differences that grounds the meaning of our lives.

Femme-transgender ties are shaped through a deep sensual dialogue that surface judgements can never grasp. To communicate these meanings is to risk raw intimacy by telling stories in public that are rarely heard beyond the ears of those close by who are interested in listening to the perspectives and secret longings of genderqueers. It is time to open up these tellings as worthy of general social recognition and cultural value, to accord the personal reflections of transgender relations the status of socially transformative knowledges.

While trans people are articulating their lives like never before in books, films, online, politically, poetically and performatively, the relational contexts and exchanges of love and passion of those erotically allied with trans people have yet to be represented. In many ways a process of transition from one gender to another (and possibly another and another), involves and changes multiple subjects who are defined, positioned and sometimes separated from those who name themselves as transgendered. Overcoming rigid divisions that isolate individuals and realms of trans experiences is a vital part of confronting transphobias. This struggle refuses to assign all responsibility and insight to a single person or group. It becomes important to redraw boundaries between trans and non-trans not out of fear and hatred, but out of respect, care and love.

The challenge is to accord trans people the interpretive power of their experiences while inviting those who are inextricably part of these experiences to converse. Framing transgender issues this way, in terms of relational dialogues, leaves room to expand the fields of community, romance and activism in which people come together and learn. It is crucial that this framework be entered from the point of self-reflexive questioning and embodied analysis, so that while broader issues of collective politics are addressed they do not displace the urgency of those whose feeling thinking bodies are on the line. If feminism is to have any relevance in this dialogue it must begin at the crux of its vulnerability — where it is cautious, tentative and unsure of how to proceed.

Connections between feminist and transgender movements are important to me at the level of my daily existence. Much more than merely expanding or altering the definition of woman, the intersection of trans/feminist/queer issues reaches into the micro details of how I engage with the world around me. These are ongoing relations and situations that are difficult to talk about theoretically, at a distance from living interactional moments and emotional process. I am spurred on by questions: How does my femme queer love for a transgender butch intersect with my feminism? Are my femme fantasies and sex play integral to my feminist consciousness? Is there a political edge to the power of my erotic explorations with a transgendered lover? What's love/pleasure/desire got to do with community and social change? Is my femme sexuality in a process of transition? Is my femininity straightened/queered through my trans lover's masculinity? Does my femme feminist identity shape my lovers transbutch identity? Does my femme female status matter within transgender politics? In what ways do I (not) belong to my lover's transgender community? Are we recognized and supported as a couple? How do others see our relationship? Do their responses influence us, inhibit us, shame us? Is trusted social acceptance impossible for us? Will we have to conform to get it? Do we want it?

To start to address these questions I try to write through a series of experiential moments, from quirky encounters of misrecognition as a straight woman, to empowering times of queer resistance, and sublime relations of desire that defy the need for categorization. I call forth feminist and queer theories indirectly while pushing them into realms of personalized erotic touch in ways that resist the abstractions of academic discourse. For me, feminism is strengthened through recognition of transgendered subjects by returning to the place where the imaginative corporeal power to love across differences exceeds the need for defensive divisions.

Transitioning from Feminine to Femme

My fem(me)ininity has emerged through contact with those willing to embrace its complexity. Combining elements from the strained legacy of feminine social ideals with the hybrid realities of women's histories, constituting a femme self is never straightforward. Sexuality marks a femme in excess of heterosexual desire, yet not in denial of its charms. Asserting sexual prerogatives to be an object of desire while affirming the simultaneous pleasures and powers of subjectivity, I criss-cross binary terms. While femme is frequently paired with butch as a complementary set, autonomy and freedom of action is the motive of a femme's identity. Refusing to follow conventional paths of romantic fulfillment, femmes have staked out an embodied narrative of resistance to heteronormativity while also refusing the regulations of lesbian feminist morality. Many femmes have written about struggles to diversify feminine sexuality against the tide of symbolic and political closures. What gets articulated is the very insurgency of femme sex/gender identifications and desires, a profound impulse to craft eroticized feminine meanings and practices in new ways.

I want to suggest the possibility that femmes experience gender as a transitional process. In between self and other, object and subject, straight and lesbian, heteronormative and queer, passive and active, feminine and fem(me)inine, femmes are cunning gender negotiators. Becoming a conscious gender mover gives rise to a situation where being a woman becomes a shaky proposition as codes, references, relations are contested. While female sex remains a constant "foundation" of a femme's embodiment, its meaning is contingent upon who, what and how this "sex" finds expression. Wearing a strap-on as a femme to fuck another femme gives rise to a qualitatively different sense of one's sex than being penetrated by a penis. Having an FTM bend over my silk-stockinged knee while I play with his pussy and cock at the same time is a deliciously trans-erotic act. There are many ways femmes not only queer straight sex through performative repetition, but twist the very paradigm of female femininity. I am not suggesting that femmes are not real women, but that they inhabit the multiplicity of that position in subtle and unique ways. At the same time that femmes enact gender fluidity, performative flux is embodied within the realm of feminine identifications. This gives rise to new approaches to femininity as a culturally open-ended practice of self-representation.

Tracing back through my own femme history, I remember dramatic variations of self-image that started with a sharp rejection of feminine appearances and moved increasingly towards a full-on embrace of the frilly glam of high-femme attire and attitude. When I came out in my twenties as a dyke, I shaved off my hair and wore second-hand jeans in an act of tomboyish disinterest in the accoutrements of consumer girl culture. I needed space to disinvest from years of looking at myself through the eyes of hetero-male desire. Stripping off layers of ideologically figured beauty signs inscribed onto my psychic-flesh, I gained a distance enabling me to resignify myself. The visible world of body fashion was a crucial realm in which I played out gender wanderings as part of my expansive body consciousness. Gradually, I reclaimed elements of feminine dress and gesture, gathering body memories of my own pleasure in wearing tight shiny fabrics, showing my flesh off in public and walking seductively in high heels. The allure of femme fashion comprised a restylization of my body and internal gaze to take hold of my own self-adoration, to wear femininity as source of personal sensual delight.

Yet my process of embracing femme identity is not only an adventure in creative self-adornment, it is deeply interwoven with my erotic relations with my transgender lover Carrie. It is through the loving eyes of someone capable of empathizing and imaginatively enjoying the richness and independence of my femme self, that I am able to feel fully at home and valued as an intelligent sexual person. My consciousness and corporeal map as a woman has been transformed as I have come to experience love and desire for someone transgendered. We both have a living memory of feeling at odds with the dull repetitions of gender expectations, of wanting to make something special out of our fantasies of gender alternatives. We share distinct dreams of becoming more than what the dominant culture offers us, excited by the courage and flair of other queers and trans folk.

I am convinced that it is a mutual appreciation and intense struggle to personalize sex-gender beyond conventional models that enables my complicated femme transitional process to be enhanced. I am able to be a seductive little girl because I know that Carrie fully understands that I am nonetheless a powerful smart woman. My trans-butch lover gets my femme differences, affirms the pluralities, ambivalence and pleasures of my fem(me)ininity. While I am not transgendered, I am someone who has gone through a long hard process of remembering and re-evaluating the gendered sexual individual I want to become. Carrie and I relate to each other's convoluted gender memories and narratives, and we meet at this place of risky willed embodiment.

Amorous Dialogues Across Transitioning Selves

My self-defined FTM trans-butch lover, Carrie, approaches me as both a man and a woman, a two-spirited soul refusing to claim either/or for the sake of ease or safety. Both are important to the sense of self that Carrie develops out of the past as a butch dyke and into the present as a trans man. Carrie is at times fully man, claiming the right to see and be seen as a guy. Physical evidence of manhood is important for Carrie. Facial hair, large cock, tattoos on muscular arms and hard leathers are vital elements of his experience. In this way gender becomes realized in space and time. It is not a parodic performance or a textual slippage, it is a forceful psychic impulse, a decisive act of self-presentation that states: "This is who I am, a hot sexually dominant man." There is no ambiguity at this moment. It is the bold directness of this demand that addresses me as a femme. I see, feel and hear its "truth," and I don't need to question its substance. I want the man that Carrie is.

The point is not to erase the mobility of Carrie's transgender self, but to allow each identity claim to be received with full attention and acknowledgement. When Carrie wants to be a woman, and sometimes my little girl, I respond with belief and love. There is a leap of faith that requires no proof or rationale. Our love is based on this ability to trust these movements and namings of self, to go to where the other feels most realized and free.

The contrasts we embody as a transbutch/femme couple go beyond queer role-play into the deep emotional core of our relational and physical identities. We don't merely perform gender distinctions with a same-sexed variation, we "are" man and woman in all the complexity of that duality. Carrie is my handsome man, my strong daddy, my sweet boy and at times my sexy girl. In turn I am Carrie's strong femme top, little girl, momma and rebellious teenage grrrl. The multiple selves we embody are equally authentic and meaningful to who we are for each other. Carrie and I meet through the recognition of who we want to be here and now, rather than the simplified mental images of what others assume we are from afar. We create an intense focus on our present desires, on the flow of our imaginative ability to perceive and anticipate them.

This ability to act out mutual recognition of sex/gender desires and differences, by accepting and adjusting the self in relation to what the other wants, is a crucial moment of our love that pushes us into new forms of transgender relations. Both of us are shaped by the work of the other to understand the identities and desires of each self. In other words, my femme self is made real and given the contours of a desirable feminine sexuality in and through the ways Carrie looks at me, touches me and talks to me.

Beginning from this place of a loving mutual recognition requires nuanced ways of understanding the transformations of transgender subjects in dynamic social relations. There is an intensely relational dimension to transgender lives that sometimes gets lost in the focus on the physical and psychological experiences of isolated trans subjects. The familial, romantic, working and friendship interactional contexts need to be integrated back into these discourses. Dialogical ways of communicating enable the intermingling of voices, changed through and against their encounters with each other. Dialogical relations involve the overlapping layers experience between self and other to collide into a meaningful picture composed of diverse perspectives.

As selves willing to enter into dialogue, we become implicated in transgendered transitions of value, identity, belonging and hope remade over and over again as alterations of body, psyche and mind are reconstructed.

It becomes necessary to ask and respond to ongoing questions: How am I transformed by your changes? What attracts me, scares or threatens me? Is there continuity in our connection across genders? How do you want me to receive you? Am I experiencing loss? Do I desire something new? What are the limits of my understanding? Am I willing to accept the unknown? It is the give and take, back and forth exchange between my transgender lover and I that opens up possibilities for gender transitioning without the denial of social attachments and support. Being able to encourage individual change within a dialogue that holds onto a secure sense of belonging, we are able to sustain our relationship over time.

PASSING PLEASURES AND DIFFICULT COMMUNITIES

> Little girl in a restaurant: "Are you a man or a woman?"
> Carrie: "I am both."
> Susan: *smiles*

While mutual learning and adoration is fostered within the private intimacy of our femme-transbutch dialogue, Carrie and I travel out into many public spaces. It is here that we must deal with the daily conflicts and contradictions of a culture fixated on clear-cut heteronormative gender relations. While our bodies communicate immense possibilities together that provide us with great pleasure, to strangers our presence can be titillating, unsettling and at times threatening. In some places we are immediately read as a straight couple, a passing that we both enjoy and use to its full potential. Viewed through a straight gaze as man and woman we blend into the crowd anonymously, enjoying the relaxation of casually fitting in.

Of course we know that this assumed sameness helping us pass is only a temporary cover. It may be Carrie's womanly voice or the queer details of our gestures that gives us away and sets us apart. Often perceived as both straight and queer, people look back at us with quizzical interest. Carrie will sometimes be called both "he" and "she" by a person in one breath, an unconscious verbal recognition of a transgendered self. When my high fem(me)ininty is the focus of attention, stereotypical heteromale desire fetishizes the complementary sexual duo that we represent. I appear to be the "normal" feminine woman anchoring us as a couple to the illusions of straight culture. We deal with the projective fantasies of what strangers want us to be, watching them do a double-take as they check to see if their first impression is right. The gaps between seeing, hearing, believing and wanting mark an uneasy passage for us as a transgendered couple.

Although we often pass as an ordinary heterosexual couple, we also like to be recognized in our femme/trans-butch uniqueness. Yet this is not an identity that most people acknowledge, and so we let go of expectations, enjoying all that we are in the face of others' indifference or incomprehension. We wear our perverse sexuality in the subtle signs of our interactions and in the more overt stylizing of our words, dress and movements, refusing to blunt the kinky edges of our relationship. The trick to inhabiting diverse contexts is to convey the comfort and strength of our passionate love and desire to others.

As sentimental as this may sound, in a world that encourages hostile devaluation of genderqueers, presenting a bold confident mutual pleasure in who we are as a couple is an effective tool against hatred. The aim is to deflect the emotional response of those hostile toward us, to recentre interest onto our positive sensual playfulness. Carrie walks and acts with a self-assurance that is astonishingly persuasive against forces that would attack his sense of authenticity and worth. We are extremely affectionate in public, kissing and caressing whenever we feel like it. This disarms people and takes them off-guard, challenging them to appreciate the warm erotic trust that we embody. These acts of amorous display are not merely strategies of tolerance, they are the essence of how we live everyday.

While we experience lots of joy inhabiting straight contexts, finding places of social belonging is complicated for Carrie and I. Our femme-transbutch combination fits into lesbian, trans, queer, straight, feminist communities with an odd and sometimes inarticulate discomfort. Carrie as man-daddy-sir rarely sits comfortably amongst my women's studies colleagues or the lesbian feminists who watch him sell leather dildo pouches to other trans men at the Michigan Womyn's Music Festival. This does not mean that Carrie is an outsider to these events but that his belonging is a selective process of give and take. In a different way, my female femininity sits awkwardly in closed communities of FTMs, where I engage from the sidelines as a supportive witness and friend. As a femme lover of an FTM, my feminist alliances are shaped through a nuanced gender politics that push me to reconsider the stakes of identifying with women-defined movements.

While both Carrie and I seek out queer spaces that are open and heterogeneous, the notion of an all-embracing community in which to easily fit is an impossibility that frees us from false ideals of unity and sameness. A vivid feeling of both being part of and peripheral to many communities offers us room to come and go, join in or stay on the margins as we see fit. The looseness of our identifications within various communities does not diminish their value and support, but enables us to connect with those excluded or invisible. An uncertain sense of community demands the same dialogical work around transgender subjects as romantic love does, and it is not something easily given or ever fully attained.

TOWARDS A QUEER FEMINIST ETHICS OF TRANSGENDERED LOVE

My specific story offers insights beyond a single romance. It provides a close-up reflection on the ways differently gendered people come together out of an intense desire to explore deeply embodied changes, to recognize how another wants to be seen and addressed. The experiences lived out in the small moments of erotic intimacy become the take off points for defining our transgendered relations. Living together within wider community spheres, Carrie and I translate our close-knit awareness to those around us.

In this essay, I have tried to sketch out an ethics of transgendered love, of coming together with no biological guarantees, few cultural symbols and little social acceptance. In the openness of this dialogue comes a chance to re-envision a queer feminist politics that takes its cue from the bonds of sexuality, care and love. It is in the act of becoming vulnerable enough to love those that we are not, that we learn most about who we are. I suggest that this flexible method of relating and learning across genders is not fast and rushed, it is a slow patient and tender approach towards mutual respect. The form best suited to this ethical knowing is reflexive storytelling, that treats experiences as the matter of theory. My feminism has been changed forever through my emotional and intellectual growth as a femme and as a partner of a trans man. In style and content I am a fem(me)inist, refusing to disown my erotic story for political security.

*

As I was completing this essay, I found out that a transgendered friend committed suicide. I feel a huge sadness for the loss of this smart imaginative young man. I wonder what was missing from his life to make him want to end it? Was he shamed by the ignorance of those who refused to see his manhood? Did this cause him to lose sight of himself? Did he want to be understood with a deeper, more expansive honesty than the world could offer? Could strong community belonging have saved him? These questions remain forever unanswered.

But it is not only this transgender warrior that moves me to tears. I also feel pain for his femme lover who believed so strongly in his beauty as a man. She will have to live with his absence. She will want to defend his spirit. She will hold the secrets he shared with her in the quiet spaces of their love. She will forever carry memories of his body in her flesh. I hope that she will be able to heal, move on and find happiness elsewhere as a powerful femme survivor. It is in life and death that an ethics of transgendered love reveals its practice and meanings.

CHAPTER 11

IT'S A LONG WAY TO THE TOP: HIERARCHIES OF LEGITIMACY IN TRANS COMMUNITIES

Alaina Hardie

I'VE KNOWN ALL MY LIFE THAT I AM A GIRL. I REMEMBER ARGUING enthusiastically as a child that I was not, in fact, the boy that people kept thinking I was. I have at various points in my life attempted to be the boy that everybody in my life seemed to want me to be. It never quite worked out. I came to terms with this several years ago, embraced my own identity and transitioned for the final time. As part of my process of identity formation and transition, I spent a great deal of time participating in trans communities. Throughout my lengthy history of interactions with various communities and groups, I have had opportunities to see the nearly infinite complexity of trans experiences and identities. I marvel at what we have in common at the same time that I revel in our diversity. I see tremendous power and potential for changing the way we think about gender.

Yet there is also a downside to many trans communities. I would think it only reasonable to expect that in a group of trans people of any kind, we should, as trans people, feel comfortable. After all, we have something in common, something that marginalizes us in the eyes of society at large. This collective marginalization could, in theory, help create a safe space for us when we are with other trans people: we could recognize one another as allies and supporters, and use our shared experiences and identities as a means to generate group cohesion. In this safe trans space, we would feel free to be who we are, to act the way we want (within the bounds of common decency and respect), to talk about how we feel and who we are and what we like. But nothing can turn safe spaces into hostile ones faster than being told that either we don't belong or that we are somehow inadequate when compared with the other members of the group. What should be a safe space suddenly becomes scary and inhospitable.

The particular cause of vanishing safe space that I would like to examine here is what I call a *hierarchy of legitimacy*, a sort of self-imposed ranking system that lets one establish oneself as superior to other trans people. It is both created and policed both within oneself and also by the community. We are complicit in the creation of this hierarchy by framing ourselves and others within it, and allowing — perhaps even encouraging — others to frame us. In many cases our need and desire to fit in leads us to do things that we wouldn't otherwise do and that we certainly would not want to have done to us.

As social animals, human beings have a completely understandable need to belong to groups. We want to be respected and well thought of by our family, friends and others in our social circles. I'm not sure, though, what aspects of the human psyche make many of us feel like we must establish our membership in these groups by excluding or attacking others; in other words, inscribing and defending the hierarchy. If nothing else, this is a strategic mistake.

*

My transition, at age twenty-five, coincided with a move to San Jose, California, to take a job with a major computer consulting company. I was thrilled to be in the Bay Area when I transitioned. After spending my entire life in the very religious and socially conservative Southern U.S., what better place to transition than the San Francisco Bay Area? I had heard the stories about how queer-friendly it was, and through my online interactions dating back to high school I discovered that the Bay Area boasted an extremely large and fairly cohesive trans community.

I joined a couple of support groups at the urging of the therapist I was seeing, and this allowed me to meet other transsexuals — in particular, other transsexual women. Through a friend I also became involved in the Educational TV Channel, NOW Transgender San Francisco, which hosts a fabulous annual Cotillion pageant in the city. So, in addition to meeting transsexual women, I also had the opportunity to meet transgendered women, cross-dressers, drag queens and a wide variety of other people from all different parts of the gender spectrum.

Over the months I was involved in this diverse community, I started to notice trends in the ways that trans people, particularly trans women, interacted with one another. As I watched and participated in social events, I observed a hierarchy of gender presentation taking shape. This hierarchy was established and reproduced in patterns of social interaction among trans people. Surgical status, "passability," attractiveness (by conventional standards) and heteronormativity were the criteria. Being "normal" was the ideal.

Thus, at the top of the hierarchy were the post-operative, passing, conventionally attractive transsexuals, usually male-to-females. These were MTFs who were, by current cultural standards, beautiful, or at least attractive. The women were trim, pretty and petite, with feminine features and feminine carriage. They tended to be closeted, not sharing their trans identities or histories with people around them. They'd had all of the surgeries they wanted. Their sexuality was heteronormative, and they would never admit to finding anything sexual about presenting as women. They were held up as models of the ideal trans woman, lofty examples to which we all should aspire. In terms of the hierarchy, they were viewed as the most legitimate, with the greatest natural right to call themselves women.

Immediately below them on the trans ladder were other attractive, passing transsexuals, but the ones who had not (yet) had surgery (the notion that someone who had not had surgery might be deliberately *non*-operative rather than *pre*-operative was, in that context, unthinkable). Then there were the rest of the transsexuals deemed less attractive, who were ranked in descending order from the most passable to the least passable. Below them were the attractive, passing cross-dressers. All the way at the bottom were cross-dressers who didn't pass, and below even them were the cross-dressers who described their cross-dressing as a fetish hobby. Also at the bottom were self-described "she-males" and sex workers.

One especially noticeable feature of this system was that people at the top of the hierarchy didn't socialize with people at the bottom of the hierarchy. In fact it operated very much like a caste system in which you rarely socialized with those outside of your caste. If people were too high up then they were too good for you; if they were too far down then you were too good for them. These issues were discussed frequently by the transsexuals in my caste, of course: we talked about how we were somehow more legitimate, more "real," than cross-dressers. If we were friends with cross-dressers then we certainly didn't want to be seen in public with them if they were dressed up. The fear was that our legitimacy as women, to the outside world, was so flimsy that the mere proximity of a cross-dresser would inform those around us that we were also trans. I mean, suppose somebody saw us together and assumed that we transsexuals were ... well, transsexuals! Shock, horror!

The connection of disclosure to value — that we are somehow devalued if we disclose our trans status or history, especially if it conflicts with a heteronormative ideal — causes all sorts of problems with our Pollyanna trans community in which everybody is happy because we're all closeted and the people around us are none the wiser. The goal, ultimately, for many transsexuals is to blend in to the mainstream. Be quiet. Not make a fuss. Pass unnoticed. We force this on ourselves just as much as other people force it on us. We are concerned about how other transsexuals feel about us because we must cling like mad to our place in the hierarchy.

I recall one particular incident during a dinner at a restaurant with two trans friends. One of them, I'll call her Tammy, was post-transition, post-surgery and at least somewhat happy in a heterosexual relationship. The other woman, whom I'll call Jane, was very out, living at the time as a transgendered cross-dresser. During the course of our dinner conversation, Jane mentioned Tammy's former wife. Tammy became agitated at Jane's comment because she didn't want the people around us to know that she had been married at one point to another woman. This exposed her as a transsexual to a Bay Area restaurant crowd that we would probably never see again and who likely couldn't have cared less about the conversation at our table, but it was important to Tammy that she keep her secret. Tammy was so annoyed with Jane that she never spoke to Jane again. A few months later, Tammy committed suicide. I felt so badly for Jane, who was struggling with the fact that her last words to her friend Tammy were an argument over being out. Jane couldn't see the problem, but it was vital to Tammy that her image not be corrupted.

I'm not sure that I would want to lose a friend over something so minor, especially given the fact that Jane's perceived slight of Tammy was completely unintentional. It's arguable that an unwillingness to be known and recognized as a trans person is based on internalized transphobia or even homophobia: why else would a woman care if someone thinks she was intimately involved with another woman? This is not unlike the protestations of some trans people who insist, "I am not gay, I am trans." I fail to see the problem with being gay in the first place.

Now, don't get me wrong: there is a completely legitimate fear of losing one's job, one's partner or one's friends if these people, who didn't know about the trans history of the person in question, were to suddenly discover that deep, dark and presumably dirty secret. I'm not saying that trans people shouldn't be selective of the contexts in which they discuss their histories. Not disclosing is a survival strategy that is often necessary. However, the social consequences of non-disclosure can take their toll on trans people who may live in fear of being outed and taken down a notch on the trans hierarchy.

I personally am not much of an in-your-face type. I've been gifted with privilege that I've not really earned. I have rounded features that come from my genetic history. I'm five foot five, a completely average height for a woman. My breasts are large simply because all of the women in my family have such generous endowments. I can afford a fabulous hairdresser and a nice wardrobe. I don't seem to need to work very hard to pass these days, though the beginning of my transition was definitely a different story. Because of all of these things, many of which are out of my control, I fit at the top of the hierarchy at the same time that I resent that location. And let me be honest: even I sometimes just want to be seen as Alaina rather than Alaina The Transsexual. Once people discover that I'm trans then that's all they can see for days, weeks or months ... maybe even for the rest of their lives. All that I am as a person gets hidden behind the fact that when I came out of my mommy's tummy and the nurses spanked me, everybody thought that I was going to go through life as a boy.

*

The struggle between being out and being closeted is a curious one. In some ways being out is a safer place to be. If I am out then the world has nothing to hold over my head any more. Being out removes the power for the world to "reveal" and shame me. Being out as trans can create other problems, though. For example, there is a chance of experiencing the moment I mentioned above, in which I stop being Alaina and become, as one particularly insensitive co-worker put it, someone who "used to be a dude." Some, at that point, refuse to grant me the descriptor "woman." "Can you believe she's really a guy?" they ask. This is an example of how my privilege within the trans community does not translate to the non-trans world at large.

Now, I have never experienced any serious problems. If the worst I receive is disrespectful language then I count myself lucky. I am keenly aware that I live in one of the most liberal cities in North America and certainly the most diverse. Being out in Toronto is a luxury that those in rural Nebraska don't necessarily have. The threat of violence for me is relatively low; for trans people such as Brandon Teena it was significant and ultimately fatal.

In my experience as an American who now calls Canada home, the political climate in the United States values integration and assimilation. Diversity itself is tamed to make difference more tolerable to a society that values conformity while giving lip service to individualism. In Canada, although there are ostensibly legal protections for minority groups, there is nevertheless similar and substantial social pressure to fit in to a heteronormative sex-gender system. Is this need to fit into rigid social structures the reason that we try to find our place in the hierarchy of legitimacy, even if it requires us to change our fundamental way of being or compromise our ideals?

Privilege within trans communities is tenuous at best. The minute we step out of the trans support group meeting, in which we smugly pat ourselves on the backs because our breasts (or beards) are real, we're back in a big, scary world. Even the most passable transsexual is still a transsexual. To many non-trans people it doesn't matter how many surgeries you've had or how pretty you are, because you're still a freak who deserves to be bashed in a back alley somewhere. Enjoy that privileged position in the trans hierarchy, folks. Gloat while you can, because the minute you step into the real world the hierarchy collapses and we're just men in dresses to the lumbering masses. The same system of value that oppresses trans people in trans spaces oppresses us in society at large: we just happen to have a more nuanced view of it from the inside. Our privilege is a sham, and enforcing it within our own group is replicating a system that is fundamentally flawed and unable to recognize the inherent value of all human beings.

*

The more voices speaking together, the louder the resulting message, which is especially important when fighting for social and political equality. A group can usually accomplish far more in terms of achieving social progress than a single person. I think it's self-evident that trans people aren't granted the agency that we deserve: we are often not allowed to make decisions about our bodies when it comes to surgical, chemical or other medical interventions because we are somehow seen as souls lacking direction. If we're not viewed as freaks to be mocked on daytime talk shows, then we are seen as tragic figures who should be pitied and will die lonely and penniless. And indeed, because of the consequences of being trans in a trans-unfriendly society, many trans people do experience economic and social marginalization, but this is a function of systems of oppression, not of being a "bad" trans person. We need to fix this situation. We need to educate those around us and show them that we're no better or worse than them, just unique and beautiful in our own ways. We're certainly no less deserving of respect and basic human decency than non-trans people are.

Liberation movements require the participation of groups of people, and it is rare that a political group will have so much in common that it can be reasonably viewed as any sort of monolithic entity. Their participating populations are broadly diverse: they involve many people from different walks of life working together towards common goals. bell hooks, the well known Black feminist theorist and one of my personal heroes, has observed on several occasions that, because of the intersections of gender, race and class, Black men can and should be her allies in political struggle even though they often stand opposed to feminist ideals and goals. Gay men and lesbian women have well-established political alliances even though the concerns of gay men and lesbian women can be wildly divergent in their day-to-day lives, simply because one thing they do share is a powerful and important aspect of their lives. Trade unions involve themselves in issues of economic equality and social justice that are not directly related to workplace issues. We see, over and over, that alliances and coalitions work and they work well despite internal challenges of managing diversity.

From a purely strategic standpoint, why, when we can observe so many examples of successful political alliances, would we build a wall between other trans people and ourselves just because we are a little different (either in an imagined or a real sense)? Difference should be celebrated! We are unique and interesting. We have our own histories and interests and ways of being who we are, and it seems to me that by understanding others a bit better we can develop more effective techniques to understand ourselves. Once we know what we want, we can go get it. We can't do it alone, though. We need help. We need the political and economic power, and the understanding of a broad range of issues, that can only come from the participation of different people.

Feminist activism is an excellent model, I think, for different groups working together for a common goal. Certainly North American feminism has had its own problems with homophobia, racism and transphobia. While feminist hierarchies aren't necessarily as well defined as the trans hierarchy of legitimacy, they do exist, and feminist movements have been around long enough to go through the growing pains of learning that they need to respect and celebrate diversity.

Early in the second-wave feminist movement, some thought that lesbian women couldn't possibly understand the issues of oppression that straight married women were facing. Black and working-class women, who have always had to work outside of their homes to support their families because of fundamental racial and economic inequalities, were seen to have nothing in common with the more vocal and privileged white women who wanted the right to have professional careers outside the home. Later, in a strange twist of history, there was open hostility from some lesbian feminists directed at straight women who were perceived as traitors to the feminist cause.

Even today we're seeing transphobia within feminist circles: rejecting trans men who were always seen as loyal feminist women before transition and not allowing trans women to join in any reindeer games because, it is whispered, we aren't "real women." The converse is also true: trans people can be antifeminist. Some trans women are in open rebellion against a movement they view as hostile to their identities. Some trans men see feminism as a reminder of something female with which they no longer wish to be associated. And sometimes, trans or not, people simply don't understand what feminism is and how it contributes to society.

With all of this said, the modern third wave of feminism does try to embrace diversity and work together simply because it is the most effective way to realize equal treatment and basic respect. Feminism is evolving into a more inclusive and pervasive political movement, one in which we can all be who we are and still be involved when we need and want to be. Because trans liberation is a relatively young movement, we can benefit from the lessons learned by more mature movements: civil rights, women's rights, gay and lesbian rights. They've made a lot of mistakes. We have the benefits of hindsight and the experiences of those movements that came before ours. We don't have to make the same mistakes in our own activism. Are we, as the cliché goes, doomed to repeat the history from which we have failed to learn? I hope not.

CHAPTER 12

MISS WHITEY SAYS:

A RANT AGAINST OPPRESSION IN MAINSTREAM FEMINISM

Ros Salvador

White feminism defines my gender
needs me to surrender
the (white-defined) masculine
bisexuality is a sin
and I can't win
cause she needs me to get with a white woman over a Black man

Man
I am tired of this
feminist supremacist "gender is the only"
bullshit

Domination
is also white women
who hold dominion
over what threatens the opinion
that gender is the most important lesson
too busy being damsel in distress[1]
to express
more than lip service

to racism
and global economic exploitation

Want to turn us away
'cause we're too brown to be gay
too tuned in to racial oppression
to be real feminist women
too concerned about racialized men
to understand woman
which we are not
'cause we're just too "dark"
and our well-justified anger's
reminiscent of Black male aggression
or some other well-constructed stereotype

And what
is this hype
about white feminist oppression-by-transgender?
Excuse me, Bio-is-besty,
last time I checked
you were the flavour
the white man savoured
enough to give you access to a few dollars
and corresponding power
all the while you do better
statistically speaking
of poverty, violence, employment
and other markers of who is winning

But Miss Whitey knows best
is the basis of colonization
and her main stream's also pathologizing Two Spirit, gender benders,
and other bin(d)ary deviations
one more notch
in her belt of condescension
that I have become complicit in

Miss Whitey
I see past your damsel in distress
supremacy dress
and on some days I can see past my own mess
to notice we hold some keys
afraid to see
our places of power
of what that might mean
to the innocence sheen
and the fortress of hierarchies
we all subsidize
while taking "others"
for a ride.[2]

NOTES

1 This image is a gender stereotype. I use it here because it is also a space of class and race privilege.

2 With sincere thanks to Roshni Narain and Vilayvanh Sengsouvanh for their suggestions and edits.

SECTION III

Inclusion & Exclusion

INTRODUCTION

Margaret Denike

SHOULD TRANSSEXUAL WOMEN BE EXCLUDED from "women-only" spaces, services and events, such as support services provided for female survivors of male sexual and physical violence? Or from a women's sports team, a women's prison or a women's music festival? If so, on what basis would such exclusion be justified? If not, on what terms? Such are some of the questions posed by various members of the feminist communities over the past few years. Similar questions enjoyed popular debate and extensive publicity in the late 1960s, in the throes of the second wave of the women's movement in North America, when Renée Richards, then a talented male tennis player, had undergone sex-change surgery and a correlative transition in gender identity and civil/sex status and sought to compete as a woman in the U.S. Open tennis tournament.

These questions of belonging continue to be debated, often at great personal cost to those challenging exclusionary policies. Two cases in particular, the Michigan Womyn's Music Festival in the U.S. and Kimberly Nixon in Canada, have become focal points. The following essays look closely at these two specific scenarios of exclusion and the politics that inform them. Rather than simply furnishing answers to these questions, these essays draw on the knowledge generated by thirty years of feminist theory and on personal and lived experiences to complicate these questions and to elucidate the complex philosophical, legal and political issues that underpin them. They turn to, and speak of, what we have learned — and failed to learn — over the decades of our collective pursuit for recognition of individual and group identities and of the relations of gender equality and inequality within and between them.

THE LIMITS OF THE LAW

Over the past four decades, feminist interdisciplinary inquiries have consistently noted that the differences between the sexes are extensively a matter of socialization; however, it still remains a standard practice to invoke biomedical and essentialist categories, such as reproductive anatomy, to distinguish and define sexual difference. In particular, the presence or absence of a penis continues to loom as the primary signifier of civil/sexual status, whether or not it is biologically furnished or surgically constructed. Many women may feel ambivalent about whether simply stating that one is a man or a woman is sufficient to affirm such identity for the purpose of participating on a sports team, volunteering at a woman's centre or being housed in a woman's prison. However, far fewer women are ambivalent about such recognition for those who undergo radical and invasive sex-change surgery and who, on this basis, have their civil status legally changed. In other words, despite feminist critiques of medicalization, and all that we have learned and questioned about the authority that we have traditionally granted to the medical profession to define our being and our identity, we continue to buttress such authority, to defer to markers of medico-anatomical definitions of sex and to allow the medical profession to define gender identity for us.

Such deference is captured in, and reinforced by, the law and specifically by legal and judicial determinations of one's civil status. As barbara findlay, a lawyer and contributor, has argued elsewhere,

> Because the law reflects the society of which it is a part, the law, too, can only "see" two genders, male and female. So the question the law has most preoccupied itself with insofar as transgendered people are concerned, is "which gender" is the person … If a person is in the process of a transsexual transition, for example, the court asks: "Has she successfully become a man?" or "Has he successfully become a woman?"[1]

Such success is measured first and foremost through the expectation that one has undergone sex reassignment surgery. Generally speaking, one is not free to define one's own gender; this is done for us, and it is often done against the best interests of those whose felt identity or expression is not consistent with the one they were assigned at birth.

With respect to defining sex and gender identity, there is no lack of case law showing the interdependence of medical and legal institutions. For example, in Ontario, under the *Vital Statistics Act*, sex reassignment surgery and medical documentation are required before an individual may change her/his birth certificate. The requirement of "official," that is, medical recognition, of gender identity strips those who do not have access to such services of the ability to be recognized and accepted as their chosen sex. Moreover there are various cases where such a law is seen to be strictly applied by various judges. For example, in *C. (L.) v. C. (C.)* (1992), an Ontario court granted an annulment of marriage for a female-to-male transsexual because he had not had surgery to construct a "likeness of male genitals." In *Canada v. Owen* (1994), a male-to-female transsexual was refused a spouse's pension, despite a forty-year relationship, because she had not had the surgery required to complete sexual conversion.

Recently, with Canadian human rights tribunals, there are indications of a recent shift away from such essentialist medical models. In the case of *Sheridan* v. *Sanctuary Investments*, the court affirmed that for the purposes of human rights legislation, "transsexuals in transition who are living as members of the desired sex should be considered to be members of that sex."[2] While this implies that all transsexuals in transition should be recognized and accepted as their desired sex, regardless of whether transition has been surgically completed, the underlying assumption remains that a "full" transition is both a realistic possibility and the end goal of all transsexual individuals. Such assumptions homogenize the contextually varied and diverse experiences of the embodiment and identity of transsexuals, and may have the most adverse impact on female-to-male transsexuals, who not only have the added constraint of more expensive surgery, but who are limited by the (in)ability of medical science to "make" male anatomy.

Furthermore, these examples demonstrate the courts' continued reliance on the medical determination and authentication of gender identity, even in the face of such shifts. Without evidentiary documentation, of either completed surgery or impending surgery, the courts have not been willing to accept self-identification as a reasonable determinant of sex. The differential outcome of this failure is clear. Not surprisingly, the trans community has voiced strong criticism of the medicalization of gender identity and its implications for human rights protections. The proposal that gender identity protections be made available only to those who can demonstrate that they are post-operative transsexuals effectively forces transsexuals to carry documentation that would verify their relationship to a medical practitioner, and to legitimize their civil status on this basis alone.[3]

In her arguments as counsel for Kimberly Nixon, barbara findlay has urged equality advocates, and particularly those who act for transsexuals, to confront the sexist and heterosexist discrimination born of biologically centred logic:

> It is important to call evidence that gender is on a continuum, rather than to treat the categories of male and female as inviolable; and to call evidence of non-transsexual and transgendered people otherwise the court may fall into the seductive trap of seeing the transsexual as someone who is stepping from one gender category to the other, leaving the either/orism — the hegemony of the existence and exclusivity of the categories themselves — unimpaired.[4]

This evidentiary foundation, she notes, would also be important in the context of Charter litigation, for the courts to find that "gender identity" should be added as an analogous ground to the list of grounds protected under the Charter. This is because, "unless gender identity is recognized as a separate ground, there is a continuing risk that a court will understand and prohibit discrimination against transsexuals (which does not threaten the gendered order) but will not understand or prohibit discrimination against other transgendered people."[5] Seeking the legal recognition of the lived experience of gender variance and human rights protections on the basis of gender identity also directly advances the substantive equality of women and sexual minorities.

NIXON V. VANCOUVER RAPE RELIEF SOCIETY

In Canada, the case of *Nixon v. Vancouver Rape Relief Society*[6] has crystallized the questions and politics of trans inclusion/exclusion concerning women's organizations. The Vancouver Rape Relief Society is a non-profit women's organization that provides counselling and other support services to female survivors of sexual violence. In 1995, Kimberly Nixon, a post-operative transsexual woman who had experience and training in counselling victims of male violence, sought to volunteer as peer counsellor at the centre. During the first training session of potential volunteers she was turned away on the basis that, as a transsexual woman, she did not meet the criteria of the centre's woman-only policy, as she had been born male and transitioned later in life. In effect, she was said not to share the "life experience" of being female that, for political purposes, was required of those who conducted peer counselling. Specifically, the centre argued that, since Kimberly Nixon had not been female from birth, she could not have "the attendant insights into the relationship between male violence and women's inequality" and would thus not be in a position to fully assist women in crisis because of that violence. It also argued that some clients of the service "may not be comfortable with a counsellor whom they may believe is not or may not be a woman."[7]

Kimberly Nixon subsequently filed a human rights complaint in which she alleged discrimination based on sex. She sought a remedy for her pain and suffering and for the affront to her dignity incurred by this exclusion. She was successful in her claim before the BC Human Rights Tribunal and was awarded $7,500 in damages;[8] however, Rape Relief appealed the decision to the BC Supreme Court. The court overturned the tribunal's ruling and affirmed Rape Relief's claim that its restrictive policy was a bona fide occupational requirement for peer-counsellor volunteers.[9] This ruling was subsequently upheld by the BC Court of Appeal.[10]

This high-profile case continues to spark debates within and between women's and trans groups and communities. It has led to personal, legal, political and philosophical interrogations of what it means to *be* a woman; in what circumstances and contexts sexual difference might matter; of what it takes to change one's gender identity and civil status; and of what similarities and/or differences exist between the forms of sex-based discrimination, oppression and violence experienced by "women-born-women," transsexual women and transgendered persons. It has prompted reviews of, and modifications to, the policies and practices of women's centres and support services across Canada concerning trans inclusion. It has led to panels of presentations at feminist and other conferences, as well as national consultations by and between trans and women's equality-seeking groups. While the case has furnished remarkably productive dialogues including self-reflexive considerations of personal and organizational "transphobia," it has also exacerbated discriminatory attitudes expressed in popular media against both feminist organizations and trans communities.

MICHIGAN WOMYN'S MUSIC FESTIVAL

In the U.S., the Michigan Womyn's Music Festival (MWMF) marks a similar site of apparent contest over trans inclusion/exclusion policies. Established in 1976, the MWMF is one of the largest and longest-running women's festivals, featuring a week-long celebration with thousands of women from over thirty countries. The festival organizers have noted that the hallmark of the festival "has always been its creation of separate, self-defined and deeply honoured womyn's space."[11] While they have explicitly expressed a deep commitment to respecting diversity as a whole, they have developed a "womyn-born-womyn" policy that excludes participation of transsexual women. "The essence of the Festival," as the organizers put it "is that it is one week a year that is by, for and about the glorious diversity of womyn-born-womyn."[12] Furthermore, they claim,

> Our intention is for the Festival to be for womyn-born womyn, meaning people who were born and have lived their entire life experience as female. We ask that the transsexual community support and respect the intention of our event ... We operate from a position of trust, expecting that people will try to do the right thing, rather than policing people to catch them doing the wrong thing.[13]

This policy has been perceived by trans groups to be transphobic, and since 1991, in response to it, transgender activists have intermittently staged a protest known firstly as Camp Trans and, more recently, as Son of Camp Trans, outside the gates of the festival. According to trans activist Ricki Wilchins, this policy "cries out to be challenged." She notes that "while the whole queer movement has embraced inclusiveness and diversity," the MWMF is engaged in little more than judgments as "who is 'woman enough' and who is not."[14]

Some feminists have expressed their frustrations with such critiques. Karla Mantilla, for example, has characterized the trans challenge to "women's spaces" such as the MWMF as a form of resistance to any gains that women have made. She notes that in the context of Western patriarchy and colonialism "women's space is a power strategy, which is evident because it is so virulently attacked both from without ... and from within." She adds, with reference to the MWMF, "it seems to me that just when women finally eke out an infinitesimal amount of space to experience one measly week away from patriarchal culture, to begin to try to even the score of five thousand years of patriarchy, the refrain has suddenly become how unfair it is to not be inclusive."[15]

While it is important for women to carve out spaces to collectively organize and freely associate as a group, it is worth considering the context and purpose of such organization and the relevance of exclusion to this purpose.

For some commentators and observers, while it may make sense to preserve such a policy for counselling victims of male violence, it is not clear why, for the purpose of gathering to listen to music, invoking a restrictive definition of womyn is either warranted or necessary, much less why gender identity matters so much. One might ask, What is it about the nature of a music festival organized by women and for women that makes the presence and participation of trans women inappropriate? What is the point of specifying a policy that explicitly and restrictively defines woman in terms of having "life experience" as a female, if it is not to exclude transsexual women simply because they are transsexual, or because they were once men? And what does this have to do with advancing gender equality? Such questions call to mind the importance of considering the specific context in which any women's group or event could give pause to the question: What do we mean by the category woman? The answers may well be as varied as the contexts, say, of a celebration of music, organized sports, or support services for victims of gender-based crimes.

In her landmark 1975 essay, "Traffic in Women," Gayle Rubin articulated a dream that imagined a society without gender hierarchy.[16] The feminist movement, she said, must dream of even more than the elimination of the oppression of women. It must dream of the elimination of obligatory sexualities and sex roles. These are inseparable goals: she, for one, is compelled by the dream of an androgynous and gender-less — though not sexless — society in which "one's sexuality is irrelevant to who one is, what one does and with whom one makes love."[17]

Such nuggets of wisdom acquired over the past three decades can help us learn to negotiate the politics of inclusion and exclusion with compassion. Through our continued and concerted efforts we will lay the evidentiary foundation and redescribe the world as it is *lived* by the many bodies and beings whose personal relationships have been rendered unintelligible, and who have been excluded and incapacitated by discriminatory rules and interpretative practices that work to keep the fiction of binary and biocentric sex and sex roles alive. We must continue challenging the judicial annulments of trans marriages. We must continue chipping away at the bedrock that sustains the sexual subordination of women, the degradation and exclusion of sexual minorities and the conservative, heteronormative sexual ethics that locates reproduction as the raison d'être of our sexual beings and personal relationships.

As we know, we remain challenged in working through and across our differences in our current substantive equality approaches. Such approaches must begin with a recognition that, for laws and social policies to have true equality as their outcome, they must take into consideration the real differences between and among the social groups as well as the contexts in which these differences arise. This includes acknowledging the difference that we create in places where they don't exist and those that we have worked so hard to make invisible, those that challenge us on our own sacred ground and that disrupt the comfort and order of our binary gendered social and political universe. This acknowledgement should animate our dreams of equality, our ability to eradicate sex and gender based violence, to rise above degrading patriarchal stereotypes and to garner mutual respect and accommodation based on the recognition the equal worth and equality dignity of every human being.

NOTES

The author co-ordinated a national consultation on legal issues concerning transgender and women's substantive equality, sponsored by the National Association of Women and the Law (2003), and agreed to address the issues presented by the contributors in this section.

1 Available online at www.yorku.ca/gilbert/tg/bc-report/pdf.

2 *Sheridan v. Sanctuary Investments Ltd.* [1999] B.C.H.R.T.D. No. 43 (B.C. Trib.) at 107.

3 Paisley Currah and Shannon Minter, *Transgender Equality: A Handbook for Activists and Policy Makers* (National Center for Lesbian Rights and National Lesbian and Gay Task Force, June 2000), 56. Available online at www. ngltf. org/downloads/transeq.pdf.

4 barbara findlay, "An Introduction to Transgender Women," paper presented at the LEAF Forum, November 1999, 16.

5 Ibid.

6 *Nixon v. Vancouver Rape Relief Society* (2005) BCCA 601, 47 BCLR (4th) 203, affirming *Nixon v. Vancouver Rape Relief Society* (2003), 2003 BCSC 1936, (sub nom. Vancouver Rape Relief Society v. Nixon) 48 CHRR D/123, (sub nom. Vancouver

Rape Relief Society v. Nixon) 2004 CLLC 230-018, 22 BCLR (4th) 254 (BCSC); reversing *Nixon v. Vancouver Rape Relief Society* (2002), 2002 CLLC 230-009, 42 CHRR D/20 BCHRT 1 (BC Human Rights Trib.).

7 *Vancouver Rape Relief Society v. British Columbia (Human Rights Commission)* [2000] BCJ No 1143 (QL) at para. 11.

8 *Nixon v. Vancouver Rape Relief Society,* [2002] BCHRTD No.1.

9 *Vancouver Rape Relief Society v. Nixon,* [2003]BCSC 1936, 48 CHRR D/123.

10 *Vancouver Rape Relief Society v. Nixon,* [2005] BCCA 601.

11 This statement appears in "Festival Affirms Womyn-Born-Womyn Space," a pamphlet handed out to participants at the 2000 Festival. Available online at www.michfest.com/Updates/handout.htm.

12 "Michigan Womyn's Music Festival Affirms Womyn-Born-Womyn Space," Press Release, 24 July 2000. Available online at www.michfest.com/Updates/pr_july24.htm.

13 "Response to Press Release by MWMF," Camp Trans Press Release, 24 August 1999. Retrieved on 17 January 2005 from www.camptrans.com/press/-post99_ mwmf.html.

14 "Protest Called For—Women's Music Festival Discriminatory Policy Still in Effect," In Your Face Pre-Camp Trans '99 Press Release, retrieved 17 January 2005 from www. camptrans.com/press/pre.html.

15 Karla Mantilla, "Men in Ewes' Clothing: The Stealth Politics of the Transgender Movement," *Off Our Backs* (April 2000). Available online at www.raperelief shelter.bc.ca/issues/menewes.html.

16 Gayle Rubin, "The Traffic in Women: Notes on the 'Political Economy' of Sex," in Wendy Kolmar and Frances Bartkowski, eds., *Feminist Theory: A Reader* (Toronto: Mayfield, 2000), 242.

17 Ibid.

CHAPTER 13

ACTING QUEERLY:
LAWYERING FOR TRANS PEOPLE

barbara findlay

I AM A FIFTY-SIX-YEAR-OLD FAT, WHITE, LESBIAN, NON-TRANS, MIDDLE-CLASS lawyer with disabilities. I was raised working class and Christian in a prairie city, by parents themselves born in Canada of British stock. English was my first language. I have three university degrees and a QC — the "Queen's Counsel" designation bestowed on outstanding members of the legal profession. In all of those ways, I am affected by the grammar of oppression in Canada that inflects some of my personal characteristics with power and status, and others with powerlessness and a lack of social status. And I am the total of all of those things: the fact that I am a lesbian affects the ways I am a lawyer; the fact that I was raised Christian modifies the ways I experience class. Each of those characteristics inflects all of the others, by magnifying them or by diminishing them. And in the world, I am a person with all of those characteristics and many more, interacting with you whose experience of oppression and dominance is different than mine.

I am Kimberly Nixon's lawyer. I have been her lawyer for the eleven years that her case, *Nixon v. Vancouver Rape Relief Society*, has taken so far. As I write, we are applying for leave to appeal the Supreme Court of Canada for the final determination.

By now the outlines of Kimberly's case are familiar to most feminists in Canada. Kimberly is a post-operative transsexual woman with an "F" on her birth certificate. After she was battered by her partner, she found help and support from Battered Women Support Services (BWSS), a Vancouver women's peer-support group that accepted her as a client without hesitation though she told the crisis-line worker in her first call that she was a transsexual.

Kimberly says that BWSS saved her life.

In 1995, wanting to give back something of what she had received, Kimberly responded to a Vancouver Rape Relief recruiting ad in the mainstream press. She had an in-person interview to determine whether she shared Rape Relief's political beliefs (all women have the right to choose their own partners; racism is never okay; abortion is a woman's right; violence against women is never the woman's fault) and was accepted into the volunteer-training program. But on the first night of training, she was expelled at the break because one of the facilitators concluded that she was a trans woman and said Rape Relief would not accept trans women. Kimberly later volunteered as a peer support worker at BWSS and became, according to the evidence, a superior peer counsellor. After that, she worked at a women's shelter.

I found it telling at the hearing when Rape Relief's star witness, a former client of theirs, testified that she knew, on the basis of looking at Kimberly in court the previous year, that she would have felt uncomfortable talking to Kimberly as a counsellor. When I asked her on cross-examination whether there were any other people in the hearing room she would feel uncomfortable talking to, she pointed to a (woman since birth) butch lesbian.

After being expelled from the volunteer training program to which she had been accepted, Kimberly filed a human rights complaint. Rape Relief went to court to argue that trans people have no human rights under British Columbia law and that Kimberly Nixon was not a real woman. They lost, and the matter went before the British Columbia Human Rights Tribunal. Kimberly won and was awarded the highest amount of damages in the history of the tribunal (the abysmally low amount of $7,500).

Rape Relief went back to court to argue that the tribunal was wrong and that *all* human rights claimants now had an additional burden if they wanted to succeed in their human rights claims. Though for decades the law has been that a complainant need prove only the fact of discrimination and that the discrimination was on a protected ground, Rape Relief argued that *all* human rights claimants now had to prove, in addition, that the treatment resulted in an "injury to her dignity." And, said Rape Relief, even though Kimberly had been given the highest award in the province for the injury to her dignity, Kimberly's dignity had not been infringed by Rape Relief's conduct. They also argued that Rape Relief should be entitled to be the ones to decide who was "woman enough" for them, and that in any case they were protected, as a women-only group, from any charge of discrimination because of the group rights protection under the BC Human Rights Code.

The Court of Appeal disagreed that Kimberly's dignity had not been affected. They accepted that Kimberly is a woman. But they said that Rape Relief was correct to say that as a women's group, they were protected from a charge of discrimination under the Code — even if they were providing a service that purported to be for all women.

*

I have spent the last thirty-five years as a feminist, the last twenty as an anti-oppression activist and the last twelve practising queer law: issues affecting lesbians, gay men, bisexual and transgender people.

The first thing I know about working as Kimberly's lawyer is that I could have as easily ended up as Rape Relief's lawyer instead. And I passionately believe that Kimberly is absolutely right that to exclude trans women from women's crisis services is to consign them to death (after all, the reason women's crisis centres exist is because of the feminist understanding that without a safe place and peer support women can and do die).

But I know that it could have been me who was arguing that this was a women's centre, after all, and we shouldn't have to accept *them*. I know, because once I took the same position myself. In the 1980s, along with most political lesbians, I believed that bisexual women shouldn't participate in lesbian groups because they "participated in male privilege."

I don't know what I meant by "participating in male privilege." I can't figure out why I was so adamant, so viscerally convinced of the rectitude of my position. In retrospect, maybe it was because I had so little lesbian-only space that I didn't want to share it with anyone. Or maybe because bisexual people seemed to be half het and half queer, I thought that meant they were only half entitled to our sacred lesbian space. They were less oppressed, our common understanding went, because they could always disappear into heterosexuality whereas the rest of us had to be lesbian all the time. Or maybe it was because no one challenged me about my opinion.

But I was completely wrong. And I passionately believed myself to be completely right.

So I cannot find fault with Rape Relief without acknowledging that I have done exactly the same thing, and *I might again, about a different issue.*

Any one of us might.

*

We all know that straight, white feminists in Canada faced very significant challenges from lesbians and from women of colour about the homophobia and racism in the women's movement. As a result many women's organizations developed caucuses for women of colour and for lesbians.

What white feminists and straight feminists have not developed, though, is an analysis of the ways that we as white women and they as heterosexual women continue to perpetuate and contribute to the racism and homophobia that we want to fight.

We women have all grown up in a culture that is sexist, racist, homophobic, ableist and oppresses people in myriad other ways. We have learned the same sexist lies that are taught to the men who continue to hold and exercise the power in the world, and we take those lies in as internalized oppression. We, members of a group targeted for oppression, find liberation through sharing our stories with each other and organizing together against sexist men and sexist institutions.

But every one of us is also part of a group or groups that are privileged by this culture — if we are white and/or able-bodied and/or heterosexual and/or rich and so on. When we share the privilege of white skin, a heterosexual orientation, an able body or comfortable wealth, we share the *dominant* role in this culture. And just as we take in society's lies about people who are oppressed in the ways we are as internalized oppression, we take in the lies about the people who share characteristics of the dominant culture as internalized dominance.

Remember for example the "white man's burden," that colonial notion that white people are superior and have the job of civilizing people of colour around the world. Consider the bedrock idea in this culture that "family is the building block of society" when "family" really means a mom plus dad plus children and doesn't include GLBT partners and their children.

Think back to what you learned about able-bodied people: this is how God meant bodies to be, this is *natural.* The myths about wealth in this culture are based in the idea that rich people earned the money they have from their own hard work, not from any accident of birth; and that one's bank account is a measure of one's "success." Those are the kind of lies we take in as *internalized dominance.*

For example, you will notice that in this essay I have opened with the legal parts of the story, as if that is the most important part. Lawyers do that. It is part of our internalized dominance.

The difference between oppression and internalized oppression, on the one hand, and internalized dominance on the other, is this: oppression and internalized oppression hurt like hell; internalized dominance generally feels good. It feels *normal.*

*

We feminists do not like to think of ourselves as part of any oppression. But we cannot escape the training we have received without active and ongoing effort. The social support of the view that I am, as a white person, superior to people of colour or Aboriginal people is just as powerful as the social support for the view that men are superior to women.

We know that when we act against our oppressor, we are taking steps to our own liberation.

But we don't think that we have to act against out internalized dominance. We certainly don't think that acting against our internalized dominance is in our best interest. We may think of it as important political work to be an ally to people of colour or trans people, but we do not really grasp how much racism and transphobia and ableism and all of the other phobias and isms constrict our own knowledge of the world and our own possibilities.

People who are oppressed in one area of their lives often have trouble understanding or believing they are part of an oppressive group — that they have enough power to be oppressors.

Oddly, the BC Court of Appeal's decision in Kimberly's case is a validation of that position: if you are a member of a women's group you can't be held accountable for discrimination. That means you can decide which women are women enough for you and, without fear of sanction, you can decide that your women's services won't provide services to Aboriginal women, for example, or to women with disabilities or to lesbian women or to trans women.

*

Going to court for Kimberly has in some ways been the least onerous part of standing up for trans people. Over the last dozen years, I have worked in feminist communities and queer communities — inside institutions like the Women's Legal Education and Action Fund (LEAF), the National Action Committee on the Status of Women (NAC), the National Association of Women and the Law (NAWL), Equality for Gays and Lesbians Everywhere (EGALE), the Court Challenges Program, Status of Women Canada, and the Pacific Disabled Women's Action Network (Pacific DAWN) — I have worked at conferences, written articles and been active in my personal and professional life to make trans issues visible. I have urged others that as non-trans feminists we need to recognize that we have been trained in the prejudices the society purveys and that we need to learn how to offer respect and support to trans people. As a feminist, I focus on the needs of trans women — but that includes pre-operative and non-operative transsexual women, as well as transgender people and intersex women. And it includes people who were treated female when growing up but who now identify as trans or male.

One woman, a friend of years' standing, told me in a fury that I had betrayed her by being trans-inclusive, that though she had always loved me and had considered me an intimate and a part of her family, she could no longer do so: I was not a part of her family any more.

Non-trans, stably gendered women are relatively privileged in relation to trans women. It is easier, more accepted, more "normal" to be a non-trans woman than to be a trans woman in this society. In this context, we must examine our internalized dominance.

*

My experience as a non-trans ally to trans women has been very difficult. It is always the case that an ally to an oppressed group will be viewed with suspicion and ostracized from the dominant group. So it should not have surprised me that many feminists I have known and trusted and worked with and supported and been proud to call my friends now revile me. It makes me extremely uncomfortable to talk about the ways I have been targeted because of my work with trans people. First, my experience of being vilified is so minor compared with the experiences of people like Kimberly: Kimberly loses another job every time she is in the newspaper. I have done six wrongful dismissal claims for her. Second, I don't want people — no, not people, *women* — to know how much they have hurt me. I don't want them to know how much power they have. But I know from my decades as a feminist that the only way to move forward is to share our stories with one another so that we can learn from the lessons of one another's lives.

I was kicked off the NAC lesbian e-list by the list moderator because I was Kimberly's lawyer, and the list was discussing Kimberly's case. There was no discussion and no recourse. I was deeply shocked at how much that hurt. But never in a million years could I have imagined being kicked out of a Canadian lesbian feminist community. I felt like I had been kicked out of my home.

A lawyer who was acting for an employer who dismissed a trans person told me it was inconceivable that when human rights legislation was passed it was intended to protect "people like them," trans people.

I facilitated a workshop at a LEAF conference in 2005 in which I was picking up a level of hatred of trans women that was venomous. Women told me that I was not a feminist. That I was using the patriarchal court system. That discussion of issues like race, homophobia, transphobia and so on were distractions from the real issues and that we should not engage in those discussions. That the only reason I acted for Kimberly was because I wanted the publicity.

Women, some women, hate me. Even as I write that, and know it to be true, my body refuses to accept the knowledge. I am in denial because I cannot take in that feminists hate me.

I have been angry, depressed, defeated, scared, exhausted and humiliated as a non-trans ally working on trans issues. But, again, the ways I have been hurt are nothing compared with the daily danger of moving through the world as a trans person, a world where there are no, or almost no, safe places.

As an ally to Kimberly and other trans women, I try to follow Kimberly's lead. My job is to translate what she tells me about her experience into the language of equality that courts understand. Of course I have made, and will make, endless mistakes. For example, Kimberly has explained to me more times than I want to admit to that what a trans woman looks like has nothing to do with it: whether someone thinks a woman "looks like a man" is simply beside the point.

*

Though the struggle for trans equality has been very hard personally on many levels, it has been enormously rewarding too. Working with Kimberly and other trans people has forced me to re-examine all of my assumptions about gender — my own and everyone else's. It has opened my mind and my heart. It has made me humble all over again to realize how, even after decades of work as a feminist, I was carrying unexamined ideas about the male/female binary. I have many wonderful and courageous trans friends. I have learned that I can survive the censure of women I had counted as friends and political colleagues.

*

Twelve years have passed since Kimberly's court case began. In those twelve years, there has been a sea change of opinion about trans women in the Canadian women's movement. Reflexive exclusion of trans women is becoming reflexive inclusion. Eighty percent of women's crisis organizations already had trans-positive policies or were working towards them by 1991. Past and current members of Rape Relief have told Kimberly that not everyone in Rape Relief supports its anti-trans policy. A training manual about trans and intersex women exists for women's sexual assault centres. Feminist conferences and books are now glaringly incomplete if they do not address trans women.

Kimberly's courage in carrying her struggle into the public eye has meant every women-only organization in the country has had to think about whether they welcome trans women.

Today, I have discussions about trans issues with all of my friends. Most are transpositive. A few are not. I hold my love for them in my heart and continue to talk with them about trans issues.

Women's organizations have changed their position, after long and often agonizing debate. West Coast LEAF, for example, supports Kimberly's case and we will urge LEAF National to be an intervenor at the Supreme Court of Canada. EGALE has changed its name to Egale ("Equality") to be more inclusive of trans members. Pacific DAWN has a trans-inclusive policy. NAWL commissioned a paper about trans issues and, after much debate, agreed with its recommendations.

Like the fight for equality for lesbians, gay men and bisexual people, the struggle for trans equality now seems destined for legal and political success.

There will be other struggles. I know that I may very well be the one who, viscerally convinced of the correctness of my views, takes positions that turn out to be oppressive and exclusive. I hope that if that happens you will challenge me, so that I can re-examine my convictions. I will do the same for you.

CHAPTER 14

WOMEN'S SPACES ARE NOT TRANS SPACES:
MAINTAINING BOUNDARIES OF RESPECT

A. Nicki

THE TRANS MOVEMENT, MADE UP OF TRANSSEXUAL AND TRANSGENDERED people and their advocates and friends, has demarcated and affirmed lives in an inhospitable, nebulous space between rigid gender categories.[1] Transsexual and transgendered people can now name feelings, identities and historical precedents; they can turn to communities of support. But the boundaries of these communities are not always clear. MTF transsexuals, for instance, have felt excluded from spaces designated as women-only and have bitterly castigated policies governing these as hateful and transphobic.[2] Some feminists indeed have been overtly hostile towards MTF transsexuals and suspicious of them.[3] However, the exclusion of MTF transsexuals from women's spaces, such as shelters for homeless women, is not simply or necessarily the result of hostility towards them. In fact, the view that pre-operative or post-operative transsexuals are women oversimplifies the unique gender identities of transsexuals. The backlash in contemporary society against second-wave feminism has resulted in an ongoing lack of attention to a variety of issues related to women's health and safety. This has made some feminists understandably anxious about the intersection of the trans movement with the women's movement. Reasonably, feminists of the second wave are worried about their further marginalization and the further neglect of their concerns.

Theorist Viviane Namaste argues that the denial of pre-operative MTF transsexuals from women's spaces reflects a cognitive error, an irrational contradictory belief that goes against a central tenet of feminist theory — namely, that one's biological sex and one's social gender are separate things. Namaste interviewed workers in shelters for women and was told that the presence of pre-operative MTF transsexuals would cause stress for women because of the sharing of rooms and bathrooms. She writes:

> It is interesting to note the slippage between the *penis* of a transsexual woman and her gender identity: this woman would not be welcome, nor would other women feel safe (I was repeatedly told), due to the presence of her penis … This position suggested that one's genitals and gender are the same … It is inappropriate to formulate feminist social policy based on their equation. [4]

Namaste oversimplifies the concerns of the shelter workers, as well as their understandings of what it means to be a woman, in caricaturing and distorting their compassion for the women in their care as panic about the penis. She neglects to relay other reasons for their belief that MTF transsexuals should not be accepted into these spaces, such as the fact that MTF transsexuals have not grown up with the publicly affirmed gender identity of a woman and with all the experiences and repercussions that this brings.[5]

Similarly, like Namaste, theorist Deke Law laments the exclusion of pre-operative transsexuals from the Michigan's Womyn's Music Festival. She challenges this exclusion:

> An organizer said she did not feel safe; she did not feel respected; she was very concerned about the women who were doing healing work around sexual abuse. "How would they respond to a penis, or to someone they thought was a man?" she asked. It is both irresponsible and disingenuous to use the red herring of women's needing healing in order to keep other women from attending a women's weekend that was organized as such. It is both irresponsible and disingenuous to talk about safe space as if translesbians make space unsafe. [6]

True, the policies and practices governing women's spaces do not address the physical and psychological well-being of MTF transsexuals. Without an understanding of the many reasons for women's spaces, one can easily be misled to perceive these policies as directly contributing to worse situations for MTF transsexuals. However, this misperception can be easily addressed. Take the example of rape crisis centres. These centres are most often designed for women who have recently been raped or are recovering from a relationship that entailed sexual violence. Very often these also are centres for victims of familial rape. Support groups may include survivors of familial rape and individual counselling is available. However, the difficulties of survivors of familial rape can be much more complex than those of stranger or partner rape. Survivors may find their needs and struggles inadequately addressed.

I have encountered this in my own experience as a survivor of father-daughter rape seeking support at centres in Canadian and American cities. Some counsellors can feel emotionally overwhelmed with survivors of child sexual assault. Sometimes rape crisis centres will recommend that a survivor see a psychiatrist, believing that her needs are too great and that she could be a source of conflict in a support group. Psychiatrists in the U.S. and psychotherapists in Canada can be very expensive and frequently have not been trained to deal with the difficulties that survivors face. Often rational behaviour is seen purely in terms of symptoms. But are rape crisis centres to blame for their limited number of programs and resources? A survivor can feel highly distressed in finding that centres are not equipped to meet her needs. But why blame the designs of these centres and not focus on the lack of alternative support centres?

Or consider this example: While children's hospitals are designed to tend to highly vulnerable members of society is it discriminatory that these do not aid other extremely vulnerable members of society, such as economically deprived adults who do not have good health-care coverage? The category "child" is just as much socially shaped as the category "woman."

It is important not to dismiss and trivialize a rape survivor's real terror at the presence and display of a penis, even though there is no potential of real threat. Recently, I attended a musical performance with a group of people that included a male acquaintance who has a PhD. I asked him what the percentage of women was in his discipline. He responded, "Too high. Eighty percent." While he spoke he very obviously grabbed his penis and let his hand stay there for a couple of moments. I tried hard not to be disturbed, to think of his penis as similar to any other bodily part he might have held. I wished with all my might that I could perceive his penis as being less powerful, that it did not have the power to create in me intense anxiety and dread. In a very simple gesture, my acquaintance was able to remind me of the power of the penis to rape, to destroy. One might say to me, "Get over it. It's just a penis. Grow up. It is the gesture that has the power, not the organ itself; the organ has no inherent significance."

When I was a child and was being raped by my father I thought the penis was a sword, a potential instrument of death. Penises are not inherent instruments of rape, and pre-operative transsexuals are not simply potentially threatening people with penises. However, our culture is rampant with rape, with penises used for destruction. It is important not to understate the harm of chronic sexual violation, and the enormous amount of courage, effort and stamina required in order for survivors to build constructive and healthy lives. Survivors face many obstacles and difficulties directly and indirectly related to the abuse. Post-traumatic stress disorder can lead to troubles with employment and relationships and to issues of trust and boundaries. The lack of justice, truly helpful therapeutic treatment and sympathetic support in society in general causes the original trauma to figure largely in survivors' lives and the penis to signify an inordinate amount of real power. As much as they would like to forget the trauma, the lack of avenues that lead away from it and the worldwide persistence of male domination and sexual violence keep survivors circling the trauma. Survivors may feel cognitively and emotionally unable to make a distinction between a benign penis and one used for harm.

It is currently in vogue to blame the second-wave feminist movement for the lack of adequate advancement of women in existing societies. This movement has been called narrow and self-serving without real appreciation for differences among women, based on class, race, ethnicity, sexuality, ability, et cetera. Women's studies departments have been judged to be *limited to* women, and many departments are renaming themselves as "gender studies." I would be curious to know if other disciplines are seeing themselves as too limited by the original designs of their disciplines. Are people in genocide studies seeing a need to rename their discipline? What about people in Afro-American or Japanese studies? With a greater intermingling and intermarrying of Japanese people with people from different ethnic backgrounds, do people think that Japanese studies should be reconsidered? These questions are not unrelated to questions about limits and boundaries of women-only spaces.

Many women hopeful for a lesbian utopia have been disappointed to find that a desire to dominate and control is not unique to men. In their disillusionment they may feel that their hours of volunteer work in women's spaces were wasted or foolish. They may feel that female counsellors at rape crisis centres displaying the smallest bit of controlling or dominating behaviour signals deficiency or untrustworthiness. They may feel betrayed and, in turn, denigrate women.

I recently attended a talk by an FTM transsexual who spoke bitterly about his former involvement in women's spaces, as if his involvement in rape crisis centres was a matter of simply "doing time." He wanted to separate completely from his previous female identity. I wondered if such hostile rejection and belittling of past activities was really necessary to ensure that others would accept his newly proclaimed male gender identity and, if it was, in what way was this new identity positive. As he mentioned, not surprisingly, many feminists felt betrayed by his transition to a male identity. In listening to him I felt not only a sense of betrayal but also a sense of sadness and disappointment at his glib downplaying of his involvement in rape crisis centres, centres that helped sustain lives. Were victimized women not worthy of attention and care?

It is not always clear when a concern with lives and socially validating personal identities becomes an over-analytical concern with "getting right," or properly categorized, these identities. Self-described identities like "half-lesbian male" or a conception of "lesbian careers," which Henry Rubin attributes to some of the pre-operative experiences of FTM transsexuals,[7] can understandably cause worry in lesbian feminists whose lives are also continually being undermined and negated. Affirming a full-fledged lesbian identity poses real perils and political challenges in a woman-hating culture that sexually objectifies and fragments women. Being a lesbian is a way of being in the world that is not reducible to a set of roles and skills.

In their quest to be socially recognized as women, some transsexuals have understood that a woman is much more complex than simply a being with a vagina and breasts. Women are not mother goddesses with pillows of full bosoms to comfort frightened men, make up for their sense of deficiency or underabundance. And women are not containers for male sperm, for some sort of excess maleness or wild masculinity.

It is, and has been, a large challenge for women's studies to determine how much attention and space to give to a variety of issues. In my own experience of teaching a course on health issues in women's studies, I found that students were much more interested in the topic of transsexuality than other issues like female reproduction, menstruation, pregnancy, breast cancer or rape. These issues to them were not trendy, but rather "too heavy" or "gross"; they were not new. One student made the point that we should not discuss menstruation because not all girls and women experience menstruation. While theorist Henry Rubin, for instance, claims that some FTM transsexuals felt, when pre-operative, uniquely repulsed by events such as menstruation,[8] negative attitudes towards menstruation persist around the world and large numbers of girls and women feel betrayed by their bodies.

Trans issues are not necessarily feminist issues. The way trans issues are framed and understood is crucially important in terms of whether they should be considered feminist issues. Women's spaces are spaces governed and occupied by women, by persons who have grown up and been raised as women. The fact that sometimes it is not clear whether someone should be considered a woman doesn't counteract second-wave feminist arguments for having women's spaces. The political and social importance of affirming and celebrating transsexual and transgendered identities is enormous, in terms of challenging rigid gender dichotomies that have served to impede human growth. These identities need their own spaces in which to grow and flourish, like any groups of oppressed peoples. It would serve no purpose, for instance, to combine Jewish studies with African-American studies on the ground that African-American people are oppressed through some of the same conceptual frameworks as Jewish people, or that African-American people and Jewish people share some commonalities in experience and biology. To include transsexual and transgendered people in women's spaces would, in fact, undermine a feminist commitment to human liberation, since it would be subsuming one category of oppression under another, and failing to maintain boundaries of mutual respect.

NOTES

1 For an excellent text on the trans liberation see Leslie Feinberg, *Trans Liberation: Beyond Pink or Blue* (Boston: Beacon Press, 1998).

2 See, for example, Pat Califia, *Sex Changes: The Politics of Transgenderism* (San Francisco: Cleis Press, 1997), 86–117.

3 One such feminist is Janice G. Raymond. See her volume, *The Transsexual Empire: The Making of the She-Male* (Boston: Beacon Press, 1979).

4 Viviane K. Namaste, *Invisible Lives: The Erasure of Transsexual and Transgendered People* (Chicago: University of Chicago Press, 2000), 178.

5 Some MTF transsexuals transition very early on in life, at a very young age. Two early transitioners with whom I consulted about this essay (who would like to remain anonymous) make a distinction between early transitioners and late transitioners. These two sources said that they consider themselves women because they grew up and were raised as women. They do not feel an affinity with late MTF transitioners whom they see as transsexuals and not women.

6 See Deke Law, "Evolution," in Kris Kleindienst, ed., *This Is What a Lesbian Looks Like: Dyke Activists Take on the Twenty-first Century* (Ithaca, NY: Firebrand Books, 1999), 139.

7 Henry Rubin, *Self-Made Men: Identity and Embodiment among Transsexual Men* (Nashville, TN: Vanderbilt University Press, 2003), 102.

8 Ibid., 109.

CHAPTER 15

THE ETHICS OF EXCLUSION: GENDER AND POLITICS AT THE MICHIGAN WOMYN'S MUSIC FESTIVAL

Susanne Sreedhar & Michael Hand

SHOULD A WOMEN-ONLY EVENT ALLOW ROOM FOR THE TRANSGENDERED, especially women who "were once men"? The controversy over the admissions policy of the Michigan Womyn's Music Festival has raged for fifteen years. Along with the interrelated theoretical problems that it creates, the festival reproduces debates that are taking place in feminist circles across the West.

The festival is an annual, women-only event that began in 1976 and draws over 4,000 women each August. The week-long music festival includes a variety of workshops and a crafts fair. It is a communal environment in which most people camp, many go topless or nude and everyone contributes to the festival by doing "workshifts." In 1991, two participants mentioned in response to questioning during a workshop that they were trans women (male-to-female, or MTF, transsexual women), whereupon they were asked to leave and were escorted out. The implication was that MTFs are not women and thus not appropriate attendees.

Within two years, organized protests against this exclusion were occurring. Responding to these, the festival organizers formulated an explicit policy barring trans women, which became known as the "womyn-born-womyn only" policy.

Two kinds of philosophical issues arise: metaphysical ones and moral-ethical ones. On the metaphysical side, the key issue is whether there are necessary and/or sufficient conditions for womanhood and thus for admittance to the Festival. For example, is possession of a penis incompatible with being a woman? Does sincere avowal of womanhood suffice for womanhood? On the ethical side, related moral and political questions concern the justice of various exclusions, the potential psychological harm to women-born women if trans women are admitted, the possibly prejudicial basis of this harm, the obligations of the Festival in light of its stated goals, the legitimacy of those goals themselves and the status of the Festival as an established exemplar or model of how a women-only space should be delimited. Until the current explicit policy was announced, the Festival was publicized as a celebration of womanhood.

It is not surprising that the current state of the controversy is a mess. We hope to shed some light on these debates by reviewing the various policies that have been suggested, critiquing the arguments that have been given and clarifying the issues at stake.

THE "WOMYN-BORN-WOMYN ONLY" POLICY

The first explicitly formulated exclusionary policy of the Festival reads as follows:

> 1. The Festival is a womon-born-womon space. That means it is an event intended for womyn who were born and who have lived their entire life experiences as female – and who currently identify as a womon.
>
> 2. We ask the transsexual community to respect and support this intention.
>
> 3. We ask all Festival-goers and staff to honor our commitment that no womon's gender will be questioned on the land. Michigan must remain a space that recognizes and celebrates the full range of what it means to be a womon-born womon. Butch/gender-ambiguous womyn should be able to move about our community with confidence that their right to be here will not be questioned.
>
> 4. We also have a commitment to run the Festival in a way that keeps faith with the womyn-born-womyn policy, which may mean denying admission to individuals who self-declare as male-to-female transsexuals or female-

> to-male transsexuals now living as men (or asking them to leave if they enter).
>
> 5. We further emphatically ask you to not question any womon's sex on this land ... Please trust that everyone who is on the land is womon-born womon.
>
> 6. Claiming one-week a year as womyn-born-womyn space is "not in contradiction to being transpositive and trans-allies."[1]

Festival organizers do not take woman-born womanhood as the *fundamental* desirable feature of participants at the Festival; rather, they emphasize "entire life experiences as female." Being a woman-born woman is a guarantee of this, and the women-born-women policy thus serves to ensure that the Festival is not *overinclusive*. The policy does not admit non-women. The complementary problem of *underinclusiveness* still threatens.

Woman-born womanhood is *sufficient* for womanhood; the controversies concern whether it is also *necessary*. What shall we make of gender-dysphoric sex-reassignment patients who profess to have been women, or to have "felt like women," having had penises throughout their childhoods and early adulthoods? What is the relevance of the fact that such gender-dysphoric individuals are, to some varying extents, beneficiaries of male privilege during their pre-transgendered lives?

Clause 3 is explicitly intended to protect butch and gender-ambiguous women. It has been interpreted to institute what is, in effect, a "don't ask don't tell" attitude towards trans women: we don't want you here, but we will not evict you if you stay quiet about being trans. The effect is to permit attendance by trans women but to require them to closet themselves as such. (As a matter of fact, it is well known that trans women *do* attend the Festival, and for the most part no one has any problem with this in practice.)

The leading objection to the standing policy is that the official exclusion of trans women is basically irrelevant to the idea of a women's space. (Careful articulation of this objection requires theorizing the notion of "women's spaces" sufficiently to bring the idea to bear on the trans issue.) In view of the fact that many trans women's claims to womanhood are at least nearly as strong as a woman-born woman's, their exclusion is unjustifiable in view of the goals of a women's space. Proponents of this objection reject the idea that *women* must have lived their entire lives as women. The objection need not rest on the assertion that all MTFs have such powerful claims to womanhood, but only that many do, and to exclude *them* from women's spaces is morally objectionable.

Another complaint about the current policy is that it overestimates the importance of womanhood in the constitution of a woman's *identity*, and accordingly dismisses other differences among women, such as race or class. In this way the policy falsely assumes a similarity among all women-born women (the Festival's version of a familiar complaint in feminist theory) *and* supports a corresponding distinction among women (denying the claim of some to womanhood).

THE "NO PENIS POLICY"

The obvious first challenge to the policy concerns the presence of a vagina (or lack of a penis) as a condition for admittance. Historically, this was the first counterproposal offered in protest to the current policy. It recognizes post-op MTFs as legitimate attendees, that is, as fully entitled to admission as women. In effect, it removes the Festival organizers' insistence on the entire life experiences as a woman and replaces it with an anatomical requirement as constitutive of womanhood. Indeed, it might be thought that a woman's having been willing to undergo the trials of sex reassignment is as sure a sign of her commitment to her own womanhood as there could be.

The proposal was first suggested in "The Michigan Womyn's Music Festival and Transsexual Women: A Statement by Transsexual Women and Their Women Friends," a document that has been endorsed by the founders of Camp Trans, including Riki Ann Wilchins, a well-known gender activist.[2] Proponents of this policy justify their inclusion of post-op MTFs but exclusion of pre-ops as follows:

> This policy cannot address issues of race and class: specifically, the exclusion of women, especially women of color, who are not able to afford sex reassignment surgery. This is simply the best and fairest policy possible, one that balances inclusion of transsexual women with legitimate concerns for the integrity of women's culture and safe women's space.[3]

This passage sounds as if it purports to provide a *practical* justification of the no penis policy, but the same document also gives the following *principled* case against penises. "Male genitals can be so emblematic of male power and sexual dominance that their presence at a festival designed to provide safe women's space is inappropriate."

It is important to see that this argument hinges on the *meaning* that the penis holds in patriarchal society. A penis can function as an emblem of male dominance in various ways. For one thing, men themselves tend to see their penises this way.[4] Second, penises can play important psychological roles for victims of sexual violence. More generally, the presence of penises jeopardizes the notion of a women's space because penises are recognized so widely as representations of masculinity.

Despite the intuitive attractiveness of these considerations, the proposal must be rejected. The Festival is hardly free of penis-as-emblems: one thinks immediately of the presence of dildos at the Festival. At any rate, the identification of vagina possession (or lack of a penis) as constitutive of womanhood is untenable. For one thing, a vagina is neither necessary nor sufficient for womanhood. One can live as a woman — *be* a woman — without a vagina. Moreover, many individuals experience themselves as men in female bodies.

Even more importantly, a no penis policy is classist and racist. To require sex reassignment surgery is unfair and callous. It is unfair because not all MTFs can afford the treatment, and callous because the transition is difficult. The no penis policy is classist in that it largely excludes MTFs who are not at least middle class, and racist insofar as the excluded group of MTFs wanting sex-reassignment surgery is disproportionately composed of women of colour.

Incidentally, the penis-as-emblem argument for the no penis policy is racist in another way. As Emi Koyama observes, "Even the argument that the presence of a penis would trigger the women is flawed because it neglects the fact that white skin is just as much a reminder of violence as a penis."[5] That is, white skin is no less emblematic of oppression than penises are.

If "safe space" means a space free from *all* power relationships, then of course Michigan is not a safe space for all its participants, even under the current policy. As Koyama indicates, it is not a safe space for women of colour. But the question at hand is not whether Michigan can provide a safe space, but what kind of safe space it can provide. The *relevant* kind of safety is the absence of patriarchal power, and this is the safety that is supposedly undermined by the open presence of trans women (especially pre-ops). Whether this is a satisfactory response to the Koyama argument depends on further theorization of the whole idea of a women's safe space, and on whether patriarchal domination can be thoroughly differentiated from other institutionalized forms of dominations and understood as a single, unitary social phenomenon.

THE SELF-IDENTIFICATION POLICY

The next step in liberalizing the policy involves rejecting a purely anatomic criterion in favour of a policy recognizing that womanhood is a constellation of anatomical, psychological, experiential and phenomenological properties, none of which is even arguably necessary or sufficient for womanhood. This means at last rejecting the apparent essentialisms of the preceding proposals.

Since there are no essences of womanhood, it is left to each individual to decide for herself what it is about herself that determines her gender identity. For instance, one woman may identify herself as such purely on the grounds of having been born with a vagina; though she's lived her life as a woman, she may not regard this as *constitutive* of her womanhood, but rather as a *consequence* of it. Another woman with a similar history may feel differently in accounting for her womanhood. Yet a third, a pre-or non-op MTF, may regard her non-vagina birth as irrelevant to her gender identity.

A self-identification policy would respect each woman's understanding of herself as a gendered person, regardless of whether other women have the same self-understanding. Such a policy requires from each participant a sincere willingness to claim womanhood on whatever grounds seem *to her* to make her a woman.

This policy has interesting practical implications. The Festival would become explicitly trans-friendly, largely preventing the self-exclusion of MTFs both post- and pre-op, yet maintaining the exclusion of those who conceive themselves as men. Furthermore, certain people who are already "stealth" participants under the don't-ask-don't-tell clause would be allowed and encouraged to celebrate their own womanhood. For example, there would be MTF workshops, discussion groups and performances oriented towards that particular mode of womanhood. This is not unimportant, since there are already at the Festival such workshops devoted to those identities that are explicitly permitted but none devoted to those permitted only under the don't-ask-don't-tell qualification. Such a policy change is the most important and palpable transformation among the various amendments proposed in the controversy. Another ramification of this policy would be the explicit recognition of the permissibility of penises. The effect of this permission on the question of nudity is probably the most despised and feared consequence of a policy change among many Festival organizers and participants.

This last consideration makes very clear the deep political issue at stake in the controversy: On whom does the burden of accommodation fall? Is it the task of the participants to get over their discomfort at the visible presence of penises, or is up to the MTF minority to shoulder the responsibility of discretion? Neither option is clearly preferable. Indeed, there are two very clear and very important values which are coming into conflict. Surely it is valuable for the majority participants to feel comfortable in the space: this is one of the very aims of the Festival. On the other hand, the importance of self-expression is certainly a fundamental good in this context, and is recognized as such by the Festival organizers.

One might hope that these problems could get worked out over time with a sharing of the burden. What happened with the S/M community is a promising sign. While many participants at the festival express reservations about the propriety of S/M activities and an S/M campground, the Festival found a way of accommodating the S/M inclinations of some participants while respecting the reservations of others by removing the S/M campground from easy access and asking that no S/M violence be performed in the general view of festival attendees. However, there is a significant difference here. The analogue of the S/M solution would be that pre-ops in particular could now *identify* themselves as such, but not *display* themselves as such, that is, not shower publicly or disrobe publicly. The key fact is that a pre-op MTFs having a penis is not an activity but a way of being a woman, and no woman should be required to hide the *kind* of woman she is (namely, a pre-op MTF woman). Moreover, the Festival's principles preclude requiring participants to disrobe or shower privately. In this way, unlike the S/M case, the MTF case brings into sharp relief the conflict between two of the Festival's goals: the non-patriarchal *safety* and *comfort* of participants and the non-patriarchal *freedom* of gender expression of participants.

This raises a further question. Which is the greater evil: the otherwise unjustifiable *exclusion* of some in order to maintain the comfort of others, or the otherwise morally obligatory *accommodation* of some at the expense of the others' comfort? Does it matter that one is the majority and one is the minority? One hesitates to impose a further burden upon the most oppressed in the group. Given the anti-patriarchal goals of the Festival, the ghettoization of any minority group among the oppressed amounts to a double oppression and should be resisted.

A virtue of the current policy is its practical success at achieving its goals as an important women's space in the U.S. Indeed, the *practicability* of the policy might justify its inadequacy as a matter of principle. However, the standing policy is metaphysically and morally unjustified in its exclusion of MTFs. The metaphysical difficulty is that it seeks a spurious unification of all women that transcends their non-gender differences, and the moral difficulty is that the excluded women, being women, are entitled to occupy women's spaces.

Adoption of the self-identification policy entails making changes to the Festival that threaten to undermine some of the Festival's original goals. Any regulation purporting to preserve the comfort level of attendees who satisfy the original requirement automatically deprives the new attendees of the treatment they deserve, constituting a double oppression. Yet unlike the no penis policy, the "self-identification" criterion strikes us as a coherent alternative. No doubt adoption of the policy would have huge effects on the atmosphere, but the burden of accommodation falls upon the majority. The self-identification policy raises practical concerns about the psychological health and comfort of all participants, and might justify rejection of the proposal despite its abstract theoretical coherence.

Thus we have one policy that suffers theoretically but succeeds for the vast majority of participants in achieving the goals of this women's space, while its competitor suffers practically in that it is far less able to achieve those goals despite its theoretical appeal. In the end, it will likely be concrete political activism that settles this debate, one way or another.

NOTES

1 "Michigan Womyn's Music Festival Press Release," 15 August 2000, retrieved 17 January 2003 from Eminism.org at http://eminism.org/michigan/20000815-mwmf.txt.

2 See Riki Anne Wilchins's account of the early days of Camp Trans in her book *Read My Lips: Sexual Subversion and the End of Gender* (Ithaca, NY: Firebrand Books, 1997), 109–115.

3 Retrieved 17 January 2003 from Eminism.org at http://eminism.org/michigan/2000809-elliott.txt.

4 Penises are regarded almost universally in our society as expressive of their owners' masculinity, if not constitutive of it. Witness the feelings of some men who for some reason or another lose their penises and consequently feel their masculinity threatened.

5 "Whose Feminism Is It Anyway?" retrieved 17 January 2003 from www.confluere.com/store/pdf-zn/whose feminism2.pdf.

CHAPTER 16

COMPETING CLAIMS FROM DISADVANTAGED GROUPS: NIXON V. VANCOUVER RAPE RELIEF SOCIETY

Joanna Harris

The complex relationship between trans rights and women's substantive equality is exemplified by the case of *Nixon v. Vancouver Rape Relief Society* — a clear example of the dilemma caused when the two concepts come into conflict. In this essay, I introduce the legal concepts of equality and the basic ideas concerning the discrimination of transgendered individuals before proceeding to discuss the case of Kimberly Nixon. Finally, I examine violence against women and the continuing need for women-only spaces.

ANTI-DISCRIMINATION LAW IN CANADA

In Canada, discrimination is addressed using various legal instruments: the Charter of Rights and Freedoms (part of Canada's Constitution) and federal, provincial or territorial human rights codes.[1] This legislation is often the final refuge of the disadvantaged and the disenfranchised. While the purposes of the Charter and human rights codes are similar, until recently the legal analysis that determines whether discrimination has occurred operated distinctly, at times leading to differing judgements on equality issues.

Under the Charter, specifically section 15, a mere distinction drawn between two people does not in itself constitute discrimination. The distinction must be based on a specified or analogous ground; the grounds specified in the Charter are race, national or ethnic origin, colour, religion, sex, age and mental or physical disability. [2] Analogous grounds have also been held to include, for example, sexual orientation. In subsequent case law, the Supreme Court of Canada established another overarching principle, namely, the prevention of violations of human dignity[3] and established a three-part test in order to determine whether discrimination has occurred.[4] The Court first considers if there is a formal distinction drawn based on personal characteristics; second, if the law or action on the part of the government fails to take into account the claimant's already disadvantaged position within Canada based on an enumerated or analogous ground; and third, if this differential treatment discriminates in a substantive sense, which would defy the purpose of remedying prejudice, stereotyping and historical disadvantage?[5]

The final step helps the Court consider whether a claimant's dignity has been infringed. Mr. Justice Frank Iacobucci, in the significant 1999 decision *Law v. Canada (Minister of Employment and Immigration)*, defined human dignity in the context of section 15:

> Human dignity means that an individual or group feels self-respect and self-worth. It is concerned with physical and psychological integrity and empowerment. Human dignity is harmed by unfair treatment and premised upon personal traits or circumstances which do not relate to individual needs, capacities or merits.[6]

In contrast to the Charter provisions, a finding of discrimination in the federal, provincial and territorial human rights legislation has not, at least historically, depended on infringement of human dignity. While the human rights codes refer generally, by way of their preambles or statement of objectives, to the concept of preservation of human dignity,[7] the legal analysis has been analytically distinct from that laid out by Justice Iacobucci in the *Law* decision. The relevant test for a finding of discrimination in Canadian human rights codes was decided in the *Meiorin*[8] decision: when a distinction in treatment between two people is made directly, or by the effect of a seemingly neutral requirement, discrimination is considered to have occurred prima facie (on its face) and the finding of discrimination will prevail until contradicted and overcome by other evidence. Therefore, the onus shifts to the alleged perpetrator who must defend their conduct based on a bona fide (genuine) occupational requirement that requires an employee to be accommodated to the point of undue hardship.

The distinction between the Charter dignity analysis and the BC Human Rights Code was at the crux of Vancouver Rape Relief's appeal to the Supreme Court of British Columbia on December 19, 2003, in the *Nixon* case. The BC Human Rights Tribunal decision of January 17, 2002, did not adopt the Charter analysis, which considers the element of human dignity. Subsequently, the BC Supreme Court overturned this decision holding that the Charter analysis should apply. However, the BC Court of Appeal reviewed this case and determined on July 12, 2005, that the "broad application of the *Law* framework in a case without governmental overtones" is inappropriate.[9]

THE NIXON CASE

Kimberly Nixon is a post-operative male-to-female transsexual. In 1987, at age thirty, she attended the Gender Disorder Clinic at the Vancouver General Hospital. Three years later, she had sex-reassignment surgery and her birth certificate was subsequently amended to change the sex designation on the registration of birth from male to female.[10] In 1992 and 1993, Kimberly experienced physical and emotional abuse in a relationship with a male partner. When this relationship ended she was referred to the services of the Battered Women's Support Services (BWSS). In August 1995, she responded to a Vancouver Rape Relief Society advertisement calling for volunteers. Kimberly explained her interest in volunteering at Rape Relief because she recognized the importance of such organizations and wanted to give something back to women who had been supportive of her.

This was a unique situation for Rape Relief, which was a small nonprofit group with only twelve members in 1995 when Kimberly contacted them. Rape Relief had never had a transgendered person seek a volunteer opportunity or volunteer training within their organization.[11] All potential volunteers are pre-screened to ensure that they agree with Rape Relief's views as a feminist, pro-choice and lesbian-positive organization. Rape Relief also requires that volunteer peer counsellors be women. Men interested in volunteering at Rape Relief are offered positions on the fundraising committee.

After passing the pre-screening interview, Kimberly was invited to attend the peer-counsellor training session. When she attended the first night of her training, she was immediately recognized by the training facilitator as an individual who had not always been physically female. During the first break the facilitator, Ms. Cormier, approached Kimberly and asked to speak with her in private. Their conversation confirmed that Kimberly had not been a woman since birth. Ms. Cormier asked that Kimberly leave the training group, and she complied.

The next day, Kimberly filed a complaint with the British Columbia Council of Human Rights. Following her removal from the Rape Relief training program, she testified that due to the distress she felt, she returned to the support groups at BWSS. In the fall of 1996, she applied and was accepted into the BWSS training program for volunteers. Kimberly ended her involvement with BWSS after she discovered that the members had circulated what she considered to be "hate" literature about transsexuals.[12] She worked briefly for Peggy's Place, a transition house for women who, in addition to dealing with male violence or battering, have mental-health issues. Kimberly was considered a very capable volunteer in her subsequent positions.

JUDICIAL HISTORY

The BC Human Rights Tribunal heard Kimberly's arguments that Rape Relief had discriminated against her on the basis of sex,[13] by denying her a service (a training program in counselling women who have experienced violence) and an employment opportunity. The tribunal ruled that the relationship between Rape Relief and its volunteers fell within the definition of employment and found that there had been prima facie discrimination — discrimination had occurred without having to provide any further evidence — against Kimberly on both counts.[14]

Thus, Rape Relief was required to justify this discriminatory treatment. Rape Relief argued that lifelong experience as a woman was a bona fide occupational requirement for peer counsellors and, in addition, Rape Relief had attempted to accommodate Kimberly by suggesting she join its fundraising committee. In effect, Rape Relief argued that it had accommodated Kimberly up to the point of undue hardship for the organization. The tribunal rejected both of these claims. In addition, the tribunal rejected Rape

Relief's argument based on section 41 of the BC Human Rights Code, which stipulates that it is not discrimination for a non-profit organization, whose "primary purpose" is promoting the welfare and interests of an "identifiable group," to give preferential treatment to members of the identifiable group. The tribunal ruled that the evidence did not establish that Rape Relief's primary purpose was "the promotion of women who fit their political definition of what it means to be a women."[15] The tribunal also held that Rape Relief did not establish that it was necessary to exclude transsexuals in order to accomplish the organization's goals.

In a controversial and highly publicized decision, taken January 17, 2002, the tribunal ordered Rape Relief "to cease denying, for discriminatory reasons, to transsexual women the opportunity of participating in their training program and the opportunity, on completion of the training, for the same group of women of volunteering at Rape Relief."[16] In addition an award in the amount of $7,500 was ordered for injury to Kimberley's dignity, feelings and self-respect. At the time of this decision, this was the highest amount in special compensation ever awarded in the tribunal's history.

LEGAL ISSUES AT THE TRIBUNAL AND BEFORE THE COURTS

Rape Relief petitioned to the British Columbia Supreme Court[17] for judicial review of the tribunal's decision. Issues considered by the court were the effect of section 41 of the Code,[18] discrimination under the *Law* analytical framework and "dignity" under the *Law* framework.

The BC Supreme Court quashed the tribunal's order. Mr. Justice Edwards held that the tribunal was incorrect in not applying the *Law* analytical framework. The tribunal's finding, that Kimberly's exclusion from Rape Relief's volunteer training was prima facie discrimination, could not stand up under the *Law* analysis. Both Rape Relief and Kimberly characterized gender as a continuum rather than a binary male/female concept. Justice Edwards accepted Rape Relief's submission that Rape Relief's community of women were located on the far end of the female continuum.

The BC Supreme Court decision also held, as was implicit in the tribunal's decision,[19] that women who were born and raised as girls and women ("non-transsexual" women) are entitled to form a group protected under the exemption provisions of section 41 of the Code. Justice Edwards held that the tribunal failed to correctly interpret and apply the leading Supreme

Court of Canada decision on section 41 in *Caldwell.*[20] The Supreme Court of Canada found that section 41 is a rights-granting provision and as such is not subject to the restrictive interpretation generally applicable to legislative provisions which place limitations on rights.[21] The *Caldwell* decision also held that it was permissible to make a preference of one member of the identifiable group over another, as long as the distinction was made honestly, in good faith and in the sincerely held belief that it is imposed in the interest of the adequate performance of the work, and if it was related, in an objective sense, to the performance of the employment.[22] Justice Edwards followed this reasoning and allowed the preference of one member of the identifiable groups over another, as long as the distinction was made for the benefit of the members of the community served by Rape Relief. Further, Justice Edwards ruled that Rape Relief did not have to prove that its primary purpose had a political dimension in light of the bona fide belief that only women born women were suitable peer counsellors for female rape victims.

The final step with the *Law* approach to section 15 is meant to be both contextual and purposeful, and its objective is to prevent the violation of human dignity. The test of whether dignity has been harmed is both subjective and objective. It is therefore necessary to consider the context of the complainant from the standpoint of a reasonable person.

Justice Edwards believed that Kimberly's exclusion from a "relatively small obscure self-defining private organization cannot have the same impact on human dignity as legislated exclusion from a statutory benefit program."[23] Because her exclusion didn't bear state approval, and hence some wider public acceptance, it was therefore judged not to be a public indignity. Although the court agreed that this was no less subjectively hurtful to Kimberly, the court distinguished the issue of the objective impact on human dignity, which was held to be unreasonably exaggerated. In particular, the court noted, "no reasonable male to female transsexual, standing in Ms. Nixon's shoes, could plausibly" argue that they "can no longer participate in the economic, social and cultural life of the province."[24] Additionally, Christine Boyle, counsel for Rape Relief, argued that a reasonable person would take into account the needs of disadvantaged groups to understand their own experience.

In essence, the court characterized the nature of Rape Relief as a political organization and the nature of the dispute as "essentially a political one over membership criteria."[25] It was not the function of the Code to provide a referee and impose "state-sanctioned penalties in political disputes between private organizations."[26] And, the court held, this was quite unlike Kimberly being excluded from a restaurant. Finally, Justice Edwards held that the reason Kimberly was attracted to the peer-counsellor training program was because it would vindicate her womanhood, because it was part of a women-only organization. Her participation was held to have a political dimension.

In the end, the tribunal's conclusion that Rape Relief's exclusion of Kimberly as discriminatory was found to be unreasonable and the order for Rape Relief to pay her $7,500 in compensation was set aside. The BC Supreme Court's decision leaves room, as the *Law* decision suggests, for different forms of disadvantage. The decision also allows and recognizes the experience of growing up as a girl and living as a woman to be a permissible basis for a group to exclusively associate.

The decision by the BC Supreme Court has been substantially upheld by the BC Court of Appeal. On July 12, 2005, Kimberly's appeal of Justice Edwards's decision was dismissed. The Court of Appeal found that although the test of "discrimination" under the BC Human Rights Code was met, Rape Relief was held to be exempt from the application of the Code by virtue of section 41.[27]

VIOLENCE AGAINST WOMEN

Oppression against women takes it most insidious form within the shocking prevalence of violence against women. The *UN Declaration on Elimination of Violence Against Women,* to which Canada is a signatory, asserts the concern about long-standing failure to protect and promote the rights of women. Also, it notes, "that violence against women is one of the crucial social mechanisms by which women are forced into a subordinate position compared with men."[28]

Many women's groups, sexual assault centres and women's interval houses insist on a women-only membership. It is seen as "essential to the struggle to restore dignity to disempowered women" and "necessary conditions to self-empowerment in a socio-economic and cultural context where access to and mobility within public space is still largely controlled by men and where women's roles and opportunities are frequently defined against their own interests."[29] Women organize as a group to share common experience and to provide support and to strategize in order to make change and address women's concerns, such as the pervasive experience of violence against women. It is a fundamental claim of feminism that women are oppressed. Members gathering from oppressed groups to organize against that oppression is a well-recognized tactic of addressing the effects of oppression and forming strategies for change.[30]

Most women's organizations, including Rape Relief, believe that gender exists along a continuum and none of the needs and desires of their groups are considered unique or exclusive to them, but, given the systemic nature of discrimination and oppression against women and the precarious nature of such groups, identity must be a legitimate basis for organizing.[31] "It is essential to the integrity and autonomy of these groups that they be able to define and control membership in their group."[32] Rape Relief thus excluded Kimberly because of the unique role Rape Relief serves for women experiencing violence.

LEGAL ANALYSIS

Ultimately, Kimberly Nixon and Rape Relief share many similar interests: both share the belief that gender exists on a continuum; both parties have experienced the threat and reality of male violence. Both support the political beliefs that violence is not a woman's fault and that women should be able to organize in women's only spaces. Rape Relief's volunteer criteria excludes not only men within the peer-counsellor training, but also many women. Rape Relief has been dedicated to providing counselling and support services to thousands of women over the past thirty years and feels that the best way to accomplish its goals is by having women that fit their membership criteria serve as counsellors and that these women have lived their entire lives as women. The reason why Rape Relief excluded Kimberly Nixon was found to be held in good faith in both the tribunal's decision and the BC Superior Court decision.

The solution to ending the "either/or-ism" construct of gender and to ending discrimination against transgendered individuals is inappropriately done by launching an action against a non-profit women's crisis centre. The crisis centre is not the source of our gender binary. Both parties supported the notion that gender exists on a continuum. It seems reasonable that women born and living as women their entire lives would exist on a particular end of that continuum and women who always felt that they were women but did not always grow up as women would exist on a different point on that gender continuum. Otherwise, inclusion of post-operative transsexual individuals reinforces the notion of two exclusive genders. As well, the exclusion of pre-operative transsexuals versus post-operative transsexuals may ultimately have a discriminatory impact on individuals who do not wish to have surgery performed or are unable to afford the cost of surgery. Forcing the admission of Kimberly serves to preserve and perpetuate the two gender categories.

The autonomy of this women's collective to set it own membership was undermined and essentially removed by an order mandating that Kimberly Nixon be admitted to Rape Relief's membership. It removed the power from a small women's group, working to assist victims of sexual violence, to decide what issues they are interested in examining and what political beliefs and services they feel comfortable offering. Disadvantage occurs in many ways in society, it occurs to many to different groups in society. The section 41 exclusion, within the Code, enables groups to meet to address their own specific needs. The law should not be used, as it has been historically, to "strike back at women's hard-won protections and benefits."[33] Moreover, to mandate Kimberly to the membership of Rape Relief also suggests that women who organize to assist one another and address sexual violence in their lives are not equally deserving of the autonomous decision to define their own identity and membership.

Feminist legal theorists and equality advocates in Canada have detailed historically sensitive and contextual theories and strategies based on the notion of substantive equality. Their approaches begin with an appreciation of the difference between people, recognizing that for law and social policies to have real equality as their outcome, they must take into consideration the real difference between and among social groups.[34] The court decision in this case appreciates a substantive understanding of equality, within the particular context of the exclusion experienced by Kimberly in this unique set of circumstances.

The BC Court of Appeal has upheld the decision of the BC Supreme Court. This appellate decision recognizes the diverse experiences of disadvantaged groups in society and affirms the right for equity-seeking groups to form independent collectives. However, the Court of Appeal may not have made the final ruling in this case as it seems destined for hearing at the Supreme Court of Canada.

NOTES

1 For non-government actors the Charter does not apply. When discrimination occurs by a private actor the complainant must seek redress under the applicable human rights code.

2 Section 15, the equality provision of the Charter, lists these nine prohibited grounds of discrimination. See also *Egan v. Canada*, [1995] 2 S.C.R. 513 (QL).

3 *Miron v. Trudel*, [1995] 2 S.C.R. 418 (QL).

4 In the 1999 decision in *Law v. Canada (Minister of Employment and Immigration)*, [1999] 1 S.C.R. 497 [Law].

5 Ibid., 39.

6 Ibid., 53.

7 Mr. Justice Walter Surma Tarnopolsky, *Discrimination and the Law* (Scarborough: Carswell, 2001), 4–100.3.

8 *British Columbia (Public Service Employee Relations Commission) v. B.C.G.E.U., 176 D.L.R.* (4th) 1, 35 C.H.R.R. D/257, [1997] 3 S.C.R. 3.

9 *Vancouver Rape Relief Society v. Nixon,* 2005 BCCA 601 at para 39.

10 Pursuant to s. 27(1) of the *Vital Statistics Act*, R.S.B.C. 1996, c.479.

11 Victoria Gray, "Vancouver Rape Relief and Women's Shelter Legal Argument Part II." Available online at Vancouver Rape Relief and Women's Shelter, www.rapereliefshelter.bc.ca/issues/knixon_vgray_argum.html.

12 *Nixon v. Vancouver Rape Relief Society* [2002] B.C.H.R.T.D. No.1, 2001 B.C.H.R.T. 1 (QL), 34. Hereafter *Nixon.*

13 Rape Relief had applied to halt proceeding on the basis that the B.C. Human Rights Code did not specifically prohibit discrimination based on transsexualism or gender identity. Mr. Justice Davies disagreed and held that the "it would be wrong to interpret the prohibition against discrimination on the basis of sex in the *Code* as not also prohibiting discrimination against an individual merely because that person or group is not readily identifiable as being either male or female." *Vancouver Rape Relief Society v. British Columbia* (Human Rights Commission) [2002] B.C.H.R.T.D. No. 1, 57.

14 The tribunal rejected the notion that the Law analysis is appropriate in the human rights context. Instead, the test the Tribunal applied was in the case of Ontario (Human Rights Commission) v. Simpson Sears Ltd. [1995] S.C.J. 74.

15 *Nixon*, 221.

16 Ibid., 231.

17 *Vancouver Rape Relief Society v. Nixon*, [2003] B.C.J. No.2899, 2003 B.C.S.C. 1936 (QL). Hereafter *Rape Relief*.

18 If a "charitable, philanthropic, educational, fraternal, religious or social organization or corporation not operating for profit and is primarily focused on promoting the interests of an identifiable group characterized by ... a common ... sex [or] political belief preference to the members of the identifiable group must not be considered to contravene the Human Rights Code."

19 *Nixon*, 208–224.

20 *Caldwell v. St. Thomas Aquinas High School*, [1984] 2 S.C.R. 603, (QL).

21 *Rape Relief*, 114.

22 *Ontario Human Rights Commission v. Etobicoke* (Borough of), [1982] 1 S.C.R. 202 (QL), 208.

23 Ibid., 145.

24 Ibid., 151.

25 *Rape Relief*, 156.

26 Ibid.,157, citing *Gould v. Association of Yukon Pioneers*, [1996] 1 S.C.R. 571.

27 *Vancouver Rape Relief Society v. Nixon,* 2005 BCCA 601, para 9.

28 United Nations, *Declaration on Elimination of Violence Against Women,* Proclaimed by General Assembly Resolution 48/104 of 20 December 1993. Available online at www.hri.ca/uninfo/treaties/ViolWom.shtml.

29 Margaret Denike and Sal Renshaw, "Transgender and Women's Substantive Equality" (paper prepared at the National Consultation on Transgender and Women's Substantive Equality, National Association of Women and the Law, February 2003), 13.

30 barbara findlay, "Real Women: Kimberly Nixon v. Vancouver Rape Relief," University of British Columbia Law Review 36 (2003), 57–76, quoting Paolo Freire, *Pedagogy of the Oppressed* (New York: Continuum, 1970).

31 Denike and Renshaw, "Transgender and Women's Substantive Equality," 13.

32 Ibid.

33 Gwen Brodsky and Sheila Day, *Canadian Charter Equality Rights for Women: One Step Forward or Two Steps Back?* (Ottawa: Canadian Advisory Council on the Status of Women, 1989).

34 Denike and Renshaw, "Transgender and Women's Substantive Equality," 5.

CHAPTER 17

STRATEGIC ESSENTIALISM ON TRIAL: LEGAL INTERVENTIONS AND SOCIAL CHANGE

Lara Karaian

USE OF THE LAW AS A STRATEGY OF RESISTANCE AND A MECHANISM FOR social change is a hotly debated subject amongst the Left.[1] Nevertheless, Canadian equality advocates, including feminists, have often turned to the law[2] for social, political and legal recognition, the granting of rights and freedoms, as well as the provision of remedies for harms done. More recently, other marginalized groups, such as gay, lesbian, bisexual, queer and transgendered communities, have made a similar turn to the law as a tool for achieving social justice. Often, this diverse group has argued for protection against sex discrimination, a category that has been deemed by the courts to include protection from both sexual orientation and gender identity discrimination.

This chapter briefly explores the intersection of feminist and transgender struggles for equality. In particular, I examine the legal arguments presented by both sides in *Nixon v. Vancouver Rape Relief Society*.[3] This case deals with whether or not a radical feminist community's refusal to include transgendered women in their organization in the interest of protecting "real" women, is unduly discriminatory. My exploration is informed by an ongoing debate among numerous feminists, queer theorists and transgender activists regarding the reliance on "strategic essentialism" as a means of resistance. I argue that while strategic essentialism may at times be useful, progressive legal activists would be more accountable to the communities they are representing if they were to incorporate greater complexity and diversity into their legal arguments.

"WOMAN" IN AND UNDER THE LAW

In order to be protected by provisions against sex discrimination, feminist and transgender legal subjects have had to fit themselves within the categorical imperatives of the law. In other words, both must argue in favour of their version of the category "woman" as well as their inclusion in that category in order to be protected against discrimination on this ground. Many feminists including women of colour, post-structuralists, postmodernists, queer theorists and transgender activists have long rejected the ideas that our identity in general and our understanding of ourselves as "women" and "men" more specifically, are uncomplicated, do not change over time and place, and consist of immutable essences. For example, gender theorist Judith Butler has argued that feminists have deconstructed or "troubled" gender. That is, they have questioned gender norms and looked critically at our assumptions about gender. At the same time Butler admits that "within feminism, it seems as if there is some political necessity to speak as and for *women*." She goes on to argue, however, that any effort to give universal or specific content to the category of women, will result in fragmentation, and that "identity" as a point of departure can never hold as the solidifying ground of a feminist political movement.[4]

When it comes down to the reality of making legal arguments we are often forced to insert ourselves into identity categories that have been labelled as protected grounds within Canada's anti-discrimination provisions. The Canadian legal framework is founded on liberal individualism and in large part continues to rely on simplified and homogeneous identity categories as well as the concept of a stable legal subject.[5] Thus, at times feminists and transgendered individuals' attempts to gain protection against sex discrimination may come into conflict with their simultaneous attempts at refiguring traditional understandings of "women" and "men" as stable and knowable categories. This, however, is not to say that the law does not play a role in shaping ideas about gender. In fact the law is not only a regulatory body, it is also a creative one, and thus part of our changing ideas about the categories of women and men have resulted from legal interventions.

There are spaces of resistance within the legal sphere. In fact, our courts have started to adopt more complex ways of understanding identity and discrimination and as such our legal strategies should both acknowledge this and continue to push the courts in this direction.

SHIFTING ESSENTIALISMS

Essentialism in social theory is the belief that one's identity is stable, has a clear meaning, and consists of fixed traits that are constant through time, space, and different historical, social, political and personal contexts. In feminist thought, according to feminist theorist Diana Fuss, essentialism is a common occurrence given that feminism presumes "a unity of its object of inquiry (women) *even* when it is at pains to demonstrate the differences within this admittedly generalizing and imprecise category."[6]

A reliance on essentialism has been thoroughly critiqued and largely rejected as reductionist and unreflective of the constructed and complexity nature of identity and experience. However, in *Essentially Speaking: Feminism, Nature, Difference*, Fuss argues that Western feminism has fostered "a certain paranoia around the perceived threat of essentialism" and that this has created an essence/constructionist binarism which feminist and queer theorists have argued is an equally simplistic framework.[7] Fuss argues that we can never securely escape essentialism and therefore it becomes useful for us to distinguish between *kinds* of essentialisms. Drawing on the work of Gayatri Spivak, she argues that "falling into" or "lapsing into" essentialism implies a problem or mistake whereas "deploying" or "activating" essentialism implies that essentialism may have some strategic or interventionary value. According to Fuss "the radicality or conservatism of essentialism depends, to a significant degree, on *who* is utilizing it, *how* it is deployed, and *where* its effects are concentrated."[8]

Queer legal theorist Carl Stychin agrees, and claims there is an increasingly apparent tension between, on the one hand, the queer desire to deconstruct and critique the categories of identity; and, on the other, the necessity of asserting coherent categories as a strategy of political reform and transformation.[9] Given that legal analysis has historically been reliant on fixed, uncomplicated and rigidly demarcated categories to define those making legal claims, Stychin argues that legal strategies might ultimately demand some sort of essentialism.

I do not doubt that strategic essentialism may at times be a successful means of resistance. Nevertheless, I remain wary of the practice and believe that there are successful alternatives. In my opinion, feminists and progressive activists too often assume that their use of strategic essentialism is necessarily radical rather than conservative because of their position as marginalized and progressive actors. In fact, the way in which the left or marginalized communities deploy essentialism, and the effects of this deployment, can be quite conservative and thus the "successes" that result from this strategy are only ever partial in nature. This, in my opinion, is what took place in the case of *Nixon v. Vancouver Rape Relief Society.*

STRATEGIC ESSENTIALISM IN THE *NIXON* CASE

In 1995 Kimberly Nixon, a post-operative male-to-female transsexual, launched a Human Rights complaint after she was denied access to volunteer training offered by Vancouver Rape Relief because she was not born a woman. Rape Relief argued that their exclusion of Kimberly Nixon from their organization did not constitute discrimination on the basis of sex, as was being argued by Kimberly. Rather, Rape Relief contended that their actions were necessary to protect "real" women within their organization as well as their right to women-only spaces. In 2002, seven years after this case was first brought to the British Columbia Human Rights Commission, a tribunal found in Kimberly Nixon's favour, awarding her $7,500 in damages, the province's highest-ever monetary award for injury to dignity. Rape Relief appealed to the Supreme Court of British Columbia, where the decision of the tribunal was reviewed and overturned in 2003. Kimberly Nixon then appealed to the British Columbia Court of Appeal and lost in 2005. The case will likely be appealed to the Supreme Court of Canada; however, at the time of publication this has yet to be confirmed.

This case provides evidence of how the legal grounds of gender identity are simultaneously crumbling below us and being reconstructed around us. Nevertheless, upon further examination of the arguments made by Nixon and Rape Relief we can see that both the transgendered and the radical feminist community resort to "strategic essentialism" when defining womanhood and advocating for the legal rights and protections that accompany that identity. Rape Relief submitted that their exclusion of Nixon was justified and protected by section 41 of the Canadian Human Rights Code.

Section 41 exempts non-profit organizations from the application of the Code if they have as their primary purpose the promotion of the interests and welfare of an identifiable group, or class of persons characterized by a common sex or political belief. In this case, Rape Relief argued that it could rely on a section 41 exemption because one of the shelter's primary purposes is the promotion of the interests and welfare of those who share its distinct and common political beliefs (read: "real" women). Rape Relief defined this as someone with a lifelong experience of being female[10] and claimed that there is a common experience of sex that includes such things as childhood socialization, lifelong experience of the cultural meaning associated with female biology, social and physical relationships to reproduction and the experience of a particular type of subordination.[11]

The tribunal chair rejected this essentialized understanding of women and wrote:

> There was no evidence before me that there is, in fact, a shared life experience that is common to all non-transsexual women, and Rape Relief called no evidence to show that it requires its volunteers, or its clients, to have such a common experience. In fact, the evidence that they did call leads me to the opposite conclusion.[12]

In opposition to Rape Relief's arguments, barbara findlay, acting counsel for Kimberly Nixon argues, "We do not assert that socialization plays no role in the acquisition of gender role. But there can be no doubt that a part of an individual's gender is determined by the time s/he has been born."[13] Both Rape Relief and findlay rely on strategically essentialist understandings of what makes a woman, understandings that are closely linked to biology and innate characteristics. Interestingly, findlay's legal strategy upholds the binary she/he as opposed to breaking it down or proposing a gender continuum advanced by many transgender theorists and activists. Instead, gender identity is largely described as innate, not chosen, and lifelong.

In addition to these essentializing arguments there is persistent presentation of Nixon as an "essential woman." For example, in her testimony, Nixon constructs herself as the ideal empathetic women. She claims, "In my experience [working with victims of violence] that [disruption or harm] never occurred. It just didn't happen … [B]ecause of my *nature*, my *compassion*, my *empathy*, and my experiences, which were similar to their experience of abuse, I'm able to connect that way with women very well on the crisis lines and in person."[14] Soon we are reassured that Kimberly Nixon is also a "good" transsexual: she has had genital reassignment surgery so that her internal and external identities correspond, she is heterosexual and she co-parents a child. This soft-spoken, heterosexual parent is described as having felt "really hurt" and humiliated. She was "distraught" and "could not stop crying." She experienced major anxiety attacks and felt "worthless," "hopeless," "helpless" and as if "everything was out of control."[15] Given this description, which reflects and reproduces dominant ideas of true womanhood, it is easy to see how the tribunal found in Nixon's favour and understood her as a traditionally feminine woman even if, as Nixon herself put it, the experience was very damaging to her sense of self and her identity as female was undermined.[16]

I would argue that while it was not articulated specifically in their decision, the tribunal recognizes Nixon's womanhood, and thus her claim of discrimination, in large part because of her dependence on essentialist portrayals of womanhood as feminine, nurturing, emotional and caring even while it goes on to reject Rape Relief's reliance on arguments that advance women as a fixed and unified category. Given these legal arguments it is not unreasonable to wonder whether the tribunal would have found in Nixon's favour had she not been portrayed as or had been an emotional, heterosexual, monogamous co-parent who — maybe most importantly — had chosen to surgically transition. Could the decision of the Human Rights Tribunal been decided in Nixon's favour without the presentation of a narrow and strategically essentialized understanding of transgendered women and the discrimination that they experience? In the next section I discuss why I believe this may have been possible and the importance of presenting legal arguments that acknowledge diversity within the category woman.

PITFALLS AND ALTERNATIVES

The legal argumentation of both sides leaves no room for complexity or dissent within the radical feminist or transgendered movement. In an effort to make the case for Nixon's womanhood, her council erases any idea of gender identity as fluid, the existence of intersex individuals as well as the realities of pangendered individuals (those that move back and forth or along a gender continuum throughout their lives).

Similarly, Rape Relief's legal strategy skirts complexity by insisting on presenting a unified voice of those in their organization and "women" more generally. It refused to recognize that Nixon had made it through the pre-screening process and was accepted for the training session and was only asked to leave by another women once the training session began. Rape Relief did not call the member who had accepted Nixon for training to the stand, nor did it explain why the member did not call her. Counsel for Nixon claimed that this suggested that her evidence would have been unfavourable to Rape Relief's presentation of a unified voice of exclusion, since at least one member of the organization knew at the time of the pre-screening that Kimberly Nixon was a transgendered women and did not exclude her on the grounds of her "sex."[17]

Feminist legal theorist Lise Gotell is critical of legal argumentation that abandons complexity in return for decisions that are inadequate in their ability to remedy social ills. Gotell claims that to really push the radical edge of "new egalitarian movements," we need to develop a more complex politics, one that does not assert, depend on or reproduce the "Truth" of a unified identity derived from the concept of the liberal legal subject as essentialized and coherent. Gotell argues that if there is to be a strategy of "partial fixity" — the reliance on a temporarily essentialized legal subject, another way of saying "strategic essentialism" in my opinion — legal activists will have to take responsibility for the construction and effects of normalized and homogenous identities that comprise the basis for their strategies.[18] Gotell further argues that, "As we develop our legal positions in these cases it is crucial to recognize that it is possible to articulate complexities and nuance within the context of legal strategies."[19]

There are alternatives to strategic essentialism. Legal theorist Douglas Kropp, for example, takes the position that we need to break from our fixation on the "grounds" of discrimination such as sex, race, age and so on, and instead we must increase our focus on the lived experience of rights claimants.[20] Only this way, Kropp argues, will the courts' approach to discrimination be able to adequately account for the social construction of individual and collective identity. Interestingly, this is the same position taken by the tribunal when it argues that the goal of the rape crisis centre might be better served if the organization recognized and incorporated into the fulfillment of its mandate the victimization experienced by transgendered women. This is a position that focuses on common experiences of marginalization and victimization as opposed to membership in the identity category "woman." It is heartening to see the courts adopt such an analysis. The tribunal's analysis shifts attention to the effects of Rape Relief's exclusion as opposed to focusing on what constitutes woman and therefore deserves protection.

The decision reached by the tribunal is reflective of the position taken by former Supreme Court Justice L'Heureux-Dubé who has suggested that the courts adopt a "vulnerable group" analysis which would "put discrimination first."[21] Thus, Kropp suggests Justice L'Heureux-Dubé may have "outlined a postmodernist model of anti-discrimination law that avoids the pitfalls of essentialist notions of identity."[22] As mentioned above, this decision may have meant the extension of protection to those that fall outside the essentialized woman, including the essentialized transgendered woman, such as to those who do not decide to transition for economic or personal reasons or those that are pangendered. Unfortunately, in the case of Nixon and Rape Relief it cannot be denied that the decision of the tribunal is arrived at in large part through a politics of exclusion, one wherein gender identity continues to be linked to problematic omissions of diversity within the category women.

While the law may be slow to change and the problems with using it to address human rights disputes are numerous, it remains a site of struggle that is not easily abandoned, nor should it be. Nevertheless, we have to make sure that our strategies as progressive legal actors continue to push the edges of our movement. Transgender activists and feminists will no doubt continue to rely on the law to address social ills. It is my hope that the future legal strategies of marginalized communities are accountable, radically creative *and* successful strategies of resistance.

NOTES

1 See Wendy Brown and Janet Halley, eds., *Left Legalism/Left Critique* (Durham, NC: Duke University Press, 2002). The debate often revolves around law's requirement that the arguments of social justice activist be forced to fit into a legal discourse that reduces the complexity of the issue into legal terms. It is also argued that the left turns too quickly to the law to eradicate social inequities when in fact other avenues of resistance are likely to take up less resources, less time and be more successful in enacting positive changes. A key element of this debate is the recognition that legal decisions that some feminists herald as successes are seen as quite the opposite by others with

the feminist community.

2 Both the Charter of Rights and Freedoms and the *Canadian Human Rights Act* are used extensively by social justice seekers. Section 15 (1) of the Charter reads: "Every individual is equal before and under the law and has the right to the equal protection and equal benefit of the law without discrimination and, in particular, without discrimination based on race, national or ethnic origin, colour, religion, sex, age or mental or physical disability." Canadian Charter of Rights and Freedoms, Part I of the *Constitution Act, 1982*, being Schedule B to the *Canada Act 1982* (U.K.), 1982, c. 11. Included in section 15 is a list of grounds of discrimination — such as discrimination in the basis of sex. These are referred to as enumerated grounds. In addition to these, the Supreme Court of Canada recognizes analogous grounds of discrimination, grounds that are related or comparable to those that are listed. Sexual orientation is an example of an analogous ground of discrimination. It has been recognized as such since 1995 decision in *Egan v. Canada*, [1995] 2 S.C.R. 513 (QL).

3 *Nixon v. Vancouver Rape Relief Society*, [2002] B.C.H.R.T. 1 (QL). Hereafter *Nixon*. The decision in this case was appealed to two higher courts; however, in the interest of space only the arguments and the decision presented in the original human rights challenge are discussed.

4 Judith Butler, "Contingent Foundations: Feminism and the Question of Postmodernism," in Judith Butler and Joan W. Scott, eds., *Feminists Theorize the Political* (New York: Routledge, 1992), 15.

5 Lise Gotell, "Queering Law by Same Sex Marriage??!!" (unpublished manuscript distributed at the Queering Political Science panel of the Canadian Political Science Association Conference, Toronto, ON, May 2002), in possession of the author. Gotell writes, "The modernist liberal equality subject is independent, unitary, coherent and fixed ignoring that social identities are culturally and historically contingent" (8–9).

6 Diana Fuss, *Essentially Speaking: Feminism, Nature and Difference* (New York: Routledge, 1989), 2.

7 Ibid., 1.

8 Ibid., 20. In *Essentially Speaking* Fuss adopts Gayatri Spivak's idea that essentialism can be powerfully displacing and disruptive when put into practice by the dispossessed themselves. See Gayatri Spivak. "Can the Subaltern Speak?" in Cary Nelson and Larry Grossberg, eds., *Marxism and the Interpretation of Culture* (Chicago: University of Illinois Press, 1998), 271–313.

9 Carl F. Stychin, *Law's Desire: Sexuality and the Limits of Justice* (London: Routledge, 1995), 140.

10 *Nixon,* para 214.

11 Ibid., para 215.

12 Ibid., para 222.

13 Submission of barbara findlay, "B.C.H.R.T. matter between Kimberly Nixon, Complainant, and Vancouver Rape Relief Society, Respondent," para 76. Hereafter *findlay*.

14 *Nixon,* para 206. Emphasis added.

15 Ibid., para 241.

16 Ibid., para 242.

17 *findlay*, para 178.

18 Gotell, "Queering Law by Same Sex Marriage??!!" 45.

19 Ibid., 46.

20 Douglas Kropp, "Categorical Failure: Canada's Equality Jurisprudence: Changing Notions of Identity and the Legal Subject," *Queen's Law Journal* 23 (Fall 1997), 219.

21 Ibid., 225.

22 Ibid., 227.

SECTION IV

Shelter & Violence

INTRODUCTION

Krista Scott-Dixon

FOR HUNDREDS OF YEARS, WOMEN HAVE SPOKEN OUT against violence and abuse by male partners and family members and have provided shelter for other women in need. Despite this historical precedent, it was not until the 1960s and 1970s that systematic feminist anti-violence discussion, action and organizing emerged. In 1977, sociologists Roger Langley and Richard Levy wrote in *Wife Beating: The Silent Crisis* that wife assault was a taken-for-granted part of North American culture, "so pervasive that it literally does not occur to people to report it or collect statistics on it. Many police officers would no more file reports on battered wives than they would on the number of telephone poles they pass on a given day."[1] Because male abuse of women happened most often within the "private sphere" of home and family (although women were also abused in public spaces), it was generally considered a domestic problem not worthy of serious legal attention. Feminists began with consciousness-raising sessions in which male violence was named and analyzed in the context of patriarchal society and family structures. Then they turned to the development of a network of shelters and services for women and their children, as well as legal and judicial activism for improved legislative and judicial tools, such as more aggressive anti-violence laws and more sensitive police practice.

Although there were differences in implementation, some broad shared principles guided collective feminist anti-violence and shelter/service analysis and action in the late twentieth century, such as the importance of grassroots organizing and the contention that gender inequalities enabled abuse to occur.[2] These principles also provided much of the foundation for subsequent anti-transphobia analyses, strategies and action. However, in practice, feminist shelters and services often came into conflict with transpositive and trans-inclusion initiatives, as discussed in both this section and the preceding one, "Inclusion and Exclusion." Thus, despite general agreement on the principles for understanding and counteracting gender-based violence, policy-makers and activists frequently struggled with how to interpret and apply these principles.

The first feminist principle involved feminists in the early shelter movement who argued that gendered power dynamics shaped women's experiences of violence and social disadvantage: men, as a group, held power over women by virtue of their physical abilities and greater access to economic and political resources. Violence and abuse were a means by which men established, exerted and reproduced their socially sanctioned control over women. Feminists critiqued the notion that male violence was a result of some individual psychopathology, arguing that this erased gendered dynamics of power between men and women. Fundamentally, feminists proposed, violence happened to women living in a misogynist society simply *because they were women.* Although later feminist analyses expanded to include same-sex violence and abuse, the diverse experiences of different groups of women and the intersection of classism, racism and other oppressions, the gendered character of violence against women remained a central theme. As a result, the inclusion of men as shelter workers and supporters was a contentious issue.

Similarly, one explanation for violence against trans people emerging in current analyses is that it is also an expression of gendered power dynamics. Anti-trans abuse happens to trans people in a transphobic, gender-rigid society simply *because they are trans.* Transphobic and misogynist violence may result from a perpetrator's desire to "normalize" his or her victim's gender. Victims may be seen as transgressing appropriate gender roles and rules of behaviour or dress. This might take the form of a wife being seen by her husband as "getting uppity" when she asserts herself or a trans woman being perceived by attackers as "too masculine" in her appearance. Perpetrators may aim to re-establish not only a proper gender order but also their own normalcy and dominance within it.[3]

There are often several gendered layers to transphobic violence. The perpetrator may "reveal" or "expose" the victim as "really" their birth gender and may engage in violence, often sexualized, against the victim in order to confirm the birth gender status.[4] The victim's perceived or actual sexual behaviour and orientation may play an additional part, as homophobia is clearly linked to both "genderism" and misogyny. In other words, like transphobia, not only does homophobia emerge from the notion that the normal gender order has been violated, but also that such a violation represents either a shameful loss of masculinity/social power by gay men, or an inappropriate claim on masculinity/social power by lesbians. Just as husbands were encouraged to "tame the shrew" in their household, trans people are "put in their (gendered) place" through violence. Yet transphobic violence is not merely a copy of misogynist violence: it can also contain elements specifically directed at the victim's trans status. Perpetrators may emphasize and direct their physical/sexual abuse at specific features of trans bodies, such as breasts/chests and genitalia. Transphobic violence may be as much a punishment for not passing as for gender transgression. In any case, as theorist Vivian Namaste argues, "those individuals who live outside normative sex/gender relations will be most at risk for assault."[5]

The second feminist principle driving the early shelter movement was that the family and household, as social institutions and microcosm of larger society, were focal points for these gendered power dynamics. Feminists argued that abuse of women by male partners was an expression of patriarchal family dynamics that positioned women as subordinate within the family structure. Likewise, sexual assault was seen as an extension of the premise that men had a right to possess and use women's bodies. Similarly, trans people have traditionally been at risk within their households and families as a result of larger gender-rigid and anti-trans social norms.[6]

Yet, although the feminist challenge to the private nature of so-called domestic abuse was important, another key feminist insight was that this "private" sphere of home and family was linked to larger "public" systems of power and oppression based on gender inequities. For instance, mainstream society not only reproduced gendered inequality but also, through the mechanisms of the state, withheld economic and social safety nets that would enable survivors to escape abusive situations, such as social assistance. Thus, the provision of safer spaces, economic assistance and various services was a major focus of feminist anti-violence initiatives. Trans people may also have limited access to economic and social resources that might enable them to escape abuse. "Coming out" as a survivor of violence may also involve "coming out" as trans, which could mean the loss of jobs, family and friends and social status. For some trans people, it might mean attempting to access resources without important paperwork and legal documentation — a no-person's land of legally gendered limbo — or with a body that is still undergoing transition (or does not pass) and does not fit comfortably into shelter spaces designed for one gender or another.

Moreover, feminists argued, public spaces were also places where gender norms were maintained and policed through various means. Verbal harassment on the street could remind women that the public space was not theirs to command. Women could be at risk (or seen to be at risk) of violence on dark streets and in "bad neighbourhoods." Some women constrained their own behaviour in order to avoid dangerous public places, although for many women, such as sex workers who walked the dark streets and poor women who lived in "bad neighbourhoods," this was not an option. If women were assaulted in public spaces, there was often swift justification for why they deserved it or had no right to be out in public in the first place.[7] This justification doesn't just reinforce gender norms by restricting women to the "proper" sphere of home and family; it hides the violence in the "safe" space of the household.

Trans people may be likewise punished with gendered violence within public spaces. For example, many trans people who are unsure of how well they pass avoid public washrooms, which are spaces that are particularly fraught with danger: trans women (and butch women) may be harassed as "really" men in women's spaces and forcibly ejected, while trans men (and effeminate men) may be revealed as "really" women and sexually assaulted.[8] Trans people who are poor, sex workers, and/or socially marginalized in other ways may experience abuse not only as a result of their working conditions but from the police as well. Crimes against trans people in general, but especially trans sex workers, are often viewed by police and broader society as justified punishment for leading a deviant lifestyle of sexual and gender transgression of norms in public spaces.

The third feminist principle of anti-violence and shelter organizing was that women's perspectives and experiences should guide feminist anti-violence policy. In the 1960s and 1970s, even granting authenticity to survivors of sexual assault or abuse was a radical act. Feminists rejected the notion that battered or raped women "asked for it," or that they were inherently masochistic or fundamentally different from other women. They substituted the term "survivor" for "victim," and sought to reframe the terms of engagement and critique prevailing cultural stereotypes of women's experiences.

Trans-positive anti-violence policy likewise attempts to destigmatize trans survivors of abuse. Because Gender Identity Disorder (GID) appears in the Diagnostic and Statistical Manual (DSM IV), the guide by which the psychiatric profession categorizes and diagnoses mental illness,[9] trans people may be negatively characterized by service providers as mentally ill.[10] Or, they may experience quite normal reactions to abuse and oppression, such as anxiety, depression or substance use, which may then be taken as evidence of overall instability. Thus, as with feminists, an individualized psychopathological approach is generally rejected by trans activists. Trans-positive shelter policies are best developed by building on the stories and lived experiences of trans people and linking them to larger systems of gendered inequity as well as to political struggles for equality, dignity and human rights.

Finally, feminist anti-violence analysis was seen as part of an overall project of advocacy for women. Feminists envisioned scholarship and research on violence as part of a broader anti-violence, anti-oppression initiative. The grassroots project of creating and maintaining shelters, safe houses and anti-violence services was an explicitly feminist political one, often based on the energy and dedication of a handful of women. Likewise, shelter and safety is now a critical component of trans-positive service delivery.

*

Feminist analyses of power dynamics are useful for understanding and organizing against transphobic violence. This is not to say that a feminist analysis can necessarily be applied directly to the specific lived experiences of trans people, but rather, that insights and lessons learned from feminist organizing can be useful in the development of trans-oriented services and advocacy.

Despite the wide range of organizations, in their early stages, the sixties and seventies feminist groups generally shared the goal of providing services and shelter for women who were survivors of male violence and abuse. Feminist literature often contained a powerful critique of the linked dynamics of oppression and identified the racial and class elements of aggression and victimization.[11] For example, some feminists critiqued the notion that some survivors were more "legitimate" than others based on their racial-ethnic and class position. Middle-class white women whose sexual behaviour was considered socially appropriate (perhaps by virtue of their dress or marital status) were more likely to be viewed by mainstream society and the justice system as more believable victims than poor women, First Nations women or sex workers. Marginalized groups of women were less likely to experience and view police and judicial bodies as helpful; rather, police and state agencies often represented harassment and further victimization.

However, despite this awareness of the links between oppressions, feminists working in collectives and shelters still often unwittingly reproduced the problem of inequities between women.[12] Shelter policies and interpersonal dynamics often repeated or reinforced the relations of oppression that they attempted to resist, either by omission (e.g., of services for diverse women) or by explicit exclusion.[13] Shelter regulations and policies often reflected a white, middle-class social order that prioritized gender oppression above other oppressions. The often taken-for-granted assumption that males could only be aggressors and women could only be victims erased both the contributions of pro-feminist men and the experiences of lesbians.[14] Shelter workers who were tired, angry, underpaid, overworked and frustrated by competing demands were often resistant to the additional labour of critical self-reflection and examination of their privileges, outreach to diverse communities, working across differences, educating others and overcoming their ingrained prejudices.

Currently, although there would appear to be natural opportunities for coalitions between feminist and trans anti-violence initiatives, shelter and anti-violence services that are both trans-accessible and trans-positive can be hard to find or absent. In addition, "few [shelters] have anti-discrimination policies that include trans people, staff are rarely trained on these issues, and those that do not deny entry may treat trans people with disrespect."[15] Women's shelters and services have responded to the issue of trans accessibility in various ways.[16] Some groups have opted to deny access to trans women altogether. In other shelters and services, access may be granted depending on role (for example, trans people may be welcome as shelter users but not workers, or vice versa), passability (using a "don't ask-don't tell" approach), or surgical status (in the case of trans women). The question of who counts as a woman is often at the heart of struggles over shelter and service policies. Shelters who do not grant open access to trans people often cite safety as a prime concern.[17]

The underlying assumption in this case builds on two elements: first, a view of trans people, usually trans women, as "really" men who carry the social baggage of male privilege and dominance (and perhaps the physical baggage of born-male genitalia); and second, the understanding of gendered violence as one-way from men to women. Thus, trans women in particular may be seen as a threat because they are "really" men who might attempt to exert their vestiges of male dominance, or because shelter clients would view them as such and feel threatened (shelters appear to have been less able to puzzle out what to do with trans men given this model). Some women's shelters attempt to deal with this challenge by insisting that trans women will be accepted if they conform to gender norms, such as feminine dress and comportment, or if their surgical status is acceptable (i.e., the removal of offending phallic genitals is complete).[18]

This position has been challenged by trans and trans-positive activists on several grounds: first, that trans women are not "men in dresses" but rather individuals with a trans identity who have likely never been gender-normative enough to enjoy male dominance and privilege — many have been genderqueer or effeminate their entire lives. Second, trans men are usually unable to access men's services, and to do so could be very risky if their trans status were known. Third, trans and gender-variant people who require shelter services are not in a position of privilege, but rather dire need. They may have had difficulty finding housing as a result of limited income, discrimination, and/or the difficulty of obtaining legal verification of their gender. For many reasons including sex work, HIV status, concurrent illnesses and poverty, shelter users typically are unable to afford or access surgery and care that would enable them to pass the stringent surgical or treatment requirements of many shelters. Finally, while violence against women and trans people is well-documented, there is little evidence that trans people are likely to assault non-trans people.[19]

Shelter and service provision remains a significant struggle for feminist and trans-positive organizing. As Julie Darke and Allison Cope argue in their publication *Trans Inclusion Policy Manual for Women's Organizations*, bringing shelter services together can be mutually beneficial to both trans and non-trans people, in that trans people would be able to access help and care, and feminist services would be able to expand and enrich their mandate and analyses: "Trans and intersex women's experiences and insights into gender and sex-based oppression can deepen our understanding of gender oppression and thus enhance services for all women."[20]

NOTES

1 Roger Langley and Richard Levy, *Wife Beating: The Silent Crisis* (New York: E.P. Dutton, 1977), 2–3.

2 Michele Bograd, "Feminist Perspectives on Wife Abuse: An Introduction," in Kersti Yllo and Michele Bograd, eds., *Feminist Perspectives on Wife Abuse* (London: Sage, 1988), 13–14.

3 Vivian K. Namaste, "Genderbashing," *Invisible Lives: The Erasure of Transsexual and Transgendered People* (Chicago: University of Chicago Press, 2000), 135–136.

4 See Namaste, "Genderbashing" and Emilia Lombardi, Riki Anne Wilchins, Dana Priesing, and Diana Malouf, "Gender Violence: Transgender Experiences with Violence and Discrimination," *Journal of Homosexuality* 42, no. 1 (2001), 89–102.

5 Namaste, "Genderbashing," 136.

6 Diana Courvant and Loree Cook-Daniels, *Trans and Intersex Survivors of Domestic Violence: Defining Terms, Barriers, and Responsibilities* (Washington, DC: National Coalition Against Domestic Violence, n.d.); Julie Darke and Allison Cope, *Trans Inclusion Policy Manual for Women's Organizations* (Vancouver: Trans Alliance Society, 2002).

7 Namaste, "Genderbashing," 147.

8 Vivian Namaste argues that when out in public, FTMs are at risk of being "revealed" as women who are then seen as transgressing both gender norms and the rules of public space; rape is a frequent consequence that is intended to violently remind the victim of these gendered rules. Fundamentally, suggests Namaste, this assault is "about policing one's gender presentation in public sites … it functions as an aggressive reinscription of the FTM individual's biological sex and social gender." Namaste, "Genderbashing," 147.

9 Courvant and Cook-Daniels, *Trans and Intersex Survivors of Domestic Violence.*

10 However, as Margaret Deidre O'Hartigan and others have argued, associating mental illness and disability with social stigma does little to challenge the negative connotations of mental illness itself. "Rather than condemning such stigmatization … GID opponents reinforce it by attacking the diagnosis rather than the prejudice

itself." O'Hartigan, "The GID Controversy: Transsexuals Need the Gender Identity Disorder Diagnosis," *Transgender Tapestry* (Summer 1997), 45.

11 Schechter, *Women and Male Violence,* 37.

12 Leslie Timmins, ed., *Listening to the Thunder: Advocates Talk about the Battered Women's Movement* (Vancouver: Women's Research Centre, 1995).

13 Schechter, *Women and Male Violence.*

14 Bonnie Murray and Cathy Welch, "Attending to Lavender Bruises: A Dialogue on Violence in Lesbian Relationships," in Timmins, ed., *Listening to the Thunder,* 109–126.

15 Darke and Cope, *Trans Inclusion Policy Manual for Women's Organizations,* 32–33.

16 Mirha Soleil-Ross, "Investigating Women's Shelters," *Gendertrash* 3 (1995), 7–10.

17 Darke and Cope, *Trans Inclusion Policy Manual for Women's Organizations; Namaste, Invisible Lives;* Soleil-Ross, "Investigating Women's Shelters."

18 Darke and Cope, *Trans Inclusion Policy Manual,* citing Namaste.

19 Soleil-Ross, "Investigating Women's Shelters," 9.

20 Darke and Cope, *Trans Inclusion Policy Manual,* 44.

CHAPTER 18

UNDERSTANDING TRANSPHOBIA: AUTHENTICITY AND SEXUAL VIOLENCE

Talia Mae Bettcher

THE PURPOSE OF THIS CHAPTER IS TO PROVIDE A NEW WAY OF UNDERstanding transphobia and transphobic violence. As almost any trans person[1] will agree, transphobia and transphobic violence are realities that impact our lives significantly. How we understand this fear and hatred matters greatly because this understanding guides our opposition and resistance.

One way of understanding transphobia involves the idea that the binary division — human into man and woman — is a social invention that inflicts great harm upon those who do not fit neatly into one of those two camps. In this view, much of transphobia may be explained in terms of negative attitudes held towards those who diverge from the binary. This account of transphobia can also be applied to people who belong to the binary by recognizing that there are specific rules that require men and women to act in certain ways. For example, a man who acts in ways that are stereotypically feminine may be viewed as belonging to the binary (as a man) but as flouting gender norms of masculinity.[2]

There is much to be said in favour of this account. Most notably, it provides an extremely general explanation that allows for a variety of possible gender identities and expressions that depart from more traditional conceptions. Yet there are also reasons for worrying about the adequacy of this view. Many trans people do not see themselves as departing from these binary categories and seem themselves to go along with the rules of how men and women are supposed to behave. They may prefer to view themselves as "real" men or women and may greet views about the social construction of gender with suspicion. Sometimes these suspicions may relate to complex issues around race and nation.[3] For example, to the extent that "queer" and "gender queer" identifications emerge from largely white, anglo U.S. cultural locations, refusals of such categories and appeals to more "binaristic" ones may partially involve resistance to a racialized discourse. Additionally, one might have feminist worries about this approach. By focusing on gender-based oppression in general, the specific ways in which women are oppressed are erased. By merely insisting that people ought to have the right to express gender however they see fit, one may forget that much gendered behaviour fits into a system that is harmful to women.[4]

Beyond these concerns, however, I fear that this "gender rebel" model cannot explain a very important sort of transphobia, which I call the "basic denial of authenticity." By this I mean the kind of transphobia whereby trans people are viewed contrary to our own self-identifications. For example, an FTM who is either "read" or who comes out may be viewed as "really a woman." Generally connected to this is the representation of trans people as deceivers, according to which we are seen as people trying to pass ourselves off as something we are not. Usually "deceiver" is reserved for trans people who pass as non-trans in the gender of our choice — but who are subsequently "exposed" as "really" another gender. By contrast, trans people who are out (either through necessity or through self-disclosure) can be represented as pretenders — people who don't necessarily "deceive" but "play" at being something that we are not.

I think that this is the basis of much transphobia and transphobic violence. For example, Brandon Teena, Bella Evangelista, and Gwen Araujo — to name a few — were all murdered when it was "discovered" that they were "really" another gender.[5] In the case of Gwen Araujo, the lawyers defending two of the men charged in the slaying (José Merel and Michael Madgison) tried to use accusations of sexual deception to argue for the lesser charge of manslaughter. In this way, the charge of deception can be used to excuse transphobic violence through blaming the victim. The basic denial of authenticity, then, not only represents trans people in ways that are odds with our own self-identity, it also constitutes an assault on our moral integrity, while helping to excuse transphobic violence. The "gender rebel" model just doesn't explain this type of transphobia.

One of the main reasons that trans people are viewed as deceivers or pretenders is because gender presentation is generally taken to communicate genital status. Notice that many people take genitalia as the basic criterion for determining whether somebody is male or female. And expressions like "discovered to be biologically female" often have to do with genital status. In general, when people use expressions like "really a so and so" they are talking mostly about genitalia. And the "really" part of the expression seems to contrast with appearance, which has to do with how a person self-presents. Trans people who are taken to "misalign" gender with sex are taken as deceivers because they have, through their gender presentation, given "incorrect information" about what is between their legs.

If this is right, then it would seem that in general, most people are symbolically declaring their genital status on a regular basis, through their gender presentation (especially their clothing). This is ironic, since we generally use clothes to conceal our "sex" in public. Yet it is precisely by "concealing" that people then go onto to disclose their genital status through their very clothes and through gender presentation more generally.

This idea has helped me understand why some non-trans people become obsessed with the genitalia of trans people: "Have you had *the* surgery?" To a large extent, this is simply a more polite way of asking what's between the legs. But no wonder people are so curious. They're used to *knowing*. They're used to everybody letting each other know through what they wear and how they act.

I don't see why it's anybody's business what's between somebody else's legs. If you translate the coded question into the *real* question you'll notice that it's nosy and rude. I resent the taken-for-granted assumption that there is a *right to know*. If there is such a right, then why wear clothes? Aren't they supposed to guarantee some sort of right to privacy about these sorts of things?

I wouldn't mind so much, if this whole business about broadcasting genital status wasn't mandatory. People can accuse you of "deception" for "misaligning" your presentation with your sex. If they "suspect," they will try their best to find out. Worse, when the going gets tough, they may physically attempt to make the determination on their own, without your consent. It's called sexual abuse. It happened to both Brandon Teena and Gwen Araujo before they were murdered. And it has happened to many other trans people too (myself included). But an issue worth considering is why unwanted questions such as "Have you had the surgery?" or "Aren't you really a man?" aren't forms of sexual harassment. Certainly, the question "What's between your legs?" appears harassing. So why shouldn't the preceding count as well, at least to the extent that these basically make the very same inquiry? And while we're at it, why shouldn't we say that the entire system of forced genital disclosure is itself abusive? If we should, then the system whereby trans people are represented as "deceivers" is based upon a sexually abusive system of forced genital disclosure.

One explanation why gender presentation should be used to disclose genital status, and why such disclosure is often mandatory, is in the case of heterosexual sexual relations. Very often, feminine attire and behaviour has been interpreted as "provocative." By this, I mean that it has been understood to "communicate" sexual interest to men, whether or not such interest exists. A woman who accepts the drink or dinner a man offers may be taken to have non-verbally "agreed" to have sex. Or revealing attire may be taken as a kind of advertisement for sexual engagement and even a reflection upon character. Such assumptions have been effectively used to blame the victim in rape cases.

Gender presentation as genital representation is part of a larger system of sexual manipulation of the type described above. The symbolic declaration of genital status is probably most important to help facilitate heterosexual sexual relations including violent ones. A man needs to know whether or not the person he is relating to has a vagina or not for basically the same reason that he needs to know that this person with a vagina is sexually interested without having to ask: the smooth facilitation of manipulative heterosexual interaction. I should add that something similar could be said about non-heterosexual contexts. The only point to knowing what's between somebody's legs in public without having to ask is to know with whom to have sex. More generally, much that goes on in dating ritual has to do with being able to make assumptions without having to ever talk about anything beforehand. The problem is that communication breakdowns are likely, and people can end up being hurt. However, I wish to stress heterosexual interactions because I am especially suspicious about the way that the heterosexual game might be set up to systematically disadvantage women and place us in tough situations. I suspect that this type of heterosexual engagement is one of the major reasons genital disclosure is so important.

Ironically, despite the fact that genitals are generally taken to be so important in heterosexual sex, it is not unheard of for straight-identified men to have sex with MTFs "behind closed doors" — even (or especially) when she "hasn't had the surgery." One of the reasons for this is that sex does not always involve penis-vagina penetration. Many people can have a perfectly good time without it — even straight-identified men. Sometimes genitals are only significant insofar as they are taken to determine sex status that has a bearing upon how somebody's sexual orientation may be regarded by others. And I think that sometimes such straight-identified men who have sex with MTFs are simply worried about what their friends might think if they knew the gender identity of the person with whom their friend was having sex.

Because of this, however, some MTFs may face tough choices. On the one hand, opting for invisibility and passing as non-trans may require that an MTF take up gender presentation that is generally "yes"-encoded with respect to the day-to-day negotiations of heterosexual sexuality. Failing to do so may leave MTFs open to "exposure as a deceiver" and transphobic violence. Yet successfully taking up this presentation may also increase sexual scrutiny and the possibility of actual sexual interaction and therefore once again open MTFs to "exposure as a deceiver." On the other hand, visibility puts an MTF at risk of accusations of "pretending" or "merely playing at womanhood" and the possibility of transphobic violence.

What happens next, however, may be partially a function of overall attractiveness viewed in terms of heterosexual male standards. If she is found attractive, she may find herself the subject of sexual advance anyway. Indeed, she may find that because she is out as trans she may be taken as "sexually available." This does not necessarily change the fact that she is still open to transphobic violence and may still retroactively be viewed as a deceiver (if the guy wants to cover his tracks). If she is not taken as attractive, she may find that she is represented as a kind of grotesque joke. Once again, however, she may be open to transphobic violence. What this suggests, at any rate, is that trans people may be vulnerable to *both* transphobia and sexism; and the fact that transphobia is itself grounded *in sexism* does not prevent this multiplication of hazards in ways that double-bind trans people in complicated ways.

Moreover, it must be recognized that this system of heterosexual engagement intersects importantly with racial oppression. Perhaps it is obvious that "presentation" is as much about race as it is about gender. Certainly "standard" gender presentation is often really just *white* gender presentation. *Barbie* isn't just *a girl*; after all, she is a *white girl*. Moreover, even genital status itself is significantly connected to racist ideology, as is evidenced, for example, by racist stereotypes of Black men as "sexual predators" and Black women as "whores."[6] Gender presentation as genital representation cannot be separated from race.

Indeed, if it is true that gender presentation represents genital status as part of a larger system of non-verbal behaviour-based "communication" system that facilitates hetero(sexist) sexual manipulation, we must acknowledge that this system is deeply intertwined with racial oppression. Notice that the myth that most rapists are strangers helps draw attention away from date and acquaintance rape. Yet also notice that the myth of the stranger rapist is connected to the myth of the Black rapist, and that myth has clearly been used to justify the imprisonment and lynching of Black men. It is a tool of racist oppression.[7] So, it is really hard to see how rape can be represented as *merely* an issue about gender and sexuality, when it is every bit as much about race. These considerations matter when it comes to strategies for opposing transphobic violence.[8] For it would seem that trans people of colour may be at a greater risk of transphobia and transphobic voilence. Any strategy designed to oppose transphobia that also (even inadvertently) strengthens mechanisms of racist oppression will fail badly.

This account helps address "gender radical" concerns that trans people who take up more traditional gender categories may be in some way complicit in maintaining an oppressive binary system.[9] What such a position fails to recognize is that by claiming authenticity as either a man or as a woman, trans people can be seen as directly opposing de-authenticating representations as deceiver/pretender. For surely to place trans people who take up more traditional forms of gender presentation as on a par with nontrans people who do so, is to simply ignore the way in which trans people are systematically denied authenticity and subjected to transphobic violence. Even the expression "really a man trapped in the body of a woman" can be seen as resistant to the basic denial of authenticity "really a woman who is dressed like a man." Rather than viewing such claims as "reactionary," we ought to view them as potentially radical.

This account is also important because it helps illuminate some of the underlying mechanisms whereby trans people themselves may be led to engage in genuinely sexist, racist and homophobic behaviour. For in addition to pressures to pass, efforts of trans people to claim authenticity in a world that denies it to us may involve the uptake of behaviour that is itself oppressive. For example, uptake of harmful gendered behaviour in order to secure authenticity may tragically lead to the perpetration of, or a vulnerability to, domestic violence.

There is work to be done to illuminate the various respects in which transphobia and sexual abuse are deeply connected. At one level, there are the mundane ways in which trans people may be subject to inappropriate questions about genital status, not to mention the deceiver/pretender representation itself. There is also the fact that a transperson's genital status may be literally verified through force. And then there are the actual rapes that occur — as in the case of Brandon Teena for example — designed to punish "the deception" and reinforce the person's "real identity." Additionally, when some trans people are coerced through economic disempowerment into sex work in visible trans-specific public space, this ought to be seen as a dangerous forced disclosure. And, in relation to this, it seems to me that some transphobic sexualized representations of trans people literally trade on eroticization of the "the shocking truth" about genitals. It may also be worth considering the ways in which trans people in intimate relationships may be vulnerable to distinctive forms of transphobic sexual abuse as well as domestic violence. At any rate, such issues should be centralized, I believe, in our struggle to make life better, safer and happier for trans people in a world that exists beyond ghostly illusion.

NOTES

1 I use trans and trans person to refer to individuals who self-identify as either transsexual or transgender and to any individual who is subject to the particular kind of phobia that I characterize in this chapter. Since individual self-identifications are complex and the terms transgender and transsexual are understood in multiply contested ways, I wish to stress, that in using these terms I do not intend to attribute identity.

2 For a classic articulation of this view see Kate Bornstein, *Gender Outlaw: On Men, Women and the Rest of Us* (New York: Routledge, 1994), 72–92.

3 For such concerns see Viviane Namaste, *Invisible Lives: The Erasure of Transsexual and Transgendered People* (Chicago: University of Chicago Press, 2000), 62–64;

and Katrina Roen, "Transgender Theory and Embodiment: The Risk of Racial Marginalisation," *Journal of Gender Studies* 10, no. 3 (2001), 253–263.

4 See Cressida J. Heyes, "Feminist Solidarity after Queer Theory: The Case of Transgender," *Signs: A Journal of Women in Culture and Society* 28, no.41 (2003), 1093–1120.

5 Brandon, twenty-one years old, was murdered by John Lotter and Marvin Thomas Nissen on December 31, 1993, in Humbolt, Nebraska. A week earlier he was kidnapped and raped by Lotter and Nissen after they had forcibly exposed his vagina. Bella Evangelista, twenty-five, was shot to death in Washington, DC, in August 2003. Antoine Jacobs, twenty-two, was charged with first-degree murder. Jacobs allegedly paid Evangelista for oral sex and became enraged upon discovering her "biological sex." Gwen Araujo, seventeen, was beaten and strangled to death by at least three men in Newark, California, in October 2003, during a party at which Araujo's "biological sex" was disclosed. Some of the men had allegedly been sexually intimate with Araujo beforehand.

6 For a good discussion of such issues, see Patricia Hill Collins, "The Sexual Politics of Black Womanhood," *Black Feminist Thought: Knowledge, Consciousness, and the Politics of Empowerment,* 2nd ed. (New York: Routledge, 2000), 123–148.

7 For the classic articulation of this view, see Angela Davis, "Rape, Racism, and the Myth of the Black Rapist," *Women, Race, and Class* (New York: Routledge, 1981), 172–201.

8 While Gwendolyn Smith's "Remembering Our Dead" website does not provide any statistics about race, an examination of the site strongly suggests that a great many of the victims are people of colour. See www.rememberingour dead.org. The same is true of GenderPac's "Hate Crime Portraits" at www.gpac.org/violence/hatecrimes.html. And while recent studies on transphobia and transphobic violence have generally failed to explore the importance of race, Emilia Lombardi has found in her as yet unpublished study "Understanding Genderism" that African-American trans people reported the highest levels of transphobic events within the year the interviews were conducted while white trans people reported the lowest.

9 See Patricia Elliot and Katrina Roen, "Transgenderism and the Question of Embodiment," *GLQ: A Journal of Lesbian and Gay Studies* 4, no. 2 (1998), 231–261; and Henry S. Rubin, "Phenomenology as Method in Trans Studies," *GLQ: A Journal of Lesbian and Gay Studies* 4, no. 2 (1998), 262–281.

CHAPTER 19

SAFE AT HOME:
REDEFINING THE POLITICS OF SEXUAL ASSAULT AND ITS AFTERMATH

Lynnette Dubois

HOME. THE WORD CAN CONJURE UP ONE'S WARMEST AND SAFEST MEMORIES, at least in theory. In practice, for transgendered women, that assurance is often lacking and home is just one more place filled with fear.

While preparing to begin my transition in early 2000, I came across the following in a newsletter about GLBT issues: "Transgendered people are often sexually targeted specifically because of their transgendered status. The sexual perpetrator will stalk them, or attack them, infuriated by their cross-gender behavior."[1]

On August 2, 2000, it happened to me. I was targeted for a violent sexual assault because of my gender status. The resulting ordeal and the lessons it taught me have become the nucleus of my views not just on my transition but also on the notion of justice. I was suddenly thrust into a different world, one populated by fears and discriminations — and that made me become a feminist.

A transgendered person is at increased risk for a sexual assault, particularly from romantic partners, according to respondents to a multi-state survey conducted by the Survivor Project, a U.S.-based non-profit organization specializing in transgender issues. The risk is as high as one in two.[2] I will let that number sink in for a moment. Fifty percent!

Sexual assault is the most personal of invasions. For me, sexual assault marked the demarcation between the falsely perceived stability of my socialization and the grim, inherent unsafeness of my gender. Since then, I have grown acutely aware of the sound of footsteps behind me and have learned in a harsh way that an elevator is not a safe place.

I became a more complete woman as a result of being assaulted (the socialization of my birth gender did not prepare me for the situation my assault placed me in), and I became something else, a feminist. Was it the abandoned and demeaned way I felt after the attack? Perhaps the way the police officers made me feel. Or was it the barely hidden condescension and derision exhibited by the Crown attorney? A little of each. As any person who has been victimized can attest, the physical aspects of the assault, while hard to bear, are often not the worst. More than my body was injured in that late summer evening. My sense of safety and self-confidence were terribly wounded.

Of all the challenges I faced in trying to rebuild my life, the hardest was dealing with the built-in prejudice that transgendered people face. Even armed with sensitivity training, the police constables who responded to the scene seemed visibly nervous. To their credit, the uniformed officers did act in a professional manner: a female constable was made available, and they went out of their way to try to preserve what little dignity I had left. The same cannot be said for the detectives assigned to the case. From our initial meeting to the actual court appearance, I felt the detectives exhibited an appalling lack of sensitivity. I was left with the very palpable impression that they resented having to deal with me. I was asked questions that seemed unfairly invasive, such as whether my breasts were real. While it is true that some transgender women rely on breast forms or enhancers, I could not see the relevance of that question. When I questioned the detectives about it I was informed that it was a standard question; they needed the information in order to document my injuries. Even if I were to grant them that, does that mean if my breasts had been artificial my assault would have been deemed less serious? Would they treat a breast-cancer survivor in the same way?

To me, the worst transgression committed by members of the Toronto Police Service concerning the particulars of my case rests with their conduct when I phoned to notify them that my attacker had violated his restraining order. I was frightened; my attacker had approached me. I assumed the police would respond. After much anguish, I was informed by one of the detective sergeants that such violations were routine and that the police could not spare the staff to deal with my complaint. I was left holding my telephone in a death grip and wondering if my very sanity was at stake. Several minutes later, the officer phoned me and offered a lukewarm apology but still did not offer to intervene. However, he did belatedly acknowledge that I sounded "very frightened."

As far too many women can attest, a restraining order has very little real value. I'm not sure that I was treated differently than any other woman would have been in similar circumstances. This disregard continued up to the trial process. I was not introduced to the Crown attorney connected with my case until the day before we were to go into court. I was supposed to be prepared by the Crown for what was about to occur but this assistance came only after I insisted on it multiple times. The Crown attorney repeatedly informed me that my choice of lifestyle would be brought up if I took the witness stand and that I would have to be subjected to defense counsel's assertions that I might be a prostitute. I was later to learn that the linking of transgender identities with prostitution is incredibly widespread.

Finally, I was able to complain about what I felt was the incompetent and disgraceful way the Toronto Police Service approached my case when it was brought to light as the case against my attacker came to trial in January of 2002. As is customary before trial, I wanted to exercise my right to review the statement I had given the night of the assault. That statement was videotaped and when I asked to review either the tape or a transcript, I was informed that neither was available and was encouraged to take the witness stand without benefit of the review. It was at that moment that I felt the most overwhelmed and frightened. Thankfully, I had my family of choice that loved me and was there for me. If one of them had not spoken up, questioning the legality of the police suggestion, I am not sure what would have happened. After my family members intervened, a copy of the tape was very provided for me within minutes, though I had been told they would have to return to Police Headquarters to locate a copy. Because of the Rules of Discovery, the defence counsel was also now entitled to see the tape. He advised his client to accept a plea bargain being offered by the Crown, which I agreed to.

Housing, Shelter and Women-Only Space

Stereotypes are not just applied to the transgendered community by some feminists; in fact, often it is members of the transgender community that engage in some of the worst examples of this behaviour. "Even after surgery and with [a trans persons'] documents changed, there are still problems in that women are particularly sensitive to safety issues."[3] This quotation by Cynthia Cousens, who at the time was the chair of the Ottawa Police Liaison Committee, illustrates the discrimination trans people face when trying to access services. On one hand many women's organizations wrestle with how to include trans-identified women; on the other, trans activists also struggle with the notions of women-only space. As a transgender rape survivor, I can attest to a woman's sensitivity to safety and I would suggest that it is a feeling mutual to all survivors of assault. Some excellent work has been done in this regard by Allison Cope and Julie Darke in their Trans Accessibility Project.[4]

The issue of transgendered women being perceived as a danger to other women played an integral part in the shaping of a pilot project in 2001 by Greenwin Properties and the Toronto Community Housing Corporation to provide affordable housing to transgendered women. I was pleased to be involved with the project as a consultant on transgender issues.

After initial favourable discussions with the management team of the building that had been selected for the pilot project, further meetings were scheduled with tenant representatives from the building in question. From the outset there were problems. One of the tenant representatives thought the proposal would distract from ongoing safety concerns the residents were having. She also disagreed strongly with the proposals on religious grounds, going as far as quoting scripture. I was deeply disturbed by her use of religion as an excuse for bigotry and I found her language and demeanour to be hostile and threatening.

Because of the above factors and others that were unrelated to the project, the building was removed from consideration. Discussions are ongoing with Greenwin Properties in the hope that alternative locations can be made available as soon as possible. I had hoped to deliver a better account of this project in this essay but such setbacks are unfortunately all too common when the needs of transgendered people are being considered. I still have great optimism that these efforts will reach fruition and that the needed spaces will be made available.

FUTURE WORK

For the struggles of countless transgendered people to truly have meaning, we have to learn from the prejudices and oppressions of the past. New ways of providing service delivery may have to be invented. Inclusive language and a zero-tolerance policy of abusive or distorting language must be enacted. Throughout this essay, I have chosen in most cases to use the term transgender(ed) to apply to all people who cross gender lines in any way. My decision to do this has much to do with the internal bias that exists in much of the transgender community about the differences between transgender and transsexual. While I do not disagree that there are differences, I refuse to discriminate by suggesting that one group is better or that identifying with one group precludes providing the rights and protections for the other. The following definition of "transgendered" was used in the final report of the Trans Health Project:

> Mostly applies to masculine dykes, but can also describe effeminate/feminine men who are androgynous psychologically and/or physically. Distinct from "transsexual" insofar as the latter desperately seek, and often obtain, a physical/sexual transformation, through medical and surgical intervention, to attain their desired level of comfort in expressing both their gender identity as men or women, as well as their sexual identity as males or females.[5]

Harmful definitions like these are a major problem, because they divide a community that is already dangerously marginalized.

Addressing these factors and adopting an inclusive policy that understands divergent needs while not relegating portions of our people to inferior status is vital. We must understand that the traditional view of women-only space can be elastic enough to preserve every woman's safety while encompassing our changing understanding of woman-only space and trans placement within women's organizations and services. This work was begun by the National Association of Women and the Law in 2003,[6] but clearly more needs to be done. It is this work that led me to establish Artemis Services (a non-profit human rights advocacy organization) and encouraged me to speak out for the benefit of all people at forums large and small. It is time to present to the world the true picture of transgender experience, not the stereotypical images that have for too long kept us isolated in fear and, for some, in extreme danger. Only then can we take a brick out of the wall of intolerance and use it to pave a road towards acceptance for everyone.

NOTES

1 Arelene Istar Lev and S. Sundance Lev, "Sexual Assault in the Transgender Communities —Transgender Victims of Sexual Assault." FORGE Newsletter (November 1999). Available online at http://my.execpc.com/~dmmunson/Nov99_7.htm.

2 Diana Courvant and Loree Cook-Daniels, "Transgender and Intersex Survivors of Domestic Violence: Defining Terms, Barriers and Responsibilities," in the conference manual of the National Coalition Against Domestic Violence, Denver, CO, 1998.

3 Glenn Crawford, "Moving Beyond Tokenism," *Capital Xtra* (November 2002). Available online at www.capitalxtra.on.ca/queercapital/cs111_beyond_tokenism.htm.

4 Allison Cope and Julie Darke, "Making Women's Shelters Accessible to Transgendered Women" (October 1999). Availiable on-line at www.queensu.ca/humanrights/tap/index.html.

5 Rupert Raj and Susan Gapka, *Trans Health Project* (Toronto: Ontario Public Health Association, 2003), 28-29. Available on-line at www.opha.on.ca/ppres/2003-06_pp.pdf.

6 Margaret Denike and cj Rowe, in National Association of Women and the Law, *Transgender and Women's Substantive Equality, Final Report* (Ottawa: NAWL, 2003). Available online at www.nawl.ca/transfinalreport.htm.

CHAPTER 20

ANTI-VIOLENCE WORK IN TRANSITION

Joshua Goldberg & Caroline White

INFLUENCED BY BOTH RADICAL AND SOCIALIST FEMINISMS, A CRITICAL outcome of second-wave feminist anti-violence activism was to "name," "break the silence" about and "make public" the widespread occurrence of male violence against women. Women's consciousness-raising groups of the 1960s and 1970s were one of the few forums where women felt "safe" to publicly disclose the male violence they experienced in their private lives. Increased public disclosure revealed the pervasive and ubiquitous nature of male violence against women, and through shared experiences women began to build theoretical frameworks for why the violence occurred, as well as what women could do to protect themselves and, ultimately, stop the violence. Feminists developed theories linking the source of male violence to the subjugated, second-class position of women. Gender and sex[1] — frequently conflated at the time — became the central analytic tools not only of theories about violence against women but also of the dominant feminist movement. As theories were built, so too were safe houses, shelters for battered women and rape crisis centres — all spaces that would offer women safety from male violence, as well as support for healing and for planning. These same spaces would also become "safe spaces" to further develop theories of male violence against women and other theories pertaining to the dominant Western women's movement.[2]

In part because the feminist movement emphasized translating one's own lived experience into universal theory, the anti-violence movement and its attendant theories largely reflected the dominant life experiences and at times racist, classist, heterosexist and ableist values and visions of its predominantly middle-class, white heterosexual and able-bodied leaders. What it meant to "name" the violence, "break the silence" or make it "public," as well as what constituted "safe space," were constructs defined by dominant Western feminism and were assumed to have value and meaning for all women.[3] This was also true for the constructs of sex and gender, which were positioned as the cornerstone of the movement, as well as for key terms such as binary (female/male, woman/man), fixed (despite how one self-identifies, or the use of hormones or surgical intervention, one's sex nor gender can never "really" be changed), mutually dependent (where physiological sex determines gender and vice-versa), ahistorical (where our understanding of sex and gender are unrelated to historical context/specificity), and universal (Western definitions of gender and sex are applicable everywhere, to everyone). Women of colour and Aboriginal women, working-class and poor women, sex-trade workers, lesbian and bisexual women, women with disabilities and other women would all come to challenge the dominant analyses with varying degree of success. Nonetheless, the core of the analyses would remain fundamentally the same.

While dominant Western feminism was shaping and strengthening its movement — and specifically its analysis of male violence against women — some Western trans people were also immersed in a growing trans movement. As with dominant feminism, trans activism included a broad range of issues such as access to employment, housing, health care and social services. Here, too, gender and sex — which were again often conflated — were the central analytic tools, as was, to a lesser degree, sexuality. However, gender and sex were neither perceived nor understood as necessarily universal, binary, fixed, mutually dependent or ahistorical. Leadership was also critically different from the dominant feminist movement in that trans activism was led in large part by trans of colour, white, poor or working-class trans sex-trade workers and night club entertainers, many of whom were in the male-to-female spectrum.[4]

Predictably, given their divergent views on gender and sex as well as differences in leadership, Western feminism and trans activism eventually intersected and came into conflict as they became more widespread and organized. Equally predictable, perhaps, was that the conflict became most obvious and consequently most contested in "women's spaces." Despite the efforts of women of colour, Aboriginal women, working-class women and women with disabilities, among others, gender and sex are still generally seen as *the* organizing principles of "women's space" and the work within this space.

Today, an increasing number of trans and non-trans activists, survivors and theorists from both inside and outside women's organizations are researching and writing on trans violence.[5] Given the historical tension between dominant Western feminism and trans activism, most of the anti-violence work to date has focused on making critical social services — specifically services for women who have experienced violence — accessible to trans women. Since few women's organizations were *publicly* accessible to trans survivors, survivors turned to trusted friends, lovers or family for support. The Survivor Project in Portland, Oregon, was a notable exception, since its mandate was to work with trans and intersex survivors specifically. More recently, however, with increasing numbers of women's and other anti-violence organizations becoming publicly accessible to trans survivors, the attention of trans activists is being directed to the issue of violence, specifically, and to the issue of service for all trans survivors regardless of gender identity.

TRANS-SPECIFIC VIOLENCE

It is impossible to discuss the extent of violence against trans people with any certainty because current tracking mechanisms are problematic. The reporting of violence focuses on interpersonal violence between adults with little consideration of institutional, systemic violence or violence against youth. Even the usual mechanisms for reporting interpersonal violence are largely unavailable to trans survivors: police and emergency medical services are compromised options because of their histories of violence against trans people, particularly sex trade workers and prisoners.[6] Gendered anti-violence organizations — often the first line of contact for survivors — are frequently inaccessible because of general public uncertainty regarding whether or not they provide services to trans survivors and, if so, under what conditions.[7] Additionally, violence against trans people is frequently monitored within the rubric of LGBT violence, with no distinction between homophobic and transphobic violence,[8] and there is no acknowledgement of violence against the loved ones of trans people as part of violence against the trans community.[9] The reporting also fails to take into account the multiple reasons for violence, including the ways that identities and experiences of trans survivors are racialized, classed and otherwise constructed.

To date, hate crimes are the most commonly tracked form of violence against trans people. Hate crimes are conventionally thought of as crimes committed against a random target by a stranger.[10] However, in descriptions of hate-motivated assaults on trans people and loved ones, it is not uncommon for the perpetrator to be someone known by the victim.[11] This challenges the conventional understanding of hate crimes as "public" and therefore distinct from family and relationship violence (conceived of as "private").

Trans-specific studies suggest that trans people are more vulnerable to violence across their lifespan than the general population.[12] At particular risk are trans people who are visibly gender-variant. When we include multiple forms of identity, our understanding of violence against trans people is altered in significant ways. In hate crimes, for example, where specific gender identity has been recorded, researchers found that 98 percent of all "transgender" violence was perpetrated against people in the male-to-female spectrum;[13] of the thirty-eight murders of trans people reported internationally in 2003, 70 percent were women of colour.[14] In other examples, where "race,"[15] class or sexual identity are considered, it is unclear whether crimes were motivated by hatred of perceived gender, "race" or sexual identity, challenging theories of violence that privilege gender over all other identities.[16]

Within the complexities of identity and violence, trans people may experience forms of violence and abuse that have specific transphobic elements. For example, physical and sexual violence may include assault, mutilation or denigration of body parts that signify specific cultural notions of gender, such as chest, genitals and hair. Economic abuse may include withdrawal of financial support related to trans-specific care (e.g., electrolysis, hormones, surgeries), withdrawal of financial support in general or exploitation of the victim's financial dependency by demanding financial compensation or payback through prostitution or the drug trade. Emotional and verbal abuse may include ridicule of cross-gendered behaviour or appearance and threats to limit or prohibit access to children or services. It can also include threats to reveal the victim's gender identity to employers, financial aid workers, health-care workers, immigration personnel or anyone else with possible influence or control over the survivor's well-being.[17] Trans people's loved ones may also experience trans-specific forms of violence and abuse, including, in the case of abuse by a trans partner, the use of societal transphobia as an excuse for abusive behaviour.[18]

BARRIERS TO ACCESS

Despite the urgent need for prevention and education, and for services for survivors of violence, many prevention and education programs do not include trans content and many services are inaccessible to trans survivors.

A key barrier is that many anti-violence services are for women only. There are some women's organizations that have made efforts to be inclusive of trans women (to varying degrees) and some human rights tribunals have upheld the legal rights of male-to-female transsexuals to access women's services. However, for the most part, women's services are not accessible to people who do not identify as women — for example, people born female who identify as male/masculine/men, androgynous people, bi- or pan-gendered people, male cross-dressers). Nor are services available to individuals who, despite identifying as women, are not able to meet agency standards of what constitutes an "acceptable" woman. Some agencies will only accept post-operative male-to-females, others accept anyone who self-identifies as a woman; decisions are often made on a case-by-case basis relating to appearance/passability. While there are some simple things women's agencies can and should do to become more inclusive of trans women (see suggestions below), these strategies do not remove the fundamental barrier created when services are specifically for women.

Even when policies or client inclusion/exclusion criteria allow for the possibility of trans access, access does not necessarily guarantee a trans-positive or trans-inclusive environment. We have worked with trans survivors who have been told not to raise trans issues during group therapy, not to discuss life prior to transition and not to discuss trans-specific/transphobic elements of the violence they experienced. In other cases, counsellors redirected the conversation every time trans issues were brought up. Other attempts to restrict trans expression have included enforcement of gendered dress codes and refusal of access to prosthetic devices such as breast forms. Assumptions about women's bodies and women's experience marginalize trans women who do not share identical experiences; pejorative remarks made by other clients and staff or volunteers about body parts thought of as "male" (e.g., the penis) reinforce shame and stigma for non-operative or pre-operative trans women.

In addition to formal or informal policies that provide trans women access to services, staff and volunteer training, procedural guidelines and other measures are needed to ensure a trans-positive environment.[19] For full trans inclusion, in addition to trans-specific policy statements and procedural/clinical guidelines, barriers that have a significant impact on trans women due to the intersection of transphobia and other forms of oppression must also be addressed. For example, shelters that have curfews are not accessible to trans women who rely on the sex trade for economic survival.

TRANSFORMING THE ANTI-VIOLENCE SERVICE SECTOR

Many anti-violence services have struggled against government and community resistance. There are constant threats to the stability of anti-violence programs in political environments where services to women and families are not considered a priority, or where anti-violence services are seen as ideological tools of feminism rather than necessary community services. In this context of an ongoing battle to establish the legitimacy and importance of anti-violence services for women, there is tremendous resistance among many leaders who challenge the predominant ideology behind anti-violence services or to consider alternative approaches. Even suggesting that the needs of survivors are varied, and hence there is a need to diversify the way services are structured, is often viewed as a threat not only to a service's funding but also to the anti-violence movement and to feminism as a whole. For example, reviewers of a trans-specific anti-violence manual asked that discussion relating to FTM access to women's shelters be removed because it could be "used by government to attack women's services." This fear and resistance make substantive transformation very difficult.

Thus far, the anti-violence sector has taken two basic approaches to diversity: transforming existing services to become more inclusive of diverse experiences, and creating services for specific populations (e.g., racialized minorities, people with disabilities, elders). Strategies for promoting inclusion in existing services include reducing physical, economic, cultural, linguistic and geographical barriers to service access; implementing affirmative-action hiring policies; educating staff and volunteers; and creating educational materials that reflect community diversity. Services targeted to specific populations have, in the anti-violence sector as a whole, been considered "specialized" services, with service for middle-class, able-bodied white women experiencing violence in heterosexual relationships still centralized as the predominant experience of violence.

It is imperative for existing services to consider how to become more inclusive of trans people. Arguably, trans survivors could benefit from the creation of a service specifically set up to meet their needs. However, the small numbers of trans people and the geographic dispersion of the trans community across Canada (including rural and remote areas) make this both financially difficult and also unrealistic. Additionally, creating "specialized" services re-entrenches the idea that the status quo is the norm, isolating survivors who don't fit the dominant system rather than changing the system to address its exclusivity.

Becoming inclusive means not only allowing trans survivors to access existing services, but devoting resources to ensuring that staff and volunteers are competent to provide services to trans people and their loved ones. This includes being fully comfortable working with people with diverse gender identities and cultural beliefs about gender; being able to engage clients in exploring the connections between violence and gender oppression; and being aware of the legal, medical and social issues that impact trans people and loved ones who are survivors of violence. It also means understanding the social, legal and economic factors that increase the vulnerability of trans people and their loved ones to violence and that make it more difficult to leave abusive relationships; reducing the barriers that make it difficult for trans people and their loved ones to report and seek services relating violence; and incorporating gender diversity in anti-violence education and prevention efforts. Finally, policy and procedures relating to safe environments for staff, volunteers, and clients who are trans or the loved one of a trans person must be developed, along with mechanisms to evaluate the agency's effectiveness in working with the trans community.

*

A significant portion of the anti-violence sector has translated a gender-based analysis of abuse and violence to a model of service delivery that uses gender-based criteria to determine access to services. We believe that the anti-violence sector, *like any other social service sector*, can best meet the needs of a diverse population when services are diverse in their structure, approach and mandate. This does not mean that gender-specific services should be eliminated: many survivors (including some trans survivors) have been, and will continue to be, well served by this approach. However, one approach cannot possibly meet everyone's needs.

As people with a commitment to anti-violence work, we need to be able to frankly discuss with one another the benefits and limitations of a gender-specific approach. For example, who is/is not well served by a gender-specific approach; which kinds of violence are/are not effectively addressed by the current model; how the current model addresses the role of factors such as racism, classism, ableism and other oppression, as well as interpersonal factors in understanding violence; and how gender exclusivity of services does/does not create physical and emotional safety for survivors.

In an era where health and social services are fighting for their survival, we know it will be difficult for anti-violence services to actively embrace this kind of discussion. Any real transformation of the sector will take time and energy as well as alliance-building across deep rifts between trans and non-trans feminists. But we also believe that a radical transformation of the anti-violence service sector is necessary not only to benefit trans people and non-trans people who are not well-served by the existing system but also to address the realities of state, institutional and interpersonal violence in Canada today.

NOTES

1 In this essay we use "sex" to refer to physiology and "gender" to refer to identity or expression of that identity — social roles, appearance and behaviours that reflect our felt sense of our own gender. We use the word "trans" as an umbrella term for anyone who does not fit the dominant norms of gender. For more on trans terminology, see Caroline White, "Re/defining Gender and Sex: Educating for Trans, Transsexual, and Intersex Access and Inclusion to Sexual Assault Centres and Transition Houses" (MEd thesis, University of British Columbia, 2002); Joshua Goldberg, *Trans People in the Criminal Justice System: A Guide for Criminal Justice Personnel* (Vancouver: Justice Institute of British Columbia, 2003).

2 See, for example, Himani Bannerji, "Geography Lessons: On Being an Insider/

Outsider to the Canadian Nation," in Leslie G. Roman and Linda Eyre, eds., *Dangerous Territories: Struggles for Difference and Equality in Education* (New York: Routledge, 1997), 23-41; bell hooks, *Feminist Theory from Margin to Center* (Boston: South End Press, 1984); Lee Maracle, "Racism, Sexism, and Patriarchy," in Himani Bannerji, ed., *Returning the Gaze: Essays on Racism, Feminism, and Politics* (Toronto: Sister Vision Press, 1993), 122-130; and Becki Ross, *The House that Jill Built: A Lesbian Nation in Formation* (Toronto: University of Toronto Press, 1995).

3 See, for example, "Disloyal to Feminism: Abuse of Survivors within the Domestic Violence Shelter System," *Emi Koyama* (February 25, 2006), available online at www.eminism.org/readings/pdf-rdg/disloyal.pdf; Leslie Timmins, ed., *Listening to the Thunder: Advocates Talk about the Battered Women's Movement* (Vancouver: Women's Research Centre, 1995).

4 Leslie Feinberg, *Transgender Warriors: Making History from Joan of Arc to Ru Paul* (Boston: Beacon Press, 1996); Gay and Lesbian Historical Society of Northern California, "MTF Transgender Activism in the Tenderloin and Beyond, 1966–1975: Commentary and Interview with Elliot Blackstone," *GLQ: A Journal of Lesbian and Gay Studies* 4, no. 2 (1998), 159–187.

5 For example, see Loree Cook-Daniels, *SOFFA Questions and Answers* (Milwaukee: FORGE, 2001); Alison Cope and Julie Darke, *Trans Accessibility Project: Making Women's Shelters Accessible to Transgendered Women* (Kingston, ON: Violence Intervention and Education Workgroup, 1999); Diana Courvant, *Domestic Violence and the Sex- or Gender-variant Survivor* (Portland, OR: Survivor Project, 1997); Diana Courvant and Loree Cook-Daniels, *Trans and Intersex Survivors of Domestic Violence: Defining Terms, Barriers and Responsibilities* (Portland, OR: Survivor Project, 1998); Julie Darke and Alison Cope, *Trans Inclusion Policy Manual for Women's Organizations* (Vancouver: Trans Alliance Society, 2002); Joshua Goldberg, *Making the Transition: Providing Services to Trans Survivors of Violence and Abuse* (Vancouver: Justice Institute of BC, in press); Joshua Goldberg and Caroline White, "Expanding Our Understanding of Gendered Violence: Violence Against Trans People and Loved Ones," *Aware: The Newsletter of the BC Institute Against Family Violence* 11, no. 2 (2004), 21–25; "The Transfeminist Manifesto and Other Essays on Transfeminism," *Emi Koyama* (February 25, 2006), available online at www.eminism.org/readings/pdf-rdg/tfmanifesto.pdf; Michael Munson and Loree Cook-Daniels, *Transgender/SOFFA: Domestic Violence and Sexual Assault Resource Sheet* (Milwaukee: FORGE, 2003); Viviane Namaste, *Invisible Lives: The Erasure of Transsexual and Transgendered People* (Chicago: University of Chicago Press, 2000); Kimberly Nixon, "Statistics on Violence Suddenly Alarming Fact for M-F Transsexuals," *Zenith Digest* 4, no. 3 (1997), 17; Northwest Network, *Increasing Accessibility/Competence for Trans Survivors of Domestic Violence Policy Packet* (Seattle: Northwest Network, 1997); Mirha Soleil-Ross, "Investigating Women's Shelters," *Gendertrash* 3 (1995), 7–10; White, "Re/defining Gender and Sex."

6 Chris Daley, Elly Kugler and Jo Hirschmann, *Walking while Transgender: Law Enforcement of San Francisco's Transgender/Transsexual Community* (San Francisco: Ella Baker Center for Human Rights/TransAction, 2000); Feinberg, *Transgender Warriors.*

7 Soleil-Ross, "Investigating Women's Shelters"; Cope and Darke, *Trans Accessibility Project;* White, "Re/defining Gender and Sex."

8 BC Hate Crimes Team, *End Hate Crime: Hate/Bias Crime Policy Guide* (Vancouver: Ministry of Public Safety and Solicitor General, 2000); National Coalition of Anti-Violence Programs (NCAVP), *Lesbian, Gay, Bisexual and Transgender Domestic Violence in 2000: A Report of the National Coalition of Anti-Violence Programs — 2001 Preliminary Edition* (New York: NCAVP, 2001); "Gay and Lesbian Anti-Violence Project Releases Report on Hate Incidents in 2001," *New York City Gay and Lesbian Anti-Violence Project* (January 13, 2003), available online at http://avp.org/publications/media/2001hcrimerpt.htm.

9 Cook-Daniels, *SOFFA Questions and Answers.*

10 BC Hate Crimes Team, *End Hate Crime.*

11 "Remembering Our Dead," *Gender Education and Advocacy* (April 24, 2004), available online at www.gender.org/remember/about/core.html.

12 Courvant and Cook-Daniels, *Trans and Intersex Survivors of Domestic Violence;* Emilia L. Lombardi, Riki Anne Wilchins, Dana Priesing and Diana Malouf, "Gender Violence: Transgender Experiences with Violence and Discrimination," *Journal of Homosexuality* 42 (2001), 89–101; FORGE, *Transgender Sexual Violence Project: Raw Data Graphs* (Milwaukee: FORGE, 2005).

13 Paisley Currah and Shannon Minter, *Transgender Equality: A Handbook for Activists and Policymakers* (New York: National Gay and Lesbian Task Force, 2000).

14 "Remembering Our Dead."

15 We use quotation marks around the term "race" to indicate that it is an inherently problematic type of socially constructed categorization. While "races" do not exist, the use of the term "ethnic groups" or "ethnicity" to replace "race" does not carry the same connotation in terms of racialization and racism.

16 Darke and Cope, *Trans Inclusion Policy Manual for Women's Organizations;* Goldberg, *Trans People in the Criminal Justice System.*

17 Goldberg, *Trans People in the Criminal Justice System;* Goldberg, *Making the Transition.*

18 Munson and Cook-Daniels, *Transgender/SOFFA.*

19 Darke and Cope, *Trans Inclusion Policy Manual for Women's Organizations;* Goldberg, *Making the Transition.*

CHAPTER 21

TRANSFORMING VALUES / ENGENDERING POLICY

Wolfgang Vachon

"HE'S GOT A COCK AND SLEEPS NAKED IN THE BUNK ABOVE ME." THE WOMAN before me was frightened and hesitant. "I can see his ...," she trailed off for a moment gesturing towards her crotch, "when he climbs into bed." The woman had been sexually assaulted, more than once, outside the shelter, by men and was feeling uncomfortable and threatened by having "a guy" in the female dorm. Her male partner, who had accompanied her into the office, was promising that he would "do something" if the shelter staff didn't.

The emergency shelter I had started working at a couple months before was in Toronto's downtown core. It was co-ed, with separate dorms for males and females. There were no policies at the shelter regarding trans people. It was 2000 and the City of Toronto was in the process of developing a new Hostel Standards guideline. It was well known that the issue of access for transgender and transsexual people was going to be included. The new policy was about a year away from being finalized, and at this shelter there was a definite discomfort when the inclusion of trans people was brought up. The approach of most staff members seemed to be to avoid the issue and hope nothing happened on their shift. Something was happening on my shift, and without any previous guidance, I was unsure how to respond.

There were three frontline staff (myself included) and a supervisor. After much hand wringing it was declared that we had to get to the bottom of this. We couldn't have "a guy" in the woman's dorm.

We agreed that the supervisor (a male) and a female staff member would speak privately to the resident in question. They took her into the nurses' office. About twenty minutes later, the two staff came back out of the office wearing expressions of relief. Don't worry, she's a real woman, they said.

The resident had offered to prove she did not have a penis. The female staff member took her into the toilets and she pulled down her pants and underwear. The woman was menstruating.

During the follow-up conversation with the complainant, she and her partner were informed that the situation had been addressed and that "she was really a she." A brief conversation took place around how the mistake could have been made. The confusion was attributed to the woman's body shape, her deep voice, and the chance of misperception when lights are out. Both she and her partner accepted that the situation was resolved and agreed to let us know if any other difficulties or conflicts arose. None ever did.

*

The incredibly disturbing nature of this experience revealed to me numerous non-conscious assumptions from which I had been operating. Entering the shelter system as a pro-feminist man I was opposed to pre-operative male-to-female (MTF) residents staying in the women's dorms. I felt strongly that it was a risk to the female residents, and as a "good man" and a shelter staff member, I needed to ensure that women had a safe space in which to live. Street-identified and homeless women are subject to numerous dangerous/abusive/violent/unsafe situations on the streets and, to a lesser extent, in the shelter system. The majority of women in the shelter system have experienced abuse, often sexual and usually from males. These women are understandably distressed when they perceive a "safer" space, such as a shelter, being compromised.

In my experience with individuals involved in the shelter system, the presence or absence of a penis defines both sex and gender for most people. Thus, if someone in the female dorm has a penis — regardless of how that individual identifies or lives — that person is considered a man. This is exemplified by the above situation where both staff and residents accepted the individual once it was "proven" that "she was really a she." Almost all the female residents and the vast majority of male residents I spoke with did not want MTFs in the female dorm (males did not want them in the male dorm either, which I attribute to homophobia as much as transphobia — although it may be hard to differentiate in this circumstance; nevertheless, MTF are read as deviant males). Their responses and concerns expressed during internal conversations with me made sense to me based upon their experiences. I overheard comments from female residents such as "I have been raped by men, and I can't sleep knowing that there is a man in the dorm"; or "This space is for women, that guy has a dick, so he ain't no woman." Men didn't want a guy in the dorm with their girlfriends.

Given the realities of life for transsexuals and the perceptions of other shelter workers and clients, how could I balance what I perceived as my responsibility to ensure women clients felt safe with the needs of MTF clients (whom I identified as distinct from the "women" in the shelter)? Most male staff expressed a great deal of resistance to the idea of MTFs staying in the shelter at all, particularly in the female dorm. Like me, they wanted to protect women from the potentially predatory nature of those with a penis. This position implied that anyone with a penis staying in the female dorm would want to have sex (even forcibly) with the women in the dorm; and that people with a penis are always driven by (straight) sexual impulses, which if not sated may be acted out in violent sexual acts against women. If we allowed MTFs into the female dorm, who knew what would happen? If something did happen (the unstated *something* being rape) then we would be legally and ethically liable. The fact that there had been no documented case of such a thing happening ever was not at issue (nor should that necessarily be the sole reason: just because something has not happened does not mean it won't). There was a rumour that a "man dressed up as a woman had been sexually inappropriate" with the female residents at the shelter, but I could not find a staff member who was actually on shift when this happened; although almost all "knew" of the alleged situation.

What surprised me was that almost all of female staff supported access to the female dorms by MTFs. I asked if they were concerned about issues of sexual violence. They responded that they were concerned with behaviours, not with gender, the way someone dressed and how someone identified. We did not refuse lesbians or gay men, nor did we refuse same-sex couples. We did not refuse individuals admittance because they were drunk, stoned or had mental health issues. Nor did we refuse them because they had just been released from jail, because they had been barred (forbidden to come into the shelter for a period of time due to behaviour) from the shelter previously. We responded to current behaviour. If someone acted in a way that threatened another resident, did damage to himself or herself, someone else or the shelter, we addressed that behaviour. We did not adhere to a policy of preventative barring. Why would it be any different for trans residents?

But what about how people felt with trans residents present? The reply: if we catered to every person's dislike/feelings/concerns/fears then we would never have more than one person in the shelter at a time.

When I protested that we needed to protect the women in the shelter, I usually got a look, a smile, a shake of the head or a turned back.

The increasing presence of trans people accessing the shelter system catalyzed recognition within the system, and the City of Toronto, that this needed to be addressed. More people are accessing shelters for many more reasons — changes in affordable-housing priorities by all levels of government; lack of supportive housing; low-income levels; limited employment opportunities and unlivable social assistance amounts. Trans people face additional obstacles —discrimination from family, potential employers, landlords, the medical establishment, shelters and most other people; the cost of surgeries; challenges around passing and the need to live for a period of time in the gender they identify in before hormone treatment or surgeries can start.

As we struggled at our shelter, many other shelters were also reacting in diverse ways to access issues. These reactions ranged from trying to do education and develop policy, to refusing service to anyone who did not identify by their biological birth sex. Most rationales for denial of services revolved around the potential disruptions and discomfort of current residents if trans folks were allowed into the shelter. This was sometimes inverted to say that the trans person accessing the shelter would not be comfortable. I often wonder about the last time these decision makers tried to sleep outside at minus fifteen degrees. Or in a park during the summer when people sleeping regularly get mugged. Really comfortable. Just walking down the street during the day can be uncomfortable for an MTF who has rapid facial-hair growth and does not have access to a razor and a sink.

In 2003, the city responded to these inconsistent practices by including a section in the new Hostel Standards (the governing document for all organizations providing shelter services) regarding policy around trans issues. Below is how that document begins.[1]

Guiding Principles

Gender identity is self-defined. Sometimes this may not correspond with a person's physical appearance. Service providers need to accept gender identity as defined by the individual rather than by the perception of staff and/or other residents.

Meeting the Needs of Transgendered /Transsexual/ Two-spirited Residents

It is expected that all shelters be accessible to the transgendered/transsexual/ two-spirited (TS/TG/2-S) residents in their self-defined gender, and that shelters will work toward improving access to this group. Shelters will support the choices of TG/TS/2-S residents to gain access to services in the gender they identify will best preserve their safety.

*

After a year and a half as a frontline relief worker, I was offered a full-time position with a new shelter that was about to open. I embraced the opportunity and volunteered to sit on the policy-development committee. After a few months, it became apparent that we needed to set out something that addressed the needs of the trans people who were accessing the shelter. All the same fears and reactions present at the previous shelter were manifesting themselves at this new location. Trans people were already accessing services and staff and residents, both trans and non trans, felt an incredible amount of anxiety and confusion. In addition, the city required us to have a policy in place.

We worked in a committee made up of a mixture of staff: frontline workers, supervisors and managers with different ethnicities, economic upbringings, countries of origins and sexual orientations, but no trans people. While everyone on the committee agreed that we needed policy around trans issues, we were all a little confused as to how to start. Given that I had spent time thinking through some of these issues, I cautiously took the lead and reached out to the trans community to educate us.

We contacted a local organization called Trans Communities' Shelter Access Project,[2] run through The 519 Community Centre in Toronto. Trans Access is funded by the city and offers workshops for staff and residents, at no cost to shelters. Their workshop was widely perceived as the most dynamic and engaging workshop that had taken place for staff at the shelter. They allowed room for multiple questions and gave a very useful primer on trans issues related specifically to homelessness and accessing the shelter system. The staff at Trans Access also agreed to work with us on our policy.

I also met with the one trans person who was then at the shelter and, explaining what we were doing, asked if she was interested in helping us to form a policy around trans access. Readily and enthusiastically, she agreed. We met over the course of two separate meetings for about three hours total; during this time she offered her suggestions, experiences and insights towards developing this policy.

After these discussions, I met with other staff members and asked for their input. I didn't meet with other residents who were not trans to speak directly about this issue. The shelter environment is a dynamic mix of people living outside the normal confines of society and of people indoctrinated by the most restrictive aspects of that same society. An indicative take on trans people in the shelter was from a male resident who had commented that he'd spent two years in prison and pointed out, "It's simple. If you've got a cock you're a guy and if you don't you're a girl. Why don't we just do that here?" I decided if I wanted to develop a policy that was progressive, I needed to seek guidance from people who were progressive around these issues while listening to all voices — including the biases and prejudices of those most resistant to a progressive policy. After discussing it with the policy committee and upper management, we decided to exclude residents from all direct policy development but we would hold weekly residents' meetings and seek their feedback informally on some issues. I accepted that this was contradictory/paternalistic/oppressive in some respects, and we had to decide how to include diverse voices in order to address the oppressions and discrimination trans residents felt.

In multiple discussions with Trans Access and the policy committee about the draft policy, it quickly became apparent that the issue was much deeper than the document — for many of the shelter staff, it was about values, not behaviours. This was an issue that touched people to the core and raised many disturbing feelings. Staff often acted out these feelings in decisions that were not helpful or supportive to trans residents. The policy committee decided that more education with staff needed to take place. We set aside time in the staff meetings to gain greater understanding of the implications and actions emanating from the document.[3]

As a way of integrating and exploring the policy, I facilitated a series of workshops based on actual and hypothetical situations that we as staff could encounter. Staff were separated into pairs and given one of these scenarios:

- What would you do if someone comes into the shelter and identifies as a female and you think they may have been born a male?
- How would you respond if a resident from the male dorm came up to you and said there was a woman staying in the dorm?
- What would your response be if someone from the female dorm approached you and said that a trans person was being loud, disruptive or stealing?

I asked each person in the pair to reflect on the question and respond from their personal values/beliefs/understanding what they "naturally" would be inclined to do, and to share his/her response with his/her partner. After this step, the pairs were asked to go to the policy and determine what the response would be based on the policy. If this was different from their initial inclination, I asked the pair to talk about this difference. This process led to long discussions regarding discordance between values, policies and procedures.

Each of us approaches the issue of gender with a long history based upon our experiences, which are informed by a range of factors, including class, ethnicities, age, country of origin, gender identification, religious background, sexual orientation and exposure to different ideas and people. The scenarios were fairly easy to respond to and, by using the policy as a template, staff were able to respond in an "appropriate" way. However, we were soon to learn that how they responded to the scenarios did not reflect how they responded in their daily practice.

With the policy written, education sessions completed, staff training done, workshops with residents run and final approval from management, we still saw transphobic situations occurring. These included speculation as to the "real gender" of a person; asking new intakes if they were a "man or a woman" when they were clearly identifying as a woman (for example, when they were referred by another shelter as a woman and asked for a bed in the female dorm); laughing when talking about trans people; when in conversation with residents, making comments that indicated that staff were not supportive of the policy; and, perhaps most disturbingly, asking a new intake if she had a penis when she came and requested a bed.

For staff implementing a trans policy, this experience raises several issues they need to be aware of. Just as staff deal with the behaviours of residents rather than with their identity, so we too must deal with our behaviours. Just as there is a range of cultures, ethnicities, religions and ages working in the shelter; so too is there a range of political and social values. A gay man is not necessarily socially progressive and trans positive; an immigrant woman from an Islamic country is not necessarily transphobic.

The role of policy is not to convert and change people's perspective, although I am incredibly grateful that mine has evolved as a result. I cannot be responsible for people's thoughts or feelings. This does not mean I don't have long, argumentative, funny, challenging, rewarding and difficult conversations with my peers. Ideas and values change; understanding develops; and we grow through learning and being challenged. We must develop and implement progressive and accountable policies to ensure a safe space to all people who need shelter.

NOTES

1 The entire Shelter Standards document can be found at www.city.toronto.on.ca/housing/pdf. shelter _standards.pdf.

2 For more information about their incredible work see www.the519.org/programs/trans/access_project/index.shtml.

3 The full policy can be found at www.the519.org/programs/trans/access_project/index.shtml.

CONCLUSION

TOWARDS TRANSFEMINISMS

Krista Scott-Dixon

> I realized consciously that one sex or one gender isn't better or more civilized or moral than the other, but that a person's relationship with his or her own body is what counts, because being true to oneself creates the integrity and self-respect we need to have if we are to extend that respect to others ... The pain inflicted by the refusal to acknowledge the lived experience is vicious and debilitating.
>
> — Jamison Green, *Becoming a Visible Man*[1]

As I was writing this conclusion in the fall of 2005, a friend of mine was agonizing over outing herself as a trans woman. She is an amateur boxer, and before her first competitive bout, she came out to her coach whom she'd met post-transition. Luckily the coach, a long-time feminist, remained literally and metaphorically in my friend's corner. However, with no firm pro-trans policies in place at the boxing commission, they both felt that they should raise the issue with the officials in order to avoid later problems if my friend were "found out."

The question of whether trans women may compete against non-trans women in boxing went before our provincial commission. Along with her fear about the repercussions of public disclosure, my friend also faced the anxiety of waiting for an institutional body to decide her fate: she did not know for a long time whether she would be permitted to compete. In the end, she was overjoyed when the commission not only allowed her to fight, but changed their policies to admit trans women in future. My friend's situation, and the example of women's participation in sport generally, ties together many of the threads spun in this book — issues of access, self-presentation, safety, bodies, institutional gatekeeping and women's spaces.

For non-trans women, access to physical activity and organized sport has been a fight spanning several decades, if not centuries. Although the debate over enabling trans women to compete in women's sports has been in the public eye in recent years, it is positioned within a context of a longer process of feminist activism. Historically, biologically based arguments were often used to explain why women, especially middle-class white women, should not undertake physical activity.[2] Such arguments ranged from women's intrinsic physical weakness to their lack of aggression to possible harm to their reproductive organs.[3] Opposition to women's sports has included constraints on girls' and women's activity choices, poor funding and resources for women's sports, minimal or negative media coverage and even open hostility. Consider the famous case of marathoner Kathy Switzer whom male officials assaulted and attempted to physically remove from the running course in 1967 when she challenged the Boston Marathon's men-only policy. Women have found it particularly difficult to compete and gain legitimacy in traditionally "masculine" sports.

Boxing provides an especially interesting case for those concerned with gender issues.[4] Boxing is a brutal sport that has cultural associations with working-class and often racialized, non-dominant ethnic-group masculinity. Success in boxing depends on strength, skill, aggression, hundreds of hours of rigorous training and the willingness to hit another person full force with the intention of knocking him/her to the ground. Boxers themselves often dance between the aggressor and the exploited. Their bodies are agents and objects of violence but are also used by others as part of larger economic and social agendas. Boxing represents a contradictory American Dream of success and class mobility through hard work and dedication, but also self-destruction. The violence inherent to boxing and its possibly illusory promise of self-actualization has led some feminists to dismiss it as a vestige of patriarchal society. Other feminists have claimed that access to *all* sports, even (or perhaps especially) the ones that aren't very ladylike, should be a fundamental right.[5]

In some regions, women's combat remains prohibited or limited.[6] Women's boxing will be a demonstration sport at the 2008 Olympics and a medal sport in 2012 (it had appeared briefly in the 1904 Olympics). The earliest recorded women's boxing match dates back to at least the 1720s in Europe, and throughout the eighteenth and nineteenth century matches were staged by women drawn from working and racialized groups.[7] However, in an official sense, women's fighting was banned in most countries until recently (for example, the UK legalized women's boxing in 1998).[8]

Women's participation in sports has also raised concerns over women's sexuality and gender presentation. Not unlike transsexual women who are often asked to conform to cultural scripts in order to "pass" and access health care, sporting women have often been pressured or forced to "prove" their femininity and heteronormativity through other means such as self-presentation and staying in the closet if required.[9] Like many clinicians who evaluate trans women, the sports media prefer straight-appearing and conventionally presented femininity.

Thus, cultural anxieties over women's sports involve not only issues of gender but also class, race-ethnicity and sexuality. Women athletes have worked hard to overcome stereotypes of biological frailty and inadequacy, along with various social prohibitions. However, the relatively new question of whether trans women (there has been little discussion of trans men) may fairly compete against non-trans women has led to debates that often return to biological essentialism. People who might not otherwise champion intrinsic biological differences may now find themselves using such differences as evidence in arguments against trans women's inclusion. Here again boxing provides an interesting case. On the one hand, it might seem sensible to reject unfair competition because of possible biological inequalities in strength and size between people born male and people born female (let us leave aside for a moment any effects of hormones and so forth). This would seem to be especially true in a one-on-one combat sport. On the other hand, boxing is full of biological disadvantage and variation: a "glass jaw," a short reach, clay feet, a right- or left-handed stance and, of course, injuries. Boxing narratives focus on overcoming innate physical disadvantages through weight classes, hard work, careful strategy and, most of all, fighting with "heart." The other interesting contradiction of boxing is that gender-essentialist arguments might be used to protect non-trans women's position in a sport that defies nearly all norms of femininity.

Feminists have often struggled with how to address and understand women's physical aggression, strength and violence. While some feminists have argued that physical development and healthy aggression in a sports setting results in social empowerment,[10] others have been critical of fitness and nutrition practices they consider "disciplining the body."[11] Social-justice activists have spoken out against violence, so often perpetrated against women, trans people and other marginalized groups. The representation and reality of violence, in every context and place from screen to street, remains dependent on gender, class, racialization and inequalities of power. Thus, while campaigns for inclusion in organized sport, particularly those that have been dominated by males, reflect feminist aims, some sports, such as boxing, represent both "atypical femininity" as well as a site of feminist unease.

I use this example of access to boxing to illustrate many themes running through this book. First, struggles over inclusion and exclusion are far from over, and such struggles have an effect on the lives of real people. This volume has drawn on people's experiences in many fields and life stages in order to emphasize the importance of grounding theory in the material world. Second, there is no single feminist position on any given issue. Lives, experiences and political positions are diverse. I have opted not to include some feminist positions (such as those that are unquestioningly anti-trans or transphobic) in this volume, but nevertheless readers should be able to see that there is variety among contributors. Feminist positions may shift as political landscapes shift, and we should be mindful that our older arguments are able to address new questions adequately. If not, we need to critique and update our theories and our activism. Third, social and political issues are complex. For people concerned with social justice, moral certainty is not always self-evident. Indeed, moral certainty itself may not always serve us well, and we may change our minds after prolonged reflection. Finally, struggles are not simply gendered; class, racialization and other power inequities shape the complex relationships between people and institutions.

*

> I don't think civil rights are in such short supply that they have to be meted out a little bit at a time.
>
> — Jamison Green, *Becoming a Visible Man*[12]

I have often spoken of trans and feminism through this book as though they were separate processes or phenomena. This is, to some degree, a false premise adopted mostly to examine various streams of theory and activism.

It is a division that is as false as speaking of anti-racist or socialist feminism as being about "race AND gender" or "class AND gender" as if these things were distinct categories that had nothing to do with one another. There is no such thing, really, as this AND that identity; there is no life lived in tidy, neatly labeled and organized little boxes. Our lives and identities are not easily divisible and neither are social relationships.

Thus, I have arrived at the possibly obvious conclusion, which is, as Kyle Scanlon has succinctly put it, "Transfeminism shouldn't be perceived as an oxymoron, but as a redundancy."[13] While it is essential to keep the complexity and particularity of people's lives in mind, it is also possible to speak of a politics that takes a broad and rich anti-oppression mandate. As Bobby Noble has written, "Transfeminism looks like any other form of committed, critical and political practice: it explores how power works in all the ways that we can see but all the ways that we can't see as well. It looks like challenges to globalization and racism, so important for those of us who are white and transed."[14] Caroline White adds that transfeminism "views gender and sex as non-binary, historically situated, impermanent and evolving, understood within the context of a colonial past and present, and seen as inextricably linked to all other forms of oppression. [It's] a feminism that practices theory by actively challenging the status quo — by actively interrogating the structure of oppression."[15] With that in mind, then, I would understand transfeminism as a politics that is both old and new: old in that it returns to some of the most basic principles of social justice and equity, and new in that we hear more diverse and freshly public voices as we continue to struggle through challenges that test the development and implementation of these principles.

This book, this conversation among many voices, feels far from complete. There are wonderful, provocative, useful ideas here. There are arguments that challenge me and make me feel — productively — uncomfortable. There are also absences that make me want to ask more questions and invite others to join the discussion. In Viviane Namaste's latest work *Sex Changes, Social Changes*,[16] she reminds readers of the often unacknowledged class biases along with the critical erasure of both francophones and sex workers in much material that discusses transfeminist issues. Racialization and disability are other major absences. When I look at organizing that is taking place across Canada, from large urban centres to tiny rural settlements, I am reminded that we need to speak (and keep speaking) about how things such as youth, aging, race-ethnicity, migration, First Nations status, ability, sexuality, family, mental and physical health, poverty, geographic and linguistic isolation and regionality inform our experiences and anti-oppression politics.

When I hear the always-eloquent trans activist Jamison Green speak, I am reminded of the importance of strategic visibility, releasing ourselves and others from shame and stigma and not buying in to phobias, our own internalized oppression and the desire to regenerate hierarchies and police boundaries. We need to demand people's safety, security and self-determination on all the terms they require, and we cannot be complacent about gains made by one group if other groups continue to suffer and be marginalized. We need to demand that scholars not use people's identities and experiences as theoretical fodder without seriously considering the consequences of this act. We need to demand that services and care be available and accessible to those who need them, and that such services and care actually do *serve and care* rather than judge, close gates, objectify and reinforce oppressive power relations.

There are also moments in reading this text when I smile, when I want to cheer and applaud, and when I am stunned by the bravery, honesty and thoughtfulness of the authors. I am excited by this collection but there is far to go. I hope that many people reading this book will throw it down and say indignantly, "Yes, but what about ...?" or even, "I can't believe they didn't ..." and then go on to write their own book or perform their own activism on the subject.

After I gave a workshop on trans and feminism at a conference in fall 2005, an elegant older woman came up to thank me and said, "I thought I was the only transsexual woman who was also a feminist. Now I know that I am not alone." This reaching out, this solidarity, these coalitions, as challenging as they may be at times, must continue. Our ongoing struggles for social justice are at stake.

NOTES

1 Jamison Green, *Becoming a Visible Man* (Nashville, TN: Vanderbilt University Press, 2004), 36, 81.

2 Working-class women and women of colour were typically excluded in practice from this, as work available to them was usually physically demanding.

3 Patricia A. Vertinsky, *The Eternally Wounded Woman: Women, Doctors, and Exercise in the Late Nineteenth Century* (Manchester, UK: Manchester University Press, 1989).

4 "Female boxing in all its different forms links the physical body with the social body and the inner with the outer self in ways which are riddled with complexities and contradictory cultural values." Jennifer Hargreaves, "Women's Boxing and Related Activities: Introducing Images and Meanings," *Body and Society* 3, no. 4 (1997), 47.

5 Ibid.

6 For example, in the Australian state of New South Wales, women's fighting remains illegal and punishable by prison time. Yvonne Lafferty and Jim McKay, "'Suffragettes in Satin Shorts?' Gender and Competitive Boxing," *Qualitative Sociology* 27, no. 3 (2004), 250.

7 Hargreaves, "Women's Boxing and Related Activities," 37.

8 Duncan Mackay, "Women's Boxing on Cards for London," *The Guardian,* 2 October 2005.

9 Pat Griffin, *Strong Women, Deep Closets: Lesbians and Homophobia in Sport* (Champaign, IL: Human Kinetics, 1998); Maria Lowe, *Women of Steel: Female Bodybuilders and the Struggle for Self-Definition* (New York: New York University Press, 1998).

10 See, for example, Leslie Heywood, *Bodymakers: A Cultural Anatomy of Women's Bodybuilding* (New Brunswick, NJ: Rutgers University Press, 1998).

11 See, for example, Susan Bordo, *Unbearable Weight: Feminism, Western Culture, and the Body* (Berkeley: University of California Press, 1993).

12 Green, *Becoming a Visible Man,* 209.

13 Kyle Scanlon, quoted in Krista Scott-Dixon, "Transforming Feminism: Trans Activism and the Challenge to Feminism," *Herizons* (Winter 2006), 45.

14 Bobby Noble, quoted in ibid., 45. This is incorrectly attributed to Joshua Goldberg in the article.

15 Carol White, interview with author, Toronto, ON, 25 May 2005.

16 Viviane Namaste, *Sex Change, Social Change: Reflections on Identity, Institutions, and Imperialism* (Toronto: Women's Press, 2005).

GLOSSARY

androcentrism
From the Greek "andro," meaning man. The notion that men's and masculine experiences, ideas and perspectives are of primary importance, and that they represent the experiences, ideas and perspectives of everyone.

androgyny
From the Greek "andro," meaning man, and "gyno," meaning woman, androgyny refers to someone whose gender is somewhere in between the binary of what is culturally defined as masculine and feminine.

bio-woman/bio-man
Denotes a non-trans person by indicating that non-trans people's gender assignment at birth matches their gender identity. Other terms used include "GG" or "genetic girl"; "natal female/male"; "born female/male." These terms are sometimes seen as *biocentric*, or overly focused on biological markers as definitive of reality.

birl
Contraction of boy-girl. Young women who prefer a masculine gender presentation without necessarily having a male gender identity.

boi
Sometimes used to refer to boyish gay men but more commonly used to refer to a woman with a boyish gender presentation. Can also connote a young butch lesbian. May be combined with other words, as in "boidyke."

butch
A masculine lesbian, or an element of masculine gender presentation, as in, "This haircut makes me look butch."

Charter of Rights and Freedoms
Part of the Canadian Constitution Act of 1982, a document that sets out

fundamental rights and freedoms for citizens, particularly in the area of equality and minority rights.

cisgender
A synonym for non-trans that highlights normative gender presentation and congruence with biological sex. The "cis" prefix plays on chemistry terminology: a "cis" molecular configuration is the opposite of "trans."

cross-dresser
One who wears the clothes, accessories, makeup, et cetera, of the "opposite" gender. Generally, these persons do not alter their bodies. A more current term for transvestite.

discourse
A system of social organization or body of thought as expressed through language.

drag
Exaggerated performative aspects of identity, particularly gender identity, such as costumes or behaviour. Generally drag is understood as cross-dressing, but it can also refer to any identity that is "put on" like a costume. As RuPaul, former "spokesmodel" for MAC Cosmetics says, "You're born naked and the rest is drag."

drag king/drag queen
Women (drag kings) or men (drag queens) who perform exaggerated and caricatured versions of masculinity and femininity, respectively. Frequently done for entertainment purposes, or to play with gender norms.

en femme
Refers to cross-dressers when they are presenting themselves as women.

Eurocentrism
The notion that European or North American (white) experiences, ideas and perspectives are of primary importance, and represent the experiences, ideas and perspectives of everyone.

femininity
Norms of behaviour, activity and self-presentation considered to be associated with women and femaleness.

feminism
A movement to end sexism, sexist exploitation and oppression.[1]

femme
Feminine gender presentation, particularly a feminine lesbian, but can apply to persons of any gender.

FTM, FtM, F2M
Female-to-male trans person; a trans man.

gender
A system of roles, behaviours and social structures that is used to organize the world. Because it has a social and cultural dimension, gender is conceptually distinct from sex. It is often said that "Gender is cultural, while sex is biological"; or, as Virginia Prince originally noted, "Sex is between the legs, gender is between the ears."[2] See also sex.

gender bending
Gender play or ambiguity, frequently deliberate and purposeful (see also genderfuck).

gender blending
The mixing of femininity and masculinity in one person such that it is difficult to determine the gender of that person.[3]

gender dysphoria / Gender Identity Disorder (GID)
Clinical terms to describe the mismatch between the gender assigned at birth, and one's internally felt gender identity.

gender identity
The deeply felt sense of oneself as having a particular gender. Trans people generally feel that their gender identity does not match their assigned birth gender/sex.

gender role
A set of activities and social behaviours that are defined as being gendered; usually either masculine or feminine.

GRS (see also SRS)
Genital reassignment surgery.

genderfuck
Intentional disruption of gender norms, through performance or behaviour.

genderqueer
A person or identity that does not fit into a binary system, or that intentionally disrupts it (for example, by combining elements of both, or refusing to identify with one or the other).

hegemony
The dominance of one group's interests over others, particularly the dominance of cultural ideas, values and practices; the process of making this domination seem justified, legitimate and normal.

hermaphrodite
An older, less preferred term for an intersexed person. From a Greek myth about the son of Hermes and Aphrodite. Hermaphroditus's female lover desired a complete union with him, and thus their bodies merged to become partially male and partially female.

heteronormative
The notion that reproductive heterosexuality that is based on two well-defined categories of male and female is the only normal, natural mode of sexual expression. Also related to heterosexism, or discrimination based on the presumption that everyone is and should be heterosexual, and that any other orientation is deviant and abnormal.

hijra
A male-to-female or intersex person in India who is understood as a third gender and may fulfill specific social duties.

intersex
People who have biological characteristics, such as chromosomal make-up, hormonal mechanisms or internal and external reproductive organs that are in some way ambiguous, indeterminate or intermediate, and are not clearly defined as male or female. May also be termed intersexed or intersexual.

LGBT
Acronym for lesbian, gay, bisexual and transssexual/transgendered. May include other letters such as a second T for transgendered, a third T for Two-Spirit, an I for intersex or a Q for queer/questioning.

masculinity
Norms of behaviour, activity and self-presentation considered to be associated with men and maleness.

mastectomy
Surgical removal of the breasts.

MTF, MtF, M2F
Male-to-female trans person; a trans woman.

non-op
Non-operative; has not had genital reassignment surgery. Non-op may be distinguished from pre-op, in that there is no implied eventual surgery. People may be non-op for various reasons: the surgery risks are unacceptable to them, the surgery rewards are insufficient, they don't feel enough or any desire for genital reassignment and so on. Although there are other types of surgery, non-op is typically used to connote genital surgery only.

orchidectomy
Surgical removal of the testicles. This may be a single surgery or as part of the process of vaginoplasty. May also be spelled *orchiectomy*.

passing
Passing refers to an individual's ability to go unnoticed. Originally, as used in North America during the nineteenth and early twentieth centuries, passing had racial overtones: blacks with light skin and Caucasian features often "passed" as white, which conferred some advantage in a racist society. In gender terms, this refers to a trans person's ability to appear unproblematically as a particular gender. Some gender clinics use passability as a criteria for granting treatment, arguing that if an individual does not pass in their gender, it would result in undue hardship for them were they to transition. Failure to pass may be referred to as "being read."

phalloplasty
Surgical construction of a penis (phallus). This may include the use of existing tissue from another location (usually from the arm or leg) as a graft, or metoidioplasty, the freeing and additional reconstruction of the clitoris and surrounding tissue.

postmodernism
A school of thought, particularly in cultural production, that rejects the notion of universal values, embraces self-referentiality and suggests that social and cultural reality is a human construction.

post-structuralism
Similar to postmodernism in its rejection of universal values and embrace of social constructions, but typically applied to discourse-based theory, and concerned with the context-specific production of meaning in language and texts.

pre-op
Pre-operative, or pre-genital reassignment surgery.

sex
A collection of physiological characteristics, such as chromosomes, genitalia and hormones, that are defined as male, female or intersex. Biological sex is generally distinguished from gender.

sexual reassignment surgery (SRS)
Also known as genital or gender reassignment surgery (GRS), or even bottom surgery, the surgical procedures that transform the body to the point where a legal change of sex designation can be accomplished. While SRS is often considered to be genital surgery only, it can also refer to other types of surgery such as breast implants or removal (aka top surgery), or facial feminization surgery.

S/M
Sexual sadism and masochism; sometimes expressed as BDSM, to include bondage and domination.

Standards of Care
A set of clinical standards established by the Harry Benjamin International Gender Dysphoria Association (HBIGDA), now the World Association for Transgender Health (WPATH), which attempt to establish guidelines for the medical and psychotherapeutic treatment of transsexuals, particularly those with the ultimate objective of GRS/SRS.

top surgery (aka chest surgery)
Surgical removal of breasts and chest contouring. See also sexual reassignment surgery and mastectomy.

trans
A broad umbrella term that suggests many forms of gender boundary crossing, whether in terms of behaviour, self-presentation or identity; or in terms of how such crossings are experienced and understood. Not all people who fit this definition will self-identify as trans.

transgender
Often used as an umbrella term in the same way as trans, particularly in North America. May also be used to denote people who do not identify as transsexual or pursue surgery, but who nevertheless engage in some form of gender boundary crossing.

transition
The process by which a trans person moves from birth gender role and presentation to chosen gender and presentation (though "chosen" implies perhaps more freedom than many people feel). This can involve elements such as name and legal document changes, full-time living in the new gender role and possible medical interventions such as hormones and surgery.

transphobia
Irrational fear, discrimination against, social rejection, hatred or persecution of trans people.

transsexual
A term used to refer to people whose gender transition included surgery. Currently, especially given a growing population of non-op people who still identify as transsexual, the term may be more loosely applied and/or used synonymously with transgender, although this usage is sometimes contentious.

transvestite
Another, older term for cross-dresser, but not typically used outside of clinical literature.

Two-Spirit
A term adopted by many First Nations people that is used to connote a "third gender" or the notion that both male and female spirits live in one body. In some First Nations communities, Two-Spirit people have special functions, such as healers or counsellors. Originally, anthropologists studying First Nations groups in North America suggested the term "berdache" for this purpose, but the term was later deemed inappropriate. The Lakota term "winkte" is more or less similar although it should be understood in its own specific cultural context.

vaginoplasty
Surgical creation of a vagina, usually either with a patient's penile tissue or with a section of their colon.

NOTES

1 bell hooks, *Feminism Is for Everybody: Passionate Politics* (Cambridge, MA: South End Press, 2000), 1.

2 Virginia Prince, "Sex versus Gender," *Proceedings of the 2nd Inderdisciplinary Symposium on Gender Dysphoria Syndrome* (Palo Alto, CA: Stanford University Press, 1973), 20–24.

3 See H. Devor, *Gender Blending: Confronting the Limits of Duality* (Bloomington: Indiana University Press, 1989).

CONTRIBUTORS

LESLEY CARTER was born in Toronto just before the start of the Second World War. She grew up living in the role that her parents believed was correct for her, but from pre-school times never fit into the role of a boy. Teasing, ridicule and persecution made grade school very difficult, and high school was only slightly better. She took her BSc in General Science at the University of Toronto and M.Div. from McGill. Her working career was mainly as a minister in two major Protestant denominations. In 2000, she identified herself as a transsexual and began to take steps to transition to her proper social role. In 2002, she had sexual reassignment surgery by Dr. Suporn of Thailand and now lives as a retired but very active woman in Toronto.

TALIA MAE BETTCHER is an Assistant Professor of Philosophy at California State University, Los Angeles. She received her PhD at UCLA and her BA at Glendon College, York University. Her research interests include early modern philosophy, philosophy of the self and philosophy of gender and sexuality. A Canadian who resides in the United States, Talia is currently active in the Los Angeles trans community and grassroots politics. She is also a community-based performance artist, using her art to explore intersections between narrative, performance, theory and identity.

MARGARET DENIKE is Assistant Professor of Human Rights at Carleton University. A former president of the National Association of Women and the Law (NAWL), she is one of the co-ordinators of NAWL's National Consultation on Transgender and Women's Substantive Equality.

SUSAN DRIVER is an Assistant Professor at York University working in-between feminist, queer and media studies. She is about to publish a book entitled *Queer Girls and Popular Culture* (forthcoming, Peter Lang) and is editing a collection of essays entitled *Queer Youth Cultures* (forthcoming, SUNY Press).

LYNNETTE DUBOIS is a writer and political activist living in Toronto. She co-founded and is executive director of Artemis Services, a non-profit human rights advocacy organization. She is also a frequent contributor to the *Toronto Star* newspaper and to "Another Side of the News" with Paul Berenson on KCSB in California. She has participated in a number of political causes and was honored to address the Commission on the Future of Healthcare in Canada and the National Association of Women and the Law.

BARBARA FINDLAY, QC, did a BA, an MA, an LLB and half of an LLM before she realized that university would never teach her what she needed to know to understand oppression. She is most interested in understanding how internalized dominance works as a glue to hold oppressions in place and in developing strategies to disrupt internalized dominance. She has been active in anti-oppression work for thirty-five years as a community organizer, as a facilitator of unlearning oppression workshops, as a writer and as a lawyer who works on cases that advance equality.

MIQQI ALICIA GILBERT aka Michael A. Gilbert, PhD, is Professor of Philosophy at York University. S/he has published extensively in the areas of argumentation theory and gender theory in journals such as *Argumentation, Inquiry, Philosophy of the Social Sciences* and *Informal Logic*. Hir most recent book, *Coalescent Argumentation*, was published in 1997 by Lawrence Erlbaum Associates. Miqqi Alicia is a life-long cross-dresser and an activist in the international transgender community. S/he is the book-review editor and a regular contributor to *Transgender Tapestry*, the magazine of the IFGE. Since coming out s/he has been written up in the *Chronicle of Higher Education,* the *Globe and Mail, Campus U. Magazine* and *Salon Magazine.* In addition s/he has made numerous television appearances to present the cross-dressing community to the general public.

JOSHUA MIRA GOLDBERG has been a grassroots organizer for fifteen years in a range of social-justice movements and has co-founded three trans organizations. In anti-violence efforts, he has been on both sides of the desk, as a client and as a crisis worker/advocate with people living and working on the streets. Since his transition from female-to-male in 1996, he has rediscovered a love of sheer fabrics.

MICHAEL HAND teaches logic, the philosophy of love and sex and other philosophy courses at Texas A&M University (College Station). The essay in this collection is his first collaboration with Susanne Sreedhar and their first foray into writing on gender issues. It was written over a couple of years, primarily in coffee shops in Chapel Hill. It took so long because Susanne and Michael only work on their joint projects when they're together in a coffee shop.

ALAINA HARDIE is a trans dyke, originally from the United States, living in self-imposed political exile in the fantastically cool urban oasis of Toronto. She shares an apartment with two adorable little dogs who run her life. Professionally she is a computer nerd. Her hobbies include cycling, martial arts, reading, gardening, watching bad movies on Friday nights, decorating and subverting the dominant paradigm.

JOANNA HARRIS recently graduated from law school at Queen's University. Prior to enrolling in the faculty of law, Joanna completed a BA in Women's Studies at Nipissing University and studied at the University of Toronto. Since 2002, Joanna has been the co-chair of Women and Law, a student organization at Queen's committed to raising awareness about women's issues in the legal profession and providing support to women in the law school and women's organizations in the Kingston community.

DARRYL B. HILL is Assistant Professor in the Department of Psychology at the College of Staten Island, City University of New York, where he teaches and studies the social psychology gender and sexuality. His current teaching and research interests and other publications based on the Toronto Trans Oral History Project can be found at http://scholar.library.csi.cuny.edu/~dhill/.

LARA KARAIAN is a PhD candidate in Women's Studies at York University and a lecturer at the University of Western Ontario. Lara's irrational fear of standardized testing (read: LSAT) has propelled her in another equally rewarding direction. In her doctoral studies, most of her work focuses on the debates within and across postmodern, queer and feminist legal theory in the Canadian context. Lara is particularly interested in Supreme Court cases coming out of challenges to the section15 equality provision in the Canadian Charter of Rights and Freedoms, and more recently cases coming out of human rights tribunals. She is co-editor of the book

Turbo Chicks: Talking Young Feminisms (Sumach Press), the first Canadian anthology on young women and feminism.

A. Nicki is a research associate at the Centre for Women's Studies and Gender Relations at the University of British Columbia. She completed a PhD in Philosophy at Queen's University and a post-doctorate in bioethics at the University of Minnesota. She has published in *Hypatia* and other philosophical collections, such as *Feminists Rereading Machiavelli* (Pennsylvania State Press). Currently, she is completing a manuscript, under contract with Broadview Press, entitled *Marginalized Moral Voices*, in the areas of feminist ethics, trauma theory and philosophy of mental health.

J. Bobby Noble (PhD, York University) is an FTM transsexual man, who is an assistant professor of sexuality and gender studies in the School of Women's Studies at York University (Toronto). Bobby is the author of *Sons of the Movement: FtMs Risking Incoherence in a Post-Queer Cultural Landscape* (Women's Press) and the monograph *Masculinities Without Men?* (University of British Columbia Press), which is listed as a Choice Outstanding Title, 2004. Bobby is co-editor of *The Drag King Anthology*, a 2004 Lambda Literary Finalist (Haworth Press) and is now working on two new book projects: *Boy Kings: Canada's Drag Kings and Performances of Masculinities* and *Strange Sisters: Genealogy of a Femme Festival.*

Alexander Pershai holds MA and *Kandidatskaya* degrees in Theory of Language from Belarusian State University, Minsk. He is a doctoral student at the Centre for the Study of Theory and Criticism at the University of Western Ontario. He also is a research fellow and lecturer at the Centre for Gender Studies, European Humanities University — International, Minsk/Vilnius. His research concerns gender, language and power, exploring technologies of constructing and archiving knowledge and related patterns of social interaction in and by linguistic resources.

Ros Salvador is a spoken-word artist, anti-racism activist and lawyer living on Coast Salish Territory in Victoria, British Columbia. Ros is a lesbian of Afro-Trinidadian and Hungarian descent, and was born and grew up in Ottawa. Ros writes to have an outlet from the cesspool of racism that is Victoria and to disrupt the myths that serve to deny the realities of oppression and preserve the status quo. Ros has a forthcoming book of spoken word/poetry entitled *Sisters Like Me.*

KYLE SCANLON is too damn busy for his own good. He currently serves as the Trans Programmes Co-ordinator for The 519 Church Street Community Centre, sits on the Sherbourne Health Centre Trans, 2-Spirit and Intersex Working Group, as well as the GLBT Police Liaison Committee and TS/TG Advisory Committee for the Children's Aid Society of Toronto. He also sings in a queer choir, volunteers for the Bereaved Families of Ontario peer support program, has two kitties who are the loves of his life and is looking for Mr. Right. (Hint, hint, hint.)

KRISTA SCOTT-DIXON has a PhD in Women's Studies and currently teaches and does research at York University. Along with trans and feminist issues, her research interests include gender, work and technology. As her secret identity Mistress Krista, she is one of the editors of Trans-Health.com, an online health and fitness zine for trans people.

reese simpkins is a trans man and PhD candidate in Political Science at York University. reese's first love is theory and he integrates his everyday life as a trans man with his intellectual pursuits. He did quite a bit of activism during his undergrad, but has taken a bit of time "off" in recent years in order to transition. His dissertation is on trans masculinities and feminism.

SUSANNE SREEDHAR is a newly hired Assistant Professor of Philosophy and Women's Studies at Tulane University in New Orleans, Louisiana. She recently finished her doctoral dissertation on the political philosophy of Thomas Hobbes in the philosophy department at the University of North Carolina (Chapel Hill). She also received a graduate certificate in Women's Studies from Duke University in Durham, North Carolina. Susanne has been to the Michigan Womyn's Music Festival four times.

WOLFGANG VACHON has recently taken a leave of absence from his work in the Toronto shelter system to co-ordinate a drop-in/counselling centre with youth in Toronto's west end. Along with several other artists, Wolfgang is developing a theatre piece with trans individuals about their experiences living in and out of the shelter system.

CAROLINE WHITE is a community-based social-justice trainer, educator and researcher. She has worked in women's organizations for over twenty years. In 1994, Caroline initiated trans-related policy and training at the sexual assault centre where she worked. Since then she has worked with both trans and women's organizations to produce policy, educational materials and curriculum, as well as deliver trans-specific anti-violence training. Caroline is currently a Program Co-ordinator at the Centre for Leadership and Community Learning at the Justice Institute of BC (JIBC). The JIBC and the Women/Trans Dialogue Planning Committee produced *Making the Transition: Providing Service to Trans Survivors of Violence and Abuse*, a training curriculum written by Joshua Goldberg for service providers. For more information on the curriculum, contact Caroline at carolinew@jibc.bc.ca.

GIGI RAVEN WILBUR follows a path of sacred sex as a prostitute priestess. Gigi has given workshops on sacred sexuality, spiritual aspects of BDSM, intersex and many other related topics all over the country. S/he creates sacred space and holds rituals in the temple of sacred sex for the bisexual movement, pagans, pansexual people, radical faeries and other alternative communities.

SHANNON E. WYSS is a radical genderqueer living with hir two cats outside Washington, DC. Ze received a BA in International Studies from Vassar College and an MA in Women's Studies from George Washington University. Wyss has also published an article on trans and genderqueer youth in U.S. high schools. Hir politics are centered around feminism, queer issues, youth rights and radical social change, and ze tries to be aware of hir own privileges and prejudices.

Other titles from The Women's Issues Publishing Program

Remembering Women Murdered by Men: Memorials Across Canada
The Cultural Memory Group

Growing up Degrassi: Television, Identity and Youth Cultures
Edited by Michele Byers

Feminism, Law, Inclusion: Intersectionality in Action
Edited by Gayle MacDonald, Rachel L. Osborne and Charles C. Smith

Troubling Women's Studies: Pasts, Presents and Possibilities
Ann Braithwaite, Susan Heald, Susanne Luhmann and Sharon Rosenberg

Doing IT: Women Working in Information Technology
Krista Scott-Dixon

Inside Corporate U: Women in the Academy Speak Out
Edited by Marilee Reimer

Out of the Ivory Tower: Feminist Research for Social Change
Edited by Andrea Martinez and Meryn Stuart

Strong Women Stories: Native Vision and Community Survival
Edited by Kim Anderson and Bonita Lawrence

Back to the Drawing Board: African-Canadian Feminisms
Edited by Njoki Nathane Wane, Katerina Deliovsky and Erica Lawson

Cashing In On Pay Equity? Supermarket Restructuring and Gender Equality
Jan Kainer

Double Jeopardy: Motherwork and the Law
Lorna A. Turnbull

Turbo Chicks: Talking Young Feminisms
Edited by Allyson Mitchell, Lisa Bryn Rundle and Lara Karaian

Women in the Office: Transitions in a Global Economy
Ann Eyerman

Women's Bodies/Women's Lives: Women, Health and Well-Being
Edited by Baukje Miedema, Janet Stoppard and Vivienne Anderson

A Recognition of Being: Reconstructing Native Womanhood
Kim Anderson

Women's Changing Landscapes: Life Stories from Three Generations
Edited by Greta Hofmann Nemiroff

Women Working the NAFTA Food Chain: Women, Food and Globalization
Edited by Deborah Barndt

Cracking the Gender Code: Who Rules the Wired World?
Melanie Stewart Millar